HOUSES

Autobiography

Matthew Caswell

World in Panorama CIC.
Quarry Court – High Street, Leeds LS27 0BY – UK
www.worldinpanorama.org

HOUSES
by Fuad Matthew Caswell
ISBN: 978-1-908509-19-2

First published in Great Britain 2021 by World in Panorama CIC.
Copyright © Fuad Matthew Caswell 2021

A full CIP record for this book is available from the British Library.
A full CIP record for this book is available
from the Library of Congress.

For permission requests, please contact: wip@worldinpanorama.org
Find out more about the author and previous
publications at www.fmcaswell.co.uk

Produced in United Kingdom.
Front cover painting by Marc Chagall

By the same author under different names:
Matthew Caswell, Fuad Matthew Caswell, F. Matthew Caswell,
and Dr F. M. Caswell

- Menashi's Boy
- The Slave Girls of Baghdad, The Qiyān in the Early Abbasid Era
- Three Master Musicians
- Voices of the Arab Streets
- Stefan and Other Plays (in parts with Daphne Thomas)
- The Khamriyyāt of Abū Nuwās (the first and only translation from Arabic language)
- Tales of the Near and Far
- Al-Khayzuran, a play in four acts

Foreword

Matthew (Fouad) and I were introduced for the first time by a mutual friend, for me, after almost forty years in Leeds, for him after a lifetime. We were at a small party given by our friend. We spoke briefly. I did most of the talking, as he did most of the listening. On the way back home, I remember thinking to myself: nice guy, but not speaking much. It took 2 – 3 meetings, before he agreed to share with me some of his experiences, views, and achievements. This time we discovered we had a lot in common. On the way back home, I kept thinking: what a great man, but so modest.

The truth of the matter is that Matthew has nothing to be modest about. His impressive record is certainly a source of pride for him, his family, and his friends.

One day, after hearing of his stories, I said to him: "You should write about all this." He replied: "I have already done". I therefore felt privileged when he showed me the first draft, which I read in no time. All landmarks of his rich life have suddenly become vivid: His beloved Baghdad, the family he left behind when he moved to England, his struggle as a newcomer in this country, the love story with his late wife, his studies, early life as a trainee lawyer, later as a barrister, his relationship with people who belonged to a very wide range of society, retirement and his time at Oxford and, last but not least his impressive publications. People, events, achievements, tales of satisfaction and disappointments are all drawn up in a continuous sequence, beautifully told, in a clear and refined style.

Writing an autobiography is not an easy undertaking. It poses before the writer many questions: am I showing off? Will anybody be offended? Is it too personal? Have I forgotten something or somebody important? What to do to avoid the feeling that the memories will not be taken as a sheer 'ego trip'? And finally, is it going to interest whoever is going to read it? After reading the book I have reached the conclusion that Matthew's autobiography is a most interesting life-story which is a pleasure to read. Moreover, its strength is that it is not 'yet another book of memoirs of a grandpa writing for his grandchildren', but an account which readers from different walks of life and backgrounds will find captivating.

Avihai Shivtiel

Contents

Sabunchiya

⟡

The house is big, very big. He loiters at the bottom of the stairs, close to the tricycle that Marcelle had got out from the *sardab* where it had lain for more than a year. It had belonged to Bertha who then grew too big for it. It is now too big for him to use unaided.

Marcelle is *bint* Mas'uda. That's how she is always referred to, daughter of her deceased mother Mas'uda. She has a brother Daniel who lives at uncle Barukh's and helps him in the shop. And there is another brother, Ephraim. He lives at uncle Sason's. They are commonly referred to as sons of Mas'uda. He had not seen either of them. He learned about them as he overheard his parents talk about them as orphans. His bed is close to where his parents slept. He has an acute hearing which is overlooked because he is always quiet.

Marcelle is in the kitchen with his mother. The kitchen is at a corner of the yard. He had never been inside it. There are three steps, then a wide, wide opening and a dark, dark interior. When he stands at the bottom of the steps, he can at times hear the sound the pestle makes in the mortar.

He has a sharp hearing; can hear the sound the wind makes in the nut-tree, the birds singing and the cooing of the pigeons. The pigeons are on the balustrade, some in the empty room up the other staircase across the yard, on the other side of the nut tree. Birds and pigeons go quiet when the loud muezzin's call to prayer is heard. It comes from the direction of the outer yard, the street and Hammudi's shop. The outer yard is big, big and dark, He had never gone into it. He was warned of getting to the street and getting lost. When sister Bertha started school she was warned of the dangers of the street, and of getting lost. She was to stick to her brothers as they returned from school. If she got lost she was to ask for help, using a mantra of which she was reminded many times: 'My name is Bertha, my father is Menashi effendi, headmaster of Mas'uda Salman School. Our house is in the Sabunchiyya near Hammudi's the butcher'.

The outer yard is big, dark and forbidding. He once saw Gourdji come in from the street with the shopping. As the street door was opened letting in a little light before it was shut, he had a glimpse of Hammudi's shop far away across the street. Gourdji says Hammudi is not good at counting. He counted the takings three times and got a different one every time. So he asked Gourdji to do a Jew count and gave him one at the end for his pains.

Marcelle comes down the kitchen steps to see how he was. He is standing by the tricycle, says he is thirsty, but not in words. He knows the words and how to say them, but does not want to say them. He signals instead silently with his lips, which

Marcelle understands. She lifts him up to the saddle and starts pushing, his feet barely touching the pedals. Marcelle wheels the cycle round the nut tree, past the steps at the bottom of the kitchen, past the next corner where the goat had been milked before, past the other staircase climbing to the pigeons balustrade, past the steps going down to the dark, damp, cool *sardab,* then comes to a stop by the *hubb* which contains the water. It is earthenware with a big opening at the top tapering down to a tip dripping into the collecting basin underneath. The *hubb* is moist and tall. When it is time to add to it Marcelle has to stand on a wooden step so she can reach the cover.

He likes the cold water that quenches his thirst. It is even better than the milk he has in the morning; much better than the goat's milk which is salty. The goat man brought it to the yard and did the milking. It was said to be good for his measles. The physician said it had to be boiled before giving it to him. Then he got out a tuning fork and told him to nod as he struck. He then said there was nothing wrong with him physically. He said it was in the mind; he will talk when he wished to talk. Afterwards, his father said it was a strange business but will perhaps be cleared in time. His mother was cross; said he was naughty and obstinate, had better answer her, else she will tell Nuri effendi.

Everyone is wary of Nuri effendi. His home is the house next door. The parents know him and are in awe of him; but no one else in the family had seen him, nor heard any sound coming from his house, even though it is summertime, and everyone spends the night in the open air on the flat roof of one's house. The mother tells the children to lower their voices so as not to upset Nuri effendi, while father and mother discuss him in whispers. The father says that Nuri effendi may regain his eminent position, come by more money, and so call to reclaim the house. The mother says she would not mind returning the house provided he came up with the money. But they both hope that will not happen since the government was now seriously considering buying the house for a school and would pay good money.

He has a sharp hearing. He can hear the sound the wind makes in the nut tree, the singing of the birds and the cooing of the pigeons. He looks at the clouds racing high up in the sky, higher than the top of the nut tree and the top of the minaret. He waits for the return of Sami from school after the afternoon call to prayer. Sami is the eldest brother and the tallest. As he comes in, he picks him up, puts him astride his shoulders so as to see the top of the minaret and be nearer to the clouds. The clouds have different shapes. He cannot make out what they all are. He can see one that looks like the white goat they had for his measles. The clouds make no noise as they cross the sky. These are white clouds going to the sea to fill up. They will be black when they returned loaded with rain.

At tea-time, his mother scolds him for not answering; says he is being naughty and obstinate. The father says he is not sure how correct was the doctor's opinion; thinks there might be some hidden defect. Later, when the parents are in bed the mother once again wonders if the real cause was the potion she had when she was carrying him. She had agreed it with the father as they wrongly expected a girl; but she could only bring herself to swallow half of it.

As he came out of his reverie, he is sitting next to his mother in the neighbourhood park. He does not know how they got to be there, nor is he conscious of the things they saw on the way. His mind must have been in another place. He does not like the park; it frightens him. There are so many bigger boys who are naughty: running about, shouting, fighting and wrestling; spoke his language but not quite the same. There were no men to be seen. All the women are in abaya, the same as his mother's; then some with hijab, others in burka, a few in *puchi* that covers the whole face behind a thin, finely perforated metal veil.

The mother is engaged in conversation with Umm Hashim. They discovered each other as neighbours, Umm Hashim's home is at the third street door after Hammudi's as one proceeds in the direction of the Maidan. She is an expectant mother desperate for a boy after the two daughters she had already. She does not know how Abu Hashim would take it if the one she is now carrying turned out to be another girl. She fears he may divorce her or try his luck with another wife. In her turn his mother explains that she had a succession of boys. Her first-born died before he was eight days old. He was followed by Sami, now her eldest, followed by Salim and then Kamal. That made her feel proud; women would then accost her to learn the secret of making boys. But next came Bertha, her only daughter. The father blamed it on her; said that her pride and boastfulness attracted envy and the evil eye. When she became pregnant again, they persuaded themselves that after a succession of boys there would now be a string of girls, evil eye working overtime. At her husband's prompting she got hold of a potion to terminate the pregnancy, but could only bring herself to drink half of it. It turned out to be a boy, pointing to him sitting now next to her listening; a happy event but only half so. Yes, she would try for another child, now the curse of the evil eye appears to have lifted. Umm Hashim implores her, for the love of Allah and his prophet Musa, to divulge to her the true secret of making boys. The mother inclines her head to tell her delicately and in confidence that the child will turn out to be a boy if the woman truly loved her man while they were engaged in making a baby. "Woe to me", Umm Hashim exclaims, "it's always us that are blamed", then adds cryptically "while he is such an unfeeling brute".

It's the day of Eid and no school. He goes to the fairground with Kamal and is excited. Kamal loves the fairground and wants money from the father for the rides. The father gives him the money for the rides and some more for the bus, and asks him to take his younger brother along, take good care of him, and not lose him. They miss the bus, which Kamal thinks fortuitous; they will walk through the market and have money for more rides.

The market is heaving with people, and full of wonder and excitement. There are rows of stalls outside the shops groaning with countless varieties of foods. As they stop outside any of them showing interest, they are given to sample the sweetmeat and the handful of grapes without being required to pay or buy. From many shops one hears the voice of a woman singing, voice and song competing with the general hubbub of the market and the voices of the traders declaiming the merits of their provisions. In a gap between the sweets and the fruit stalls stands a man in a red coat, white *dishdasha* and a red fez, a pile of pomegranates next to him in a hamper. He picks one which he slices in two then places each half in a press to squeeze the juice into a cup which he gives to them in turn.

At the fairground he stands waiting for his brother who returns after having had and paid for several rides, keeping just enough for the big wheel and the bus. The wheel is made for little children; a simple wooden structure with four hanging baskets. Kamal pays the money and wants to lift him into one of them. But the younger brother lifts his eyes, sees the boy in the basket stuck at the top in a swaying basket, takes fright and shakes his head, obstinately ignoring the coaxing of brother and operator. On the way back they sit on the last bench of the bus, Kamal in the middle and he next to the door. As the bus lurches at a street corner, the door flings open and a passenger screams. Kamal grabs his young brother and continues to hold him tightly after the door is re-shut securely. As they get off, Kamal implores him not to tell their father, and he nods. It had been a wonderful Eid day, added to which is the wonder of sharing a secret with an older brother.

It is the twilight, the furniture had been carted away, the house was swept clean, the street door locked as they stand in the empty street waiting for the conveyance that would take them away. The talk is of money and of the new home on the other side of town. He has an acute hearing but does not listen. He is thirsty and misses the hubb and the cool water in the basin underneath. He wonders if the tricycle was carted away with the rest or might have been left behind. He thinks of the pigeons cooing on the balustrade and the birds singing in the big, big nut tree stretching up in the sky towards the clouds. He lifts up his eyes to look at the speeding dark clouds come back from the sea carrying rainwater. A lightning followed by thunderclap brings him out of his reverie. He looks around and realises that he is all alone in the empty street, while twilight had now turned to dusk. Hammudis's shop is closed and shuttered. He starts walking in the direction of the Maidan, goes past two street doors, then enters the third that is ajar. Umm Hashim emits a cry of surprise as she sees him. "What happened?" she asks, "Poor boy, are you lost? Have they gone and left you?" Abu Hashim goes out to look for them. Umm Hashim exclaims: "How could they do this?" before noting his distress and his being close to tears and adds words of comfort: "Do not worry, little boy, they will send to look for you, and Abu Hashim will bring them to you" then adds ruefully as an aside: "But what could she have been thinking, forgetting her darling little boy!"

Abu Hashim returns with Salim who comes towards him sheepishly and takes his hand, while Umm Hashim puts her arm round him and exclaims: "Such a darling little boy; how could she bring herself to do it!" and he can no longer contain his tears. He raises his tiny fists to swipe them aside, and straightaway finds his voice: "My name is Fouad, my father is Menashi effendi, headmaster of Mas'uda Salman School. Our house is in the Sabunchiyya near Hammudi the butcher."

Basoos

***

September is the cruellest month of the year to the boy's head teacher father. It is the start of a new school year with the myriad of problems that attended upon it; some of the plans meticulously put together and gone over many times in the long hot summer months would now be seen to unravel under the daily stress: What with the new syllabus, new teachers, arguments and rivalries old and new, setting a new budget and exceeding it. There was also the intake of new pupils and having to deal with their parents; also, the odd importuning father or mother turning up at the last moment pleading for the enrolment of the mischievous child to a class already filled to capacity and wanting the child to be disciplined as much as taught: "You may take the flesh, just leave me the bones!"

That is also the season for the manifestation of a stigmatic inflammation in the palms of the headmaster of Mas'uda Salman School. That is particularly bad this year, what with having to deal with a new school accommodation and a new home for the family, both used as stopgaps.

For many generations Baghdad had one main thoroughfare, Rashid Street which traversed it from end to end. Now with the growth of the population and the increase in the volume of traffic, coupled with the availability of public funds, it was decided to create another thoroughfare, Ghazi Street, to run roughly parallel with Rashid Street. The line of the new thoroughfare ran over the father's school which was then taken over by the authorities under a compulsory purchase order. The compensation money was set aside for the acquisition of a new site for the construction of a new school. But it would be a year or more before the new building would be finished and made ready for use. An alternative accommodation had to be found for the intervening period, and a big Ottoman house in the Basoos district was rented.

At the same time the sale of the family house in Sabunchiyya to the government had been completed and the proceeds were received by the boy's mother, the owner. The money was then invested in the purchase of building plots in the new suburbs of Battaween and Saadoon. One of the plots was set aside for the construction in due course of a new house for the family. It would take a long time to complete, pending which, the family went into occupation of a rented house next to the Basoos school.

That arrangement was a mixed blessing for the boy's father. It meant he could never feel free from work. Complaints and requests now often came knocking on his door, and in the holidays the letters addressed to the school were routinely delivered by the postman to the house. As against that was the benefit of no travelling between home and school, being able to keep a close eye on both, and the ability to spend more time with the children.

It had suited the boy's brothers and sister well: The house was in a predominantly Jewish district at a short walking distance from their respective French Jewish boys and girls schools; they enjoyed more social life as they met their friends out of school, visited each other's houses and, contrasted with the wary watchfulness of the Muslim Sabunchiyya they freely experienced and added to the boisterous activity and noise of a Jewish street in which everyone was seen as a friend, many greeted as relatives. The brothers participated in the pastime of flying paper kites from the flat rooftop. That could not have been done in a place like conservative Sabunchiyya where flying kites from rooftops in full sight and view of the women in the neighbours' courtyards would have hardly been tolerated.

The making of a serviceable paper kite is not as simple as one may imagine. The boy watched as his brothers made several abortive attempts before they got one up in the air. You would start by getting thin, pliable strips of bamboo from the shops; they are to form the head and spine. You next attach the coloured sheet to them by fastening and gluing, taking care not to cause the thin sheet to tear. Then you get down to attaching the tail. That's where it gets tricky; tail long and heavy and there might be no lift-off; short and lightweight and the kite once in the air would spin and fall in a heap. Every neighbourhood with serious flyers would have informal local customary laws to govern the incidents and situations that may arise: What is your right to retrieve your kite fallen on another person's property? In what manner, and subject to what requirements before you may exercise that right? What the ownership of the kite of an unknown owner? Or the kite captured in an aerial duel?

The boy's mother was contended. The stopgap house was within an easy walking distance to her mother's house in Liquorice Corner and to sister Hannah's in Abu Sayfain. The house was a small, traditional family house, very small compared with the one they had left. It was easy to look after with the help of Marcelle. That allowed the mother the time to go visiting, to receive visitors; or just to idle the time away and to take up knitting again. And she was expecting another child. She was no longer exercised by thoughts of the evil eye and misfortune. She felt that with the move to a new house at the other end of town, those could be said to have been left behind. The last thing as they left the Sabunchiyya house was Marcelle flinging the content of the water basin in their wake, thus to efface the real or virtual impressions their feet made on the tarmac, thereby so confuse the spirits that lurked in the sardab as to make them lose their tracks.

The boy now felt closer to his mother. He had her all to himself, with brothers and sister at school, father at work, while there were periods when the mother, being at ease, would be aware of his presence, engage him in reading from the syllabaries, or in learning the multiplication table, or just by keeping him close to her at the knitting, tied to her by the string of wool between the ball held in his hand and the needles in hers. The fact that his mother misguidedly tried to end his life while he was in her womb was now a distant, dim memory, and long forgiven. He could now speak freely with no physical impediment, nor mental block, but he had still retained a measure of reticence that would last him a lifetime. Thus, mother and child at the knitting with nothing said; mother dreaming of the new child she is carrying, boy concentrating on the length of string that he cautiously fed from the ball of wool in his hand -- not too freely which would cause it to entangle, nor so taught as might cause it to snap.

The mother enjoyed her enhanced status within the family brought about by the bearing of another child at her age, and by the demonstration of her financial worth. She was now the owner of readily marketable plots of land increasing in value by the day, while she provided, more than a headmaster's salary could, the means to construct a brand new modern family home in a modern trendy suburb. She was envied by sisters, cousins and friends, which pleased her. The stopgap house was kept clean and tidy all the time, while she took good care of her appearance and was always dressed as for going out. You never knew who might drop in at any time for a chat. She could allow herself the occasional self-indulgence of going out during the day shopping for clothes and personal adornment, or as on one occasion going to the *hammam*. It was a Wednesday, ladies day; she laid down the knitting at a whim and took the boy by the hand across the street to Haidar's bath house. They were stopped at the entrance and refused entry, the manageress objecting to the child, a male. The mother remonstrated with her, pointing out that an innocent five-year old boy could hardly be thought capable of impure thought. The manageress was unmoved. She did not expect the boy to be an initiator of mischief; her concern was for some of the women becoming excited and scandalised at the sight of him.

"She is ugly", said the father and walked out of the room. The mother cried. The boy approached the mother, touched her arm and gazed in wonderment at the baby that she was cradling. His new sister. The father was a good man at heart and noted for fairness. After the second cigarette he went back to console his wife. She told him how sorry she was that she could not present him with a boy. He told her it's no one's fault, just the luck of the draw. She said it was a gift from God which one accepted whatever it was. He was an agnostic and said it was nature's way to perpetuate the human race; it would not do to have only boys. She thought that the human race would have still survived if the bundle in her lap had been a boy, but did not say that out of regard for her husband's feelings; said instead that she will make sure that the girl will look pretty as she grew up. He consoled her by saying that she already had four sons in addition to himself. He then stood his ground by saying that the new child was ugly and there was not much that could be done about that, "she is ugly, ugly" he insisted. "She is not ugly, she is beautiful", said the boy. Father and mother smiled benignly and were somewhat cheered on by his intervention.

The headmaster started an exposition on social developments and the changing place of women. He could imagine that by the time this girl attained full age, some women could be at the forefront of the relentless advances in the arts and sciences.

There were signs of that already. The mother said that everyone knew that a girl is more helpful to her parents in their old age; as the saying went, "your son is yours until he marries, your daughter is yours for life". The headmaster brushed that aside and started to talk about Madame Curie who had died not long before. She was a Polish chemist who studied and worked at the University of Paris. She specialised in the study of radioactivity and discovered two new elements, radium and polonium, the first becoming helpful in the treatment of cancer. She was the first woman to win the Nobel Prize, and more remarkably to win it twice. The mother listened to that exposition with rapt attention, mixed with deep admiration for her erudite husband. That showed on her face, which induced him to embark on another example of female achievement that would have been rated daring when achieved by any man. It was the case of the British aviator Amy Johnson, the first female to fly solo from Britain to Australia. The mother looked down on the little bundle in her lap and wondered if she would ever grow to be a scientist or an aviator.

He liked his new little sister who paused no threat to his standing in the affection of the father who ever favoured whoever happened to be the youngest of his sons. The mother was now busy and had no time for knitting, and the boy spent hours by the cot gazing at his sister's black eyes, black hair and shiny olive skin, holding her little hand and counting the fingers. He recalled snatches of a lullaby describing the sun shining on the "cot of Aisha, daughter of the Pasha, playing with the *khishkhasha* rattle". Amy turned her head towards him and smiled. He was smitten. A sibling love that will last a lifetime.

Taht al-Takia

The family rents a house in Taht al-Takia where uncle Sasson is the landlord. He calls once a month to collect the rent; and every month the mother is heard to say how stingy he is. His avarice is demonstrated by the hungry look and careful way he counts and pockets the money. When it is time for him to leave, he gets up, straightens the folds of his trousers to check for any elusive coin that might have fallen accidentally, would next sit down to feel in the turn-ups, then get up again to scan the floor. Uncle Sasson is hard of hearing.

The mother had argued against renting his house. There were several houses available in the market; Sasson was charging a full market rent; so she could not see why her husband would favour his brother with no benefit in return. The father had other considerations in mind which he applied in all his dealings. Anticipating the possibility of a disagreement or dispute in the course of a transaction he would wish it to be such as can expeditiously be resolved, give or take, within the confines of the family rather than suffer it to be dragged out in public, which may lead to the involvement of an outsider as arbitrator, or worse still, the courts. That was in line with his entrenched nepotism. Whether the occasion was choosing a new teacher or employing any of the general staff his principle was to prefer in descending order the relative, the friend and the one recommended by a friend. He would justify that principle by saying that the one you know is better than the one you do not know.

Uncle Sasson's meanness was notorious in the family. On the day of Purim, the brothers would stalk him as he tried to avoid them. He missed the evening reading of the Book of Esther coupled with the rowdy noises in the synagogue as in the street celebrating the people's deliverance and the humbling and dispatch of the evil Haman. Instead, he attended the service the following morning when it was less noisy with fewer people about. Salim spotted him coming out of the Grand Synagogue, rushed over to him and wished him a (happy) *megillah* which is usually acknowledged by the exchange of gifts, or giving money to children. Uncle Sasson returned the greeting cautiously by wishing his nephew the same, and made for turning away. Salim intercepted him again, wished him a (happy) *megillah,* this time with extended arm and upturned palm for emphasis and clarity. The uncle got out a wallet from his inner breast pocket. As if at a signal the other brothers came rushing out of the side street shouting 'Uncle, uncle, *megillah; megillah*'. Uncle Sasson made them a gift of one fils each. He would hold the coin tightly in his fingers as if not wanting it to part from him, and would then be seen to wince as he dropped it.

On one of Uncle Sasson's monthly visits Marcelle was bold enough to ask him about Ephraim. He said that Ephraim had left him, now that he was grown up, and went instead to work for a draper in the bazaar. He did not know where he was living, but conjectured it was a room in some rooming house. He then added deprecatingly that Ephraim was a spendthrift, went often to the cinema and was even known to bet on racehorses. His brother Daniel was kneaded in a different clay. He still worked for Barukh in the goldsmith business, but having finished his apprenticeship, was now an employee receiving a wage from his uncle while living on his own. He lived frugally and knew the value of money. Sasson added darkly that he often wondered if Ephraim may have taken after his father. Marcelle was puzzled; and Sasson said no more.

It is August and the father spends it in the Lebanese mountains. He does that to avoid the stifling heat of Baghdad and to build resistance to the approaching new school year with its anxieties and the flaring up of the stigmatic inflammation in the palms of his hands. He always stays at Umm Raji's in Bhamdoun. There are many holiday mountain resorts in Lebanon. Most of the Baghdadis go to Bhamdoun so you find them greeting each other as they arrive; a coterie of familiar faces with familiar tastes and the same familiar topics of conversation: the weather, politics, money and health; health complaints most of all. In the early years the mother accompanied the father on holiday, but with the growing of the family, new babies, more responsibilities and the demands of the big house in Sabunchiyya, the mother now stayed behind.

There were already early signs of the flaring up of the father's seasonal stigmatic inflammation, and he took the bus ride down the mountain to consult a dermatologist in Beirut. The latter would see many Iraqi patients during the summer holiday season and thought most of their complaints were psychosomatic. He now concluded that the father's condition was caused or aggravated by mental stress. The doctor had a jar containing a solution of manganese which he had recently received as a sample. He thought it harmless and gave it to the Iraqi complainant as a new drug for him to try. The father rode the bus back up the mountain with a miracle in his pocket. The solution soon cleared all inflammation, rash and skin irritation. Thereafter, he would not go anywhere without a good supply of the solution produced in an English laboratory, contained in a clear jar bearing the label "Colossal Manganese: Oral". A Samaritan at heart he accosted anyone showing signs of eczema or rash to give him the good news; and otherwise to impart it with a missionary zeal to all who would listen.

There were several Jewish schools serving a Baghdadi Jewish population of 130,000. One such was the Mas'uda Salman School for boys, of which the father, Menashi Zelouf (Menashi effendi), was the head. It had been founded by the widow Mas'uda (another Mas'uda) in memory of her husband Salman. She had no children and lived on her own occupying one wing of the school building; the schoolboys were the sons she never had. But for the elite of the Baghdadi, the places of learning were two French language 'Alliance' schools established under the direction of the Paris-based Alliance Israelite Universelle, with the twin aims of the advancement of Jewish youth as well as the propagation of French secular culture and colonial influence. One of the two was the boys school founded in 1864 (first of the Alliance schools) named 'College Albert David Sasson' in recognition of the Sassoon bequest. The other was the girls' school founded after the boys' school and named 'Laura Kedourie'. It was funded by the other eminent and successful Baghdadi Jewish family of Lord Kedourie of Hong Kong. The syllabus of the Alliance girls' school was identical to that of the boys.

Menashi himself was a product of the Alliance school in which he received his education and later taught. When a third Alliance school was opened in Hilla he was appointed to be the head. But that was an inauspicious venture. Hilla was at the centre of the tribal area of Southern Iraq, a world apart from the culture, sophistication and standard of health of middle class life in Baghdad; so it was difficult to tempt those teaching in Baghdad to go to Hilla and take their families with them. Not long after the opening of the school by Menashi, his wife left him and went back to her family in Baghdad. That came after their first born child, a son, had died from an infection. Salvation came in the form of a disastrous fire that consumed the school, while there was no subsequent desire to re-establish it. Menashi rejoined his wife in Baghdad and assumed the headship of the new Mas'uda Salman School. He chose not to have his children as his students; they were admitted to the Alliance schools.

It was the boy's first day at school. His father took him by the hand and they walked together with his sister Bertha to the Alliance girls school where the kindergarten was situated. Madame Sabbagh ran the kindergarten by herself applying the Montessori method. Every day, after finishing the classes, she would walk to the Alliance boys' school to meet her husband who taught French language and literature.

Menashi and Mrs Sabbagh knew each other and could be said to be professional colleagues.

To the boy, the experiences of the day were overwhelming: being in a class of boys and girls, not knowing any of them, listening to his father speaking in French, Madame Sabbagh speaking to him in a strange language interspersed with a few Arabic words, reinforced by sign language. Even at his tender age he felt embarrassment at what he perceived to be his father's importuning, particularly when he expressed concern at his darling little boy going through the whole school day without proper nourishment. He brought along a packet of biscuits, and Madame Sabbagh was to give the boy some to take with the milk. Before going away the father pointed to the teacher's study to which the boy was to go for the biscuit. He was exhorted most of all to wait at the end of the lessons for his sister who will come to walk him home. The father had a thing about nourishment. He not only saw it as indispensable for good health, but had a delusional fear of the dread calamity of a child missing a meal. There was an occasion when after a spat with his mother the boy refused his food and went to sleep without having his supper. When the father came home and was told about it, he insisted on waking up the child to get him to eat before going back to sleep. The boy was too embarrassed to go to the teacher's study to claim his biscuit; and when at the end of the lessons he saw the other children being collected while there was no sign of Bertha, he went out to the street and made his way back home on his own. A little while later Bertha came sobbing and screaming: "I've lost him, I've lost him"; then, seeing him, stopped, slapped him on his upper arm, then resumed crying, tears of relief this time.

The father was a francophone to his fingertip. He gloried in French culture, language and grammar; and he was well versed in French literature. The boy was his favourite not only for being the youngest son but also because he liked to be engaged in the stories that his father told him about the luminaries of French literature citing, among others, Victor Hugo, Anatole France and the Alexandre Dumas, father and son. He would talk of Corneille and Racine, recite from memory passages from *Le Cid* and *Andromaque*. But his favourite was the Count of Monte Cristo. There were evenings when surrounded by the family the father would sit to read from that book, all the family savouring the dramatic tale of betrayal and retribution, victimhood and despair turning to the possession of untold wealth and boundless power.

The father was also a romantic. He believed in human progress, the inexorable advances in science and medicine; saw the good side of any of his fellow men; and believed, shades of Tolstoy, in the curative effect of countering hostility with love, doubt with faith, and fear with trust. That was to be illustrated by the case of the tonsillectomy that the boy needed to have. The father made inquiries and ascertained that the best surgeon to approach was Sa'ib Shawkat, a young graduate of a German medical school who was now recommended as the best in Baghdad. However, the recommendation came with a serious caveat. The Shawkat family was notorious for its association with the fascists; Sa'ib himself was reported attending a fascist rally at which he spoke in glowing terms of the social and political developments in Germany that he observed and experienced in person. That did not deter the father; he would not accept that an educated, cultured practitioner of medicine who

25

had acquired such a high reputation would allow political and racial prejudice to have any part in the discharge of his professional duty. In the event the father's trust was vindicated, the operation was successful and carried out with sensitivity and amiability extended to the parents who were present in the course of the procedure. The condition in which the operation was carried out would have horrified the surgeon's erstwhile teachers in Heidelberg. Next to his consulting room was his so-called operating theatre containing a table and a few surgical instruments. The boy was laid flat on the table restrained physically by the male nurse while a gag kept his mouth open allowing the surgeon to remove the tonsils with quick neat cuts. The nurse later explained to the parents that it had been safer to carry out the operation without anaesthetic. On the last visit to the consulting rooms the eminent surgeon gave boiled sweets to the boy, told him how brave he was, and wished that his own new-born son would grow to be as brave.

The big event of the family's life in Taht al-Takia was the wedding of Marcelle. It began with the parents discussing the matter and agreeing that it was time for them to find her a husband. They needed to approach the matter as one would a military operation. A most important thing to discuss was the size of the dowry that they would be prepared to offer. The father suggested a figure which the mother forthwith knocked down to half, pointing out in the process that there was no room for a dowry to come out of her husband's monthly salary of twelve dinars. It would have to come out of her own money, being the marriage dowry that had been provided for her by her wealthy wool merchant father. She also pointed out that they now had two daughters, hence the need to allow for two more dowries in due course.

They employed a woman matchmaker who made a list of Marcelle's assets and drawbacks: a good figure; light reddish hair which could be referred to as blond; white complexion with some freckles that one would ignore; hazel colour of eyes which were not set too close. A great asset was Marcelle's family background, maternal uncle a headmaster. That put in stark relief the great negative; nothing was known about her father or indeed about any paternal relative. The parents confronted that in the seclusion of their private discussions. To their knowledge sister Mas'uda's husband was one Isaac who could hardly provide for her and the children in her lifetime, so she had to resort to her brothers for help from time to time. Isaac was not a bad sort and Mas'uda felt a lot for him, which he reciprocated. It was just that all he was fitted to do for a living was to play the fiddle that he carried to celebrations of weddings and circumcisions. As Mas'uda was dying Isaac took the three young children to her deathbed for a last look. After she died he knew that he was in no position to look after and provide for the children, so he agreed, and it was a relief, that the children be taken over by their uncles. Mas'uda's brothers saw the arrangement as a fulfilment of a family obligation; not that it was entirely altruistic: Sasson would have someone to help him in running the shop; Barukh needed someone to help him in the goldsmith's workshop and use the blowpipe, while the teacher's wife could do with the services of a healthy young girl who would do her bidding. Within days of Mas'uda's death Isaac had one last look at his children then disappeared. Afterwards there were unconfirmed rumours that he went to live among the tribes of Diyala, that he was in a relationship with a Muslim woman, or may even have converted. None of that would be disclosed in the search for a husband. All that was disclosed was that Isaac left after the death of his wife and was neither seen nor heard of after that.

Marcelle was looked over by Yahuda's sisters and found acceptable. Yahuda expressed himself willing after receiving their report. Marcelle had no part in the discussions or negotiations. The last thing that was to be agreed was the size of the dowry. Yahuda's sisters and the matchmaker came over, and there was a long discussion, at one point quite heated, before the figure was agreed at 450 rupees with 30 more for the matchmaker. The choice of the rupee for currency was odd in the circumstances. The then official currency of the Iraqi state founded in 1922 was the dinar. The official currency until the end of Ottoman rule had been the lira. There was a small gap between the two periods when Iraq was occupied by the British army and administered by the British India Office; that was when the currency in use was the Indian rupee. One suspects that the use of the out-of-date rupee as the dowry currency may have been a ruse by the matchmaker to have the dowry so represented in order to produce a bigger number, or cynically to confuse. Later that evening while the boy was asleep, Marcelle stole over to stretch herself next to him and, full of excitement, told him that she was going to get married, would have money, and asked him how much was 450 rupees.

The wedding reception was held in the house, and the family was unstinting in the preparations. The house was cleaned from top to bottom, the yard swept, scrubbed and set with tables, and with some extra help in the kitchen. All afternoon deliveries were received of the fish, the lamb, the drinks, the fruits and everything else that was fitting for a middle class wedding reception. The last delivery was of the bread. The baker arrived with the twelve loaves on order; and a date pie decorated with the name Marcelle. They thanked the baker for his kindness and generosity. He disavowed the generosity; said by way of explanation that two days before, a strange man came to his shop, enquired about the wedding, placed the order for the pie, paid the money, and left. He did not give a name nor leave an address.

Battaween

⎯⎯⎯ ⌇ ⎯⎯⎯

I t was a big event, moving the family from Taht al-Takia to a rented house in Battaween. Until then all the houses had been in the centre of Baghdad; now they were going to savour life in a European style house in a new modern suburb. That coincided with an explosive increase of the population of Baghdad, the rise of a new middle class that came out of the 'Dark Ages' of Ottoman rule and was now looking to the West for cultural inspiration, technological advances, and material wellbeing.

The family was pleased with the amenities of the new home in comparison with the old ones: tiles easy to wash and sweep instead of harsh flag stones, modern plumbing that one could rely on, modern kitchen and a modern electricity installation with many plugs and power points. The whole was suffused with optimism. That was marked by the fact that instead of blank walls looking inward to a discreet central yard, the new house had no yard but boldly looked out to the world through doors and windows. The new world was also competitive and rife with a new class system. Battaween looked down on the backwardness of the old Ottoman houses in the city, while it envied the opulent individually designed villas on big plots in Saadoon.

To the schoolboy the main drawback of the move to Battaween was that he had to use public transport to travel to and from school. There was as yet no regular public bus service run by the government or the municipality. Instead, there were small independent operators using small-size buses. In the morning one had to stand at the crossroad and wait for one, not knowing when it will come. In the afternoon, coming out of school tired and hungry, one had to wait with a crowd of youngsters waiting for a bus, then join in the melee to secure a place when one turned up. The boy had the first stirring of what will mark him a life-long socialist. That was when seeing limousines go past with the odd schoolboy looking smug and haughty as he was being driven home, and with no concern for the others.

Grandma Khatoon, father's mother, came to spend time with them. She was very old and poor. Her marriage had started as a union of money on her husband's side and the rabbinate and erudition on hers. She may have been the only woman in Baghdad who, brought up on the Hebrew bible, could still read it in her seventies then to lay it down to relate to any grandchild who would listen the strange tales and episodes of the history of the world. The arrangement in her widowhood was to live most of the year at her third

31

son Barukh's home. When Barukh's first wife died leaving three young children it was she who cared for them. Barukh remarried and his second wife produced children who it was said received preferential treatment. Khatoon who continued to see to the upbringing of the first family defended Muzli, "she is not a bad woman, one cannot feel for a step-child the same as for one's own flesh and blood."

As it was time for Khatoon to be taken to Battaween, the boy's father entrusted him with a cardigan that belonged to her to take on the bus. Knowing of his predisposition to carelessness the father impressed on him not to forget and lose it. But the boy did just that. After the long hot school day, he shoved and pushed to gain room on the bus; then got off leaving the cardigan behind. That was one of several episodes in which he was seen to be distracted and absent-minded, which gave rise to the speculation that the disposition may have been natal.

Khatoon's husband Eliahou had come from the well-to-do Zelouf family with a sizeable inheritance of his own, but he was like the proverbial prodigal son, wasting his money on drink, women and associating with disreputable people. The biggest scandal in the family was when he formed a relationship with an unknown Muslim woman that the family accused, rightly or wrongly, of being of low morals and a predator. When he would not terminate the relationship Khatoon applied for the marriage to be annulled and she secured that through the influence that her uncle wielded at the upper reaches of the rabbinate. Thus, Khatoon was free from a troublesome marriage, but not from the bitterness that was left in its wake. She went to the Grand Synagogue, prayed, and then added a wish that the other woman burnt in hell to requite the burning hatred she felt in her heart. Not long after, news reached her that the other woman died of burns which she sustained when a primus exploded. Khatoon was full of remorse; went back to the Grand Synagogue, prayed, and declared from the bottom of her heart that she had not intended her earlier incantation to be taken seriously. Then Eliahou came back to her full of contrition, and they were remarried. They were happy for a spell before Eliahou slid back to his bad old ways. Khatoon went back to the Great Synagogue, prayed, and pleaded with her Maker to grant her one last wish, which was for her to survive her husband, then have ten years of trouble-free widowhood. Afterwards, every day, she counted the days and what was left to her in this world.

There was grim news coming from Europe; the preparation of war between France and Britain on one side opposed by Germany and Italy on the other. On his way home the boy stopped at the corner shop for some sweets. He overheard a conversation between the shop keeper and another man; and they appeared to rejoice in the proposition that Germany was strong enough on her own to overwhelm Britain and France, and can assuredly do so with Italy as a bonus. The boy's father thought that a delusion. He had an absolute faith in the France of Clemenceau and Foch, the Marne and Verdun, and now with the benefit of the Maginot Line and of millions of citizens and republicans marching to war fired by patriotism and the Marseillaise. He taught the boy the words of the Marseillaise and stressed in particular the rousing emotion that is evoked by a ferocious enemy advancing right up to one's arm to cut the throats of one's son and companion, that is one's woman. The boy was left ignorant of the meaning of the word 'tyranny' as used in the song; it was beyond the father's ability to explain that abstract notion to a seven year old youngster.

A street of new houses, it was not yet a community. There were interesting neighbours. As the boy walked from the bus stop Yousef came out of his house with a tray of small ice cubes that he extended to him while Yousef's son Jacob looked on smugly. It was the first refrigerator in Battaween. Narayan, the builder, lived a little further along; he was Armenian, and a fascist. There was an instance when the boy witnessed an argument that his father Menashi had with him about the developments in Europe and the impending war. Narayan defended Hitler, saying he was a patriot safeguarding his own people while seeking to correct the injustices of Versailles. Narayan followed that by accusing the American and European Jews of provoking hostilities, Menashi reminded him that the Turks had used the same racist argument in the World War to justify the persecution of the Armenians.

Fascism and admiration of Hitler were rife in Iraq at that time; and there was a suspicion that another neighbour Tariq was also a fascist, but he will say if asked that he was a nationalist wanting to set the country free from British domination. He appeared to bear no ill feeling towards his Jewish neighbours, would greet them with a smile even as they avoided him. His house was just across the street from the boy's family's; he had three women in his household whose relationships with him were uncertain. His profession was also subject to speculation. He conveyed the impression of a hard man of action, as someone who had a military training which he was now deploying in one way or another, and for which he was due admiration and respect. That was put to the test one starless night when the whole street was awakened in the early hours by a woman's scream of 'burglars' which was taken up by other terrified voices and women adding their screams. The commotion was stilled as suddenly as it had begun by the discharge of a firearm from the direction of Tariq's house followed by Tariq raising his voice to announce that he was taking full charge of the situation and to add, by way of challenge, that he will sort out whoever might be foolish enough to try to break into any house in the street. At the rising of the sun it became clear that there had been no forcible entry anywhere, nor any other signs left by the so-called intruders. Tariq claimed an enhanced prestige backed by the revelation of a working revolver in his possession.

The boy's mother Nusha made friends with Layla whose house was quite near. Layla was a Lebanese married to Abdallah. They had first met when he was studying at the American University of Beirut. He was now making a lot of money running a big restaurant in downtown Baghdad. Not much was seen of him since he spent all his days at the restaurant and only returned home late in the evening. Layla spent her days in an elegant house that combined her good taste and her husband's money. She was pleased to welcome Nusha for a chat; they talked of their husbands, Nusha also referring to her children and to the next one that she was expecting, while Layla bemoaned her fate that would not allow her to have a child. They would play the bagatelle then have thick Turkish coffee in small cups, drink it, overturn the cup on the saucer and let the dregs slide down, wait for them to dry leaving lines, shapes and images that they would see as symbols presaging the future. Layla had a fertile imagination; she would see more in the dregs than Nusha whose devination was limited to the sex of the child that she was carrying. On one occasion Layla saw the shape of a box which she interpreted as a coffin; she next saw a small splodge that could arguably be a body. That upset Nusha who related the matter to her husband

Menashi. He cursed Layla, accused her of envy and mischief, and told his wife to avoid her. The coffee dregs did not alert Layla to the calamity that would befall her. When Nusha called on her next visit, she was in tears and almost choking with the words: Abdallah was threatening to do the very thing she had feared since she married him. Now that his business was thriving with a big bank balance he was minded to take another wife. After all, he was allowed four. And he wanted to have a child, perchance a son, who will continue the business and keep his name alive. Layla could not think what to do; so she was going to Beirut to spend a few days with her family and to work out her future.

Menashi was in Bhamdoon for his annual holiday when Nusha delivered their fifth son. Menashi, overjoyed by the news, rushed back in time for the circumcision on the eighth day and he named the boy Eli in memory of his father Eliahou. The breastfeeding went wrong, a lump appeared in one breast. It was removed surgically by Sa'ib Shawkat and found to be benign. However, the incision turned septic and the doctor's nurse came to the house several days to nurse the mother to recovery.

Happily, none of the negative divinations in the coffee dregs came to pass. Nor did the dregs presage the family's next move, back to the city and grandma Ini's house at Liquorice Corner.

Grandma Ini's House

They were now living at Grandma Ini's house. The boy's mother, Nusha, had left it twenty years before as a newly-wed bride; now she was back with five sons and two daughters to live with her own old and fragile mother Rifqa who needed looking after. Nusha was a name that she had assumed in preference to her real name, Ma'tuqa, which was old and obsolete, one hardly ever came across it in modern times, its derivation and meaning obscure. Yet it is of important historical significance; it translates as 'May He set her free from bondage', harking perhaps to as far back as the 6th century BCE when Jerusalem was sacked by the Assyrians under Nebuchadnazzar, and some Israelites were carried off as captives to Babylon where they sat by its waters and wept in memory of Zion.

Grandma's house was at 'Liquorice Corner' being the T-junction where the street of the Grand Synagogue came down to touch the long thoroughfare and market known as Suq Hannun. It was called 'Liquorice Corner' because there was always in living memory a man squatting there on a cushion, selling liquorice from a big tray in front of him as he declaimed its health benefits.

The house was at the heart of the Jewish civic district of Baghdad, just beyond the bustling and historic market known as the Shorja. That is a long, straight thoroughfare with small shops on both sides used in modern times for the sale of household goods. But the name insinuates other uses it would have had over the years. The word 'shorja', in its Abbasid historical context, referred to the 'brine' that was scraped from the salty lands of southern Iraq, by the employment of mostly African slaves; the term would later be used to refer to salt generally.

As one approached the civic area from the direction of the Shorja one would have walked past the school for the blind next to the community offices, then past the two Alliance French schools, 'Albert Davide Sasone' and 'Laura Kedourie'. The Sassoons and the Kedouries were among the most eminent and celebrated of the Baghdadi Jewish community. Sir Albert Abdallah David Sassoon was a British Indian businessman and philanthropist, born in Baghdad in 1818. His father, David Sassoon, had been a leading Baghdadi merchant and a treasurer to the Ottoman governor. Implicated in a corruption scandal, he fled with his family to Persia, thence to India where he founded large banking and mercantile businesses that served the British imperial administration of India, while he flourished under it. As for the Kedourie family with its vast commercial interests in the Far East, the most notable was Sir Ellis Kedourie, businessman and philanthropist, who was born in Baghdad in 1865. He established Laura Kedourie School in 1919 in honour of his wife Laura.

After passing the schools one would come next to the Grand Synagogue. There were many synagogues in Baghdad at the time catering to a Jewish population of about 130,000. But the Grand Synagogue was in a class of its own, held in high veneration by the community. A big old building, a long line of metal cylinders, each holding a copy of the Torah or the Talmud ranged against the wall of the long entrance corridor testified to its age. It had a large interior with a raised covered platform (the Bimah) where the Torah was read during the service. The hazzan conducted most of the services from the Bimah, and it is where the shofar was blown on High Holy Days. The synagogue would be full on the special evening of the Day of Atonement which even non-observant Jews attended. A central part of the service is the 'Kol Kinidrei' declaration that provides an opportunity to raise money for charity. The Kol Kinidrei would be auctioned, and the highest bidder would have the privilege of rising to the Bimah to recite it. The hazzan would have conducted the auction and spiced up the bids by loudly announcing the amount of the last bid and adding an exhortation: 'Kol Kinedrei, may he increase the life of him who increases'. The Bimah was surrounded by the rows of pews for the men; the women's section was in the balcony.

The last building as one came to Liquorice Corner was Prayer House Zilkha facing the street of the Grand Synagogue. Except that it was not a prayer house nor a synagogue. It was what later came to be known as a *yeshiva*, that is an institution for the study of religious texts. Grandma Ini's was its neighbouring building facing Suq Hannun.

The removal of the family to grandma Ini's house was a shock to the family. It meant foregoing the easy life and comfort of a European type house in the new suburb of Battaween to be replaced by the confined living space of half the sleeping accommodation while sharing the basic amenities of an old traditional Ottoman house. But there were compensations: living in an inner city while observing, as well as participating in, a multitude of human activities and events unfolding within a few hundred metres. Next to the seller of liquorice was a kiosk for the sale of Jewish devotional objects, the owner suspected of being a crypto communist. In addition to the tallit (prayer shawl), tefilllin (phylacteries) and mezuzah (doorpost with holy writing identifying a Jewish home) the man would also receive every month copies of an Arabic left-wing Palestinian periodical which he would pass on to special clients. Across the street was the tailor's shop next to the grocer's. Whenever the grocer received a delivery of a barrel of 'amba, a very hot bright mango pickle, several people would rush out of their houses with bowls, bottles and other receptacles to get some for the price of one 'ana (four fils). A garrulous cobbler next door was once seen and heard celebrating a lottery win by standing at the front of his shop waiving the banknotes for all to see and envy. Further along there was the seller of chickens; the customer would choose one to be pulled out from the bamboo cage; one would then take it to the shohet standing close by to have it certified as kosher. The shohet would run his fingers expertly over its legs and wings to feel for bumps and deformities, followed, once satisfied, by his slitting the throat, then twisting the neck, leaving the warm crimson blood to drain into the heap of sawdust on the floor. The shohet would be given a fils or two for his pains, which he was supposed to account for as a gabelle, that is the communal tax levied on anything (mostly lamb) certified as kosher. The gabelle provided the major part of the funds required to maintain the communal Jewish institutions, and to help the poor. Further along, of particular interest in the street, was the scribe inscribing the text of the Torah or the Talmud on parchment. That work would have had to be done with extreme care and concentration since one slip and the whole thing would have to be discarded as "unclean".

Grandma Ini was treated with deference by the inhabitants of Liquorice Corner. That was due as much to the dignified way in which she conducted herself towards every trader as to the reputed wealth of her family. Her late husband Ezra was a successful wool merchant, a scion of the rich Tweg family, his brother Meir was reputed to be one of the four richest men in Baghdad. On her family side were the Inis, successful merchants with international ties. When her husband died leaving her with five daughters, having had no son, Rifqa's brother Jacob took all of them under his wing and made all the decisions for them. He was erudite, had travelled in Europe, and was the owner of several enterprises including an import business managed by his son Frank. When Jacob came to visit his sister everyone was in owe of him; his grave manner and the self- assurance with which he carried his wealth and assumed social superiority that dominated the conversation to the discomfort of even the headmaster. When it became known that Baghdad was to grow exponentially with thousands of new houses, Jacob and his son Frank bought a sheet glass factory in Belgium to meet the demand. Frank was later reputed a philanthropist, founder of a new Baghdadi synagogue that bore his name; also a school run along the upper class English public school system that was to overtake then supplant the French alliance schools. Another son of Jacob was a horticulturist. He had a big estate planted with orchards. Every year a horseman would come to Liquorice Corner with panniers of fruits for his auntie Rifqa.

The boy was happy at Grandma Ini's house. He would sit for hours next to her in an upper storey bay looking down on the people coming and going about their businesses. He also observed the funerals on the way to the Jewish cemetery.

There would be the deceased wrapped in a white winding sheet carried in an open coffin that would be used for a succession of funerals. When it was the funeral of a lady the open top of the coffin would be covered by her dresses and shawls spread over it so as to conceal the body from view.

The boy did well at the kindergarten and he liked Madame Sabbagh. She had no children of her own and treated him tenderly. She recognised an acuity which she mentioned to his father. That induced his parents to push him harder to progress in his studies to the extent of skipping the first year as he moved to the boys' school. He was beginning to read, and when he had a cold that kept him at home his father brought him a small children's book containing the adventures of Sinbad the Sailor. That was his first book and which he thereafter would cherish over all others. His father also brought him an exercise book. The father wrote the son's name in the book, in Arabic on the first page, Hebrew on the next, and asked him to practice copying them.

Grandma Ini is seriously ill. She is bed-ridden and receives several visits by the physician. At the suggestion of the headmaster, three doctors were called together for a joint consultation. After they had examined her in turn, they retired to the next room to compare their observations and to come up with a joint diagnosis. They concluded that the illness was terminal, a case of cancer that had spread, and for which there was no remedy. They left pain killers in ampoules.

The boy happened to pick one marked 'strychnine' which he showed to his father who was horrified and told him he must stay clear of all medicines and not to touch let alone pick any that was lying loose. Later, recounting the incident to his wife, the headmaster conjectured, citing Louis Pasteur, that the doctors' formula may have been intended to use a poison to overcome a worse one. Aunt Naʿima came to minister to her mother in the last days of her life. A few nights later everyone was awakened by the scream of Naʿima announcing the death of Grandma Ini.

The house was sold but with the sale delayed until the completion of the family's new house in Saadoon. In the meantime the buyer wanted to make a few changes, and an Arab builder arrived to carry out the work. He was genial, respectful and anxious that his work did not intrude too much on the family's daily routine. He was seen to be wilting in the afternoon of a hot summer's day, but he politely declined the offer of a drink of water, saying that he was a shiʿi, and said it with a gentle, genial smile. As he knocked the plaster off parts of a dividing wall a concealed niche was discovered containing an old ceramic set of dish, inkwell, sand holder and quill. There was then the question about the ownership of the set; whether it formed part of the house and belonged to the buyer, or was a chattel belonging to the family. The issue was resolved by an agreement to present it as a gift to Prayer House Zilkha.

It is summertime and everyone spends the night sleeping on the flat roof of their houses. Likewise, at Prayer House Zilkha the top Talmudic sitting is held on the roof illumined by a single electric bulb where the senior rabbi Yohanan sat, and two hurricane lamps for the others. There was a history about hurricane lamps. It was said that a fire once broke out caused by one that was knocked over; that the whole building was damaged, but not the room of Rabbi Yusuf of the blessed memory, and which contained his valuable library that was saved. Some onlookers claimed to have seen two angels warding off the flame; others said the angels were in the guise of firemen using buckets of water.

The boy was now a pupil at the Sassoon school and the owner of a French exercise book of which he was proud and which he carried everywhere. One evening he climbed the low roof boundary wall and landed on the neighbouring roof of Prayer House Zilkha. They told him that it was wrong to have a foreign book in a Jewish house of prayer, so he returned the book to his house then climbed back to see what was going on.

They were studying the gemara which comprised components of the Torah with rabbinical analyses and authoritative rulings. The gemara covered a large number of topics, the one under consideration on this occasion was 'The Egg' dealing with a number of situations such as: How kosher is an egg laid on the Sabbath? Is it permissible to pick it up on the Sabbath? If not then, when? What would be the position if the Sabbath happened to coincide with a High Holy Day such as the Rosh Hashana (New Year's Day)? Rabbi Yohanan led the discourse, and did so with a serene air and measured words that captivated the boy, while the others listened to the analyses accompanied by the Rabbi's own commentary with appreciation and respect. The boy sat at the head of the stairs keeping an eye on the copies of the gemara, and setting them together as a neat pile even as he listened avidly to the discussion. He gathered that for every question there were two answers or authorities, the one by Hillel the Babylonian, the other by Shammay of Safed. He also got the impression that Rabbi Yohanan favoured Hillel for being less strict. When the following day the boy related that to his father, the latter, a graduate of the Alliance with its generally secular liberal tradition, exclaimed that Shammay was 'mad', meaning a religious fanatic.

The second evening was a repeat of the first. But on the third Rabbi Yohanan, seeing the boy arrive, stopped in the midst of his discourse and told him he should go down to where Rabbi Moshe held a class for youngsters in the afternoon, and which would be more beneficial to him. The boy felt unhappy, took the instruction to be a demotion, but he had to comply. The boys at Moshe's class were older than him and received him raucously; one wag called out if he had come for his tea; another asked him if he wanted his milk with sugar; Rabbi Moshe could not control his class and did not even attempt to restrain them. Instead, he asked the boy his name. The boy said it was Fouad, and the teacher asked him what was his real name, insisting that he must have had a Jewish name, and told him to speak to his mother to find what it was. The boy said he would but in the event he forgot. When he turned up the next day Rabbi Moshe asked him his name. He repeated that it was Fouad and that he had no other. The teacher asked him if he had spoken to his mother, and he said that he had forgotten. The teacher was displeased with that answer and the other boys, noting the master's displeasure mocked the boy with the cry 'He forgot, he forgot'. Rabbi Moshe reminded him to ask his mother, and not to forget.

The boy was given to distraction, absent-mindedness and forgetfulness, a reminder of how he was in the first three years of his life. That was when he refused or was unable to speak, and which was hazarded to have been due to the time when he was an embryo and his mother tried to abort him. He went back to Rabbi Moshe's class the next day having again forgotten to ask his mother. Rabbi Moshe asked him if he had spoken to his mother. He could not face the derision and disgrace of owning up to more forgetfulness; he had to think of a name on the spot, and came up with the name Mattana that he had heard being called in the street. The master was delighted with the name, said what a good Jewish name it was. For the rest of the lesson he kept on addressing the boy as Mattana which caused him confusion and distress. He reported that experience to his mother when he returned home, and she rocked with laughter. A woman would have gone for years without being able to have children, then as she despaired of ever having any, she miraculously conceived and was delivered of one that she would acknowledge as a gift from the Almighty, a 'Mattana'. The boy's mother thought his choice of name hilarious as she already had six children, and with another on the way.

The boy had only one other day at Rabbi Moshe's class. At the end of the lesson, and as he was going down the stairs on his way home, Rabbi Yohanan came out from another room, and they walked down together. As they reached the threshold an Arab woman in black abaya holding a swaddled baby close to her chest prostrated herself before the Rabbi, took hold of the hem of his caftan, kissed it and begged the man of God to pray for the recovery of the child that was ill. The doctors had told her there was no medical cure, so she made her way to the mosque, and now to the synagogue for reinforcement. Rabbi Yohanan recited the 'Bless and heal Shabarach'. The woman said she will be walking next all the way to the house of the nuns to beg them to invoke the help of the mother of Jesus.

As in the case of all expectant mothers, the boy's mother was consumed by the thought of the one she was carrying and by the speculation whether it was a boy or a girl. It was the only topic for conversation when women friends and relatives called. There were opinions, theories, titbits, and tales that circulated widely at large while having no basis in reality, such as: the carrying position: high for boy, low for girl; the craving: salt or savoury for boy, sweets for girl; the way the mother walked, her moods and how she felt in the morning. To those general speculations there was another that absorbed the boy's mother, all alone. That related to the death of her mother. Should the baby turn out to be a girl then the desire to name her Rifqa will be overwhelming. She wondered whether fate cognisant of that fact would decree a girl to answer to that desire and keep the name of the deceased alive.

The arrival of another son was received with jubilation, a confirmation that the mother could still produce a child to present to her husband and, thinking back to the discussion with Umm Hashim in the days of Sabunchiyya, a validation of her and her husband's unscientific method of producing boys.

The father got busy employing a mohel to perform the ritual of circumcision of the new boy to be named Sabah, and he invited relatives and men friends to come witness it performed in the afternoon of the eighth day in fulfilment of the brit milah covenant. That would be followed by a celebratory party in the evening. It was a hot summer and the mother, since she gave birth, kept herself and the child down in the cool sardab. On the morning of the brit milah she noticed that the baby was not well which gave her concern. When the moment came for the child to be taken up for the procedure she handed him over with reluctance, but her concern at that stage was not to an extent that would impel her to call off the proceedings. The condition of the child Sabah worsened the following day, it so happened that a new doctor arrived in town, a Jew by the name of Doctor Aaronsohn, who had left Germany to escape racial persecution. The father always had a bias in favour of European culture and medical expertise. He took the child to Doctor Aaronsohn who diagnosed a summer cold and fever. A medicine was prescribed. The child died from suspected pneumonia. He was three weeks old. Two months after his arrival in Baghdad Doctor Aaronsohn, a victim of persecution, unhappy, lonely and sad committed suicide. The headmaster spent every remaining day of the school holiday overseeing the building work of the house in the Saadoon to expedite the work and bring it to completion.

Saadoon

It was built on a plot belonging to the mother, one of many plots of a new development that was to become a sought after new suburb boasting several embassies and the state hospitality 'White House'; as well as the open spaces, fountains and smallish lake of Saadoon Park. The plan for the house was approved by the father, the main feature distinguishing it from the old traditional Ottoman house was that this one was principally a closed box sitting in a garden while the other was blank walls surrounding an enclosed roofless courtyard open to the sky. The new house had a central lobby or hall with rooms off it, and it ended in a loggia and four steps leading down to the garden. The main part of the house consisted of one storey, but the father saw to it that the weight-bearing walls were of a sturdiness that would allow for another floor to be added in due course, such as to hopefully provide a home for one of the children. Beside the main part of the house there was a wing on two floors. The lower floor was at garden level and consisted of kitchen and utility rooms, while the upper floor was accessed from the main part of the house by a flight of stairs leading to the maids' room and a smaller end room off it with a balcony overlooking the garden. The end room was the boy's room. He was the only one who had a room all to himself, an acknowledgment of his being an assiduous solitary reader, would-be writer and collector of books. Another reason was that he was still his father's favourite since the last 'Battaween' child was not yet old enough to engage attention and sentiment such as to supplant him as the youngest son in the father's affection. Yet another reason was that the mother saw less moral hazard in his being at close proximity to the maids sleeping arrangement than might be the case with any of his older brothers.

The plots were uniform, each measuring 500 square meters. At the time that the family's house was being constructed there were only two other houses in the street, leaving open spaces which the *mu'dan* and *kasiba* occupied in the times of the flood. They were a low-grade urban proletariat that had no regular employment but sought a precarious living by doing odd jobs as and when required. They inhabited the mud and shanty town covering the plain behind the embankment that protected Baghdad from the seasonal surge of water that would rush down the Tigris and threaten to overwhelm it. In order to ease the pressure, breaches would be deliberately made in the levees and river banks upstream so as to divert the water to the vast open plain part of which was occupied by these poor people, in the process destroying their dwellings and forcing them to seek temporary shelter in whatever vacant space could be found on the city side of the embankment, and with a daily struggle to find drinking water to fill the buckets that the women carried on their heads. After the floods receded, they would go back behind the embankment to rebuild their mud houses and shanty huts, to crudely yet lovingly and proudly decorate them and inhabit them as their homes and so using them for weddings, circumcisions, religious festivals and devotional anniversaries as they waited resignedly for the next deluge.

The garden was made by the Iranian Ehsan. He was a brilliant landscape gardener, his expertise highly sought by the owners of the big imposing villas, the rich and the eminent. That he was now working on the relatively small garden of an undistinguished suburban house was due to his friendship with a merchant, father of a pupil at the headmaster's school, who made the introduction as a favour. Ehsan spent odd times designing the garden and seeing to it being well stocked, in part by cuttings, saplings and bedded plants from the other gardens that he was tending among which were the Italian and Belgian embassies nearby. The end result was a garden in the 'bagh' style of a walled Persian garden consisting of a central lawn field surrounded in turn by floral borders, a path, then by trees hugging the brick boundary wall. Ehsan managed to 'borrow' the sapling of an aromatic Australian eucalyptus that he planted at one corner and which will grow to its full height after ten years. For the rest there were fruit trees planted alongside the perimeter including apple, orange, lemon, prune and pomegranate. There was also a sunny corner planted with loofah which would come in handy for scrubbing and in the bathroom for exfoliating. When the garden was finished it had the look of the Kashan rug hung in the guests' room, which wasn't surprising since the Kashan style was derived from that of the traditional Isfahan garden. Some time after Ehsan had left, a strange cluster of plants appeared in a flower bed. After the poppy flowers had shriveled under the hot summer sun poppy seed pods were revealed. The mother made a cut in one of the pods and collected the latex to use as balm to toothache. And there was more to Ehsan than met the eye. His landscaping and gardening days were cut short by his arrest, conviction, imprisonment and deportation as a secret agent in the employ of the German legation; some who were close to the action would whisper in your ear that he had really been a double agent all along.

The Saadoon years were a period of exceptional political upheaval and shifts in social attitudes leading to a prevailing general sense of anxiety and insecurity. There were the wars in Europe and the Far East; Iraq was not directly involved but felt the repercussion. That was mirrored at home by insurrections, political assassinations, invasion and, worst of all, an armed conflict. That was when a nationalist Iraqi regime with a fascist leaning rose in defiance to Britain. The involvement of the army in shaping government policy can be said to have begun by an army coup led by General Bakr Sidqi in 1936; that was in the days of the Grandma Ini's house. The boy was at morning school assembly when two airplanes passed overhead close to roof top level followed by two muffled explosions which the boy heard but which meant nothing to him or to those near him. Later that morning as he was in class his father's school attendant Gourdji came to take him home. That was followed by his father himself coming home accompanied by a baggage carrier bearing two bags of rice and wheat from the grains warehouse.

As far as the family was concerned the war in Europe was not going well, and there was the disaster of the fall of France which filled them with foreboding and the father with despair. But that was not the general popular feeling. The boy would often accompany his father to the open- air tea house where Jewish men would sit in a knot in one part, while the others, Muslims, sat in groups in the other parts. The boy was free as a boy to walk all over the ground and so be privy to what was being said by the different groups. There was much elation at the setbacks being suffered by the English, and admiration for Hitler and his invincible armies sweeping with lightening speed all that stood before them, and getting ever closer to Iraq. After invading and occupying Crete all that stood between Hitler and Iraq was Syria then held by his erstwhile enemy now his ally, Petain. But while many of the Iraqis were cheered on by the news after decades of English direct and indirect domination which they loathed, none of that fascist leaning appeared to be directed against the Jews. In the teahouse Muslims and Jews treated each other with civility, while keeping themselves at a respectable distance apart. When all was said and done, they were all people of the same quarter. On one occasion the boy happened to find an unoccupied table with a set of dominoes. He played with the tiles setting them together and next to each other making different patterns. A man who came past asked him if it was a swastika as he patted him on the shoulder approvingly.

It was summertime and much of the living was in the open air on the flat roof top. Some airplanes were seen flying in the direction of the airport, German insignia clearly visible. That was followed soon after by a coup to overthrow the royalist pro-British regime. With the Regent and the prime minister in flight, Rashid Ali al-Gailani, nominal head of a fascist, nationalist political group, became the new prime minister. That spread alarm in the Jewish community; friends came over to discuss the event with the boy's father. He related to them what he was told by Sasson Khedhouri, Chief Rabbi and head of the Jewish community. Some time before, a son of al-Gailani fell seriously ill; Sasson Khedhouri called and prayed for the recovery of the child. Al-Gailani assured him that as long as it lay within his power no harm will ever come to any Iraqi Jew. Al-Gailani was a scion of a noble religious family and was not thought to have any personal animus towards the Jews, so he was thought likely to honour his promise; which was yet of limited comfort since the real rulers of the new insurgent regime were four colonels self-styled 'the golden square'. In the event there were no official measures affecting the Jews during the month that the insurgency and al-Gailani's premiership lasted. Several fascist measures were initiated at government level, but the insurgency did not last long enough to see any of them activated. There was a decree designating schoolboys as civil militia, their teachers as officers. The headmaster of Mas'uda Salman School stepped out one morning in the new uniform of a militia major. That was in compliance with the edict which was ignored by nearly everyone else. The same edict specified that any schoolboy who adhered to the militia code would have his bus fare reduced by half. To prove his entitlement a boy would need to have an identity card bearing his photograph and the signature of a school director. But the cards were rejected with contempt by the privately operated buses since the government did not provide any fund to compensate for the discount. The greatest alarm to the Jewish community was a proposal to introduce an identity card system albeit that it was stated to be applicable to everyone; there was not the time to incorporate that into law. The one measure that the junta successfully implemented was to require the schools and colleges to start every morning assembly with a heroic, some would say sentimental, military song:

> Behold the tips of spears shining amidst those hillocks
> Behold phalanxes of young men
> Of youth going forth to *jihad*
> O our mother you'll see us return victorious
> Else we would have been slain
> And if I should be martyred
> Rise, and call out the youth to *jihad*

It was at this time that the boy had his first love, puppy love, with Eveline of the same age, the youngest of three K sisters. The eldest was Louise, Margot came next, then ten year old Eveline. Theirs was a big corner house at the end of the street. The boy could no longer remember the first time he went inside it, but he was soon a frequent caller in the afternoon after school. He hardly ever saw Mr K who was in business, while Mrs K was always welcoming. She would start a conversation while the maid fetched the fruit juice and patisseries, while Eveline sat to listen and be enthralled by the boy confidently engaging her mother in what seemed like adult talk, the mother amused at his youthful boastfulness which she did nothing to diminish. She would then leave the two young ones to enjoy each other's company. Him saying that he would grow up to be a writer, her saying she will do the same; or he would talk of travelling to far-away lands, and her asking if he would take her along. One day an odd thing happened. He was sitting with the mother and the girls; the maid brought tumblers of some fruit juice on a tray. The boy lifted his to the light and said: "Its colour is the colour of amber". And they laughed. He had no idea what it meant, the words were of an advertisement that he had seen on a hoarding in town. The mother asked him what he did at school that morning – and it happened! He started to explain then stopped abruptly, a strange sensation came over him and his ability to talk was frozen, the same as it had been in his early years in Sabunchiya. The others did not know why he stopped talking and the mother said she understood what he was saying and encouraged him to continue, which he could not do, nor give a reason. He put down the tumbler and went home. He returned three days later and was welcomed by the maid and the mother with the same amiability as before. When left alone with Eveline she asked him if she had done anything to upset him; he reassured her; and she asked him if he would still marry her.

Then there was the insurrection and after, the K family went away for their summer holiday in their favourite mountain resort of Zahle in Lebanon. There was a big change on their return. The maid stopped him at the front door saying that Louise was not well and they did not want to have visitors while she was in that condition. When that

HOUSES

happened again, and then a third time the boy took it as a rebuff and stopped calling. Then it began as a whisper, but before long became known in the neighbourhood that Louise had gone incurably mad. That was followed by Bertha coming home from school one day saying that Margot had missed attending, while rumour had it that Louise had hit her on the head which also made her insane. It would be six years before the boy saw Eveline again.

The house was at a stone's throw of the army academy, and that attracted the attention of the English air force. One could differentiate between the warring airplanes -- white Iraqi, black or half-and-half English, the latter not coming to bomb but overfly to observe. Every time an English one appeared, anti-aircraft batteries opened up from the academy. After one such engagement the boy found a shell casing on the roof of the house which he kept to show to his father who was alarmed to realise how close they were to the war front.

The war was not going well for the fascist junta. The end when it came was sudden. The British army that had come to restore the royalist regime reached the outer approaches beyond the river and halted. The junta was now in flight. There was no government in control. Law and order had ceased to exist. The last of the insurgent to flee took the road to Tehran. Interviewed on his arrival he said that he left Baghdad awash with blood. That was very much the hyperbolic bluster of a defeated leader. But real blood was now being shed accounting for more than a hundred Jewish lives. The fascist cadres and some of the supporters of the junta may well have wanted to unleash a general massacre; but no sooner did they start to put their plan into action than it was overwhelmed by what was to be known as the Farhud or pillage in which wave upon wave of *kasiba* and *shargawis* descended into the city, braking into shops and homes and taking away whatever could be carried. Killing Jews may not have been intended but would have happened as a collateral activity. That no more lives were lost during the two days of the Farhud was due to geography and the general decency of the Arab inhabitants. Baghdad could then be said to be a Jewish metropolis in the sense that New York was talked of as a Jewish city. The Jewish community measured more than one hundred thousand or a fifth of the total population. In recent years a large part of the community, generally the more affluent, had moved out of the city centre to new, almost exclusively Jewish suburbs of detached villas and wide streets. The rest continued to live in the old parts with their narrow streets and unbroken lines of tenements and houses leaning against each other – some in the old Jewish quarter, others in mixed but predominantly Arab streets. The Jewish shops and homes in the old parts took the brunt of the Farhud. The shops were singled out by a process of elimination. The shutters of almost all the Arab shops were over-painted by words writ large declaring the owner to be an Arab, a Muslim, a nationalist. The Arab houses were identified by their owners standing guard over them. And there were cases when an Arab householder would point to the houses of his Jewish neighbours as much to divert the wild mob hungry for pillage away from his property as out of malice. In many cases, as a Jewish home was broken into those who were able-bodied took to the roof, then climbed over one or more low boundary walls until they were received and given sanctuary, in many cases by an Arab householder. Such an escape from peril was all but impossible for those living in the outer suburbs. Each house was an island unto itself. At the approach of danger there would be no avenue for escape, no sanctuary, nor even the physical and moral support that those living in the inner city derived from each other. But for the two days of the Farhud the suburbs were in remission. It was the turn of those in the old parts. Every time a Jewish street was attacked a blood chilling scream was let out which was carried far into the evening stillness of a city that had stopped working and playing, in which anyone who was not involved in the Farhud stayed at home behind locked and bolted doors.

Those living in the suburbs heard the succession of screams and the cries of women and children coming ever louder and nearer as a death sentence. They were helpless. There was no way of defending themselves. Nor of getting out of harm's way. All thought, action and reason were submerged in the panic. The boy was told by his brother Sami, voice quivering with terror: "When they come, you hide under the wardrobe". In the house next door an old man could no longer bear the suspense. He went out to the balcony and emitted a shrill blood curdling scream as of an animal at bay. The father was concerned for the Persian carpets and rugs; he had them piled up and stowed in the void beneath the stairs. The bigger boys then contrived to close the opening by a crude panel of board and mud so bizarre that it would not have fooled anyone. The only one who had a residue of resolve was the mother; seeing a group of some five *shargawis* sauntering outside she said she was not afraid of 'that lot' and will fight them.

On the third day of the Farhud a soldier in uniform carrying a rifle appeared in the street. Some years before, uncle Moshi had befriended a military man and done him a favour. The man was now a high ranking army officer and the time was opportune for him to repay the favour. He sent his orderly to protect Moshi. By then the Farhud had all but ended. The royalist army had entered the city; some shots were fired, some rioters killed, the rest returned to their streets, homes and shanty town while law and order were beginning to be restored. When the Farhud started, sister Bertha was staying at uncle Barukh's house in the city centre and there was no knowing what may have happened to her. The father then arranged for the soldier to accompany the boy and go look for and hopefully bring back the girl. With no transport, the armed soldier and the boy walked all the way from Saadoon to Taht al-Takia where there was an emotional reunion with Bertha. She was unharmed and had lived in trepidation not knowing what would happen to her nor what might have befallen the rest of the family. All three walked back to Saadoon along streets devoid of life, an eerie silence enveloping the city. They could see some shops that had been vandalised, while all the others were closed with shutters over-painted with words indicating that they were not Jewish property. There was not a single policeman in sight.

The following day uncle Sasson and his wife Lulu came to stay and relate their Farhud experience. Their house in Hayderkhana was broken into and all the contents gone. As the mob was breaking the door, they took the stairs to the roof then climbed several low walls until they were received by Abu Ahmad who offered them sanctuary, the same as two other Jewish families before them. The Jewish families shared a room apart from the host family and were provided to eat what the host family had to eat. On the third day Abu Ahmad came covered in embarrassment. He said that they were about to run out of food and that he did not have enough money to send one of his sons to see if he could buy ought in the street. He asked if any of his guests were in a position to contribute, and a small collection was raised. The banks were closed during the Farhud.

Things calmed down. The Regent came on the radio to describe his near-death experience as the treasonable coup started, and to reassure the people that things had now returned to normal, and to urge everyone to be calm, attend to their jobs, businesses and tasks with renewed vigour as they contemplated the future with confidence. People started to emerge from their houses and you would find the odd corner shop selling provisions, also the odd privately operated bus. As the boy was walking with his father close to their house three men saw them and came across. They were regular customers of the tea house and were known to have pro-German sympathies. One of them was the man who had congratulated the boy for what he mistook to be a swastika. They expressed their shame for the Farhud and the loss of life, looked forward to the criminals being brought to justice, while they reaffirmed their solidarity with the Jews – their cousins and neighbours. The schools were reopened after the Farhud, and the boy took the regular privately operated Saadoon to town bus. As he tendered the fare the driver told the conductor not to accept it, "It's on me today" he called out. A vicarious expiation for the communal wrongs? Relief that normal business was resuming? Perhaps a mixture of both!

On one spring day's morning, bright as the day of festival with a clear blue sky and a light breeze. Two pigeons pecking for their breakfast, and oleander was in bloom adding colour to Eastern Gate. The square at the Eastern Gate was milling with people, serious looking men on their way to work and school children with satchels on the way to school. There was a gibbet in the middle of the square. A man in the uniform of a middle ranking officer gesticulating, urging the Jews to feast their eyes, and they avert them. He gets hold of the schoolboy and turns him to face the hanged man who was condemned for murdering Jews in the Farhud. The boy disengages himself and turns away. No, not a murderer but a miserable lifeless body at the end of a rope, feet not touching the ground.

Then there was the German invasion of the Soviet Union and new voices were now to be heard in the tea house. A small knot of men, effendis and socialists including a lawyer and a teacher talked animatedly of the great leader, comrade Stalin. They would hug the radio when the news bulletin was read and seemed anxious at the inexorable advance of the Hitlerites deep into Russia in the face of a heroic resistance by the Red Army. That mirrored the dread of the Jews at the news that a German army had already plunged deep into the Caucasus, hence just a short step to Iran and Iraq. Then there was a great jubilation as the tables were turned with the momentous defeat of the German armies at Stalingrad and the reversal they suffered in North Africa. They were forced to pull out of the Caucasus; Iraq was saved and the Jews felt reprieved. The socialist group grew bigger with more joining it, newcomers listening avidly to the news from the front, of daily successes of the Red Army announced as orders of the day of Generallisimo Stalin. Also listening to talks of Marxism, Lenin, the Bolshevik Revolution and the constitution of the Soviet Union. The boy now a youth loved to pull a chair and sit to listen to their discourses, take in their enthusiasm and hopes as they spoke of the future. They were going to create a brave new world in which everyone was equal. Muslims, Christians and Jews all treated the same and living in amity, each with socialist each. Where there will be no rich and poor, no privileged few with cars while others struggled for a bus; where the resources will be plentiful so that it will be a case of from each according to his ability and to each according to his needs. All of that would be unfolded the moment capitalism was abolished and replaced by a free socialist society. A newcomer asked what was capitalism and that was explained; another took the discussion further by asking how capital was created and was answered by a reference to Karl Marx's great foundational book 'Capitalism' (*Das Kapital*) and the chapter dealing with 'surplus value'. That passed over the heads of the youth and many of the others.

The youth was smitten. He went to the corner bookshop near his school which was known to handle left wing literature, and got a book in Arabic written by a member of the Syrian Communist Party comparing the respective economic models of capitalism and socialism. The reactionary media lauded the liberal -- that is capitalist -- economic and social model. Some categorised it as the best, others as the least bad, model that was ever devised, its bedrock being an open competition that would lead to the improvement of the product and the lowering of the price.

In the same breath socialism was derided as economically inefficient while failing to take account of human nature. Contrary to those views the Syrian communist postulated that the socialist model was more efficient economically and more moral socially. To him competition was wasteful. Taking a broad brush approach he posited that a lot of human resources and endeavours were wasted when manufacturers and traders resorted to advertising in order to promote one brand ahead of other brands in a field in which there was little to differentiate between them. Thus, competition did not create value in itself, and added nothing to economic progress and human happiness. The youth was impressed by that simple but potent argument which he could illustrate by an example close to home. His brothers were now traders in the Shorjah market, dealing in, inter alia, imported disposable safety razor blades. They handled more than a dozen competing brands of what was essentially the same article. Thus, the socialist system would be more beneficial, obviating the need for people to fight each other for space. Treated as equals in what they offered and what they received there would be no big gap between the strong and the weak, the rich and the poor – hence no urge for people to struggle against each other, while anti-social evils such as egoism, exploitation, and envy would be held in check. Most of all, the socialist model was more moral for being more just.

The youth was seduced by the socialist exposition and carried it to his school mates and there was soon a cell of crypto revolutionary youngsters committed to the cause. But nobody knew what that cause was, while they elected a committee with the boy as leader adopting for the purpose the hated democratic, reformist, conservative electoral system of casting votes in secret. But once constituted they had to find a cause for which they would fight to vindicate their revolutionary pretensions. They made the mistake of choosing a wrong target. The school day was determined by the exigencies of the climate, the summer in particular. It would start at seven in the morning and end at two in the afternoon with one short break at midday. No food was provided nor could it be had other than from a small school tuck shop that offered few unappetising items, while the students were not free to go out to the street during the break to look for better choices. That was an unsatisfactory state of affairs fit to engage the attention of rebels looking for a cause. It was capable of stirring malcontent, particularly coupled with the fact that the prices charged by the tuck shop were alleged to be more than could cost on the outside. The true target of the malcontent should have been the school administration. Instead, the troublemakers, the youth at their head, initiated a boycott of the tuck shop, the instruction going forth by word-of-moth. The tuck shop was in fact independent of the school, the business owned and operated by a family of modest means who were affected badly by the boycott. They complained to the headmaster as they pleaded with the boys to lift the boycott which was threatening their livelihood. The boy and another close follower and friend were hauled to the headmaster's office where they received a severe dressing down. With the youth identified as the ringleader of the communist misadventure he now faced the ultimate sanction of expulsion which was only averted by the intervention of his father. The boycott collapsed with ignominy to the leadership; and it marked for other students the end of their flirtation with radical politics. But not entirely. Years later, the youth by then a law-abiding university student in London was mortified to learn through the grapevine that some of his school revolutionary mates had joined the ranks of the Communist Party, which he himself never did, and that one of them had left the movement after finding himself exposed to mortal peril as a member of the Central Committee. The ill-conceived boycott taught the youth a bitter lesson which was the need to be quite sure in one's own mind what one was seeking before taking the first step.

The youth's deep involvement in that little thought-out juvenile political activity did no good to his studies. He could always be counted on to produce a good Arabic essay or short story which the teacher would read to the class as a model. But as for the rest his marks were abysmal. He was shamed every time his father came home with a glum expression after he had met one of his teachers and asked about his progress. The worst was the French teacher who answered that the lad could not sink any lower. Against all expectations including his own he passed the official French *Brevet* which marked the conclusion of his French school years. It was in the middle of the *viva* that the news was received of his winning the intra-school short story competition; his entry featured a poor, hungry waif named Tamata disputing a loaf of bread with the scurvy dog of the neighbourhood. His immediate reward was some money for books, but more significantly the intimation that upon finishing his studies and passing the *Matriculation* (University of London external examination) he will be favourably considered for an English scholarship. That was provided out of a bequest set up by Lord Khedourie of Jewish Baghdadi origin that was entrusted to the Anglo- Jewish Association. The income would be used to fund scholarships to study in England, to be awarded to young men and women of the Iraqi Jewish community, and recommended for the award by the Community Board of Education, The following year the youth was to go up to the top secondary school where the majority of the subjects were taught in English. He went to McKenzie's bookshop with the prize money and came out with Plato's Republic. He went to a coffee house, sat at a table next to the street and started to leaf through it. He was engrossed in the Socratic dialogues and dialectic exchanges when he was suddenly jolted by "What are you reading?" He got up and Eveline was standing next to him. She asked him if he was still writing, and congratulated him on winning the short-story competition. She looked sad, said the family were planning to emigrate to Palestine. And it happened again! There was a lot he wanted to say but could not find his voice. 'So long' she said and walked away. Forty ears later he was on a visit to Israel, his very first, and on his last day in Tel-Aviv it occurred to him to ask about Eveline. He was told that she lived in Jerusalem on her own, did not marry, but spent all her days writing. Jerusalem was only forty miles away, which was tempting. But he was then in his late fifties. He had been happily married for thirty years, had many children and grandchildren. He looked in the mirror, pondered it, and the distance became unbridgeable. A regret he took to his grave.

The youth now a young man started well at the 'English' school almost catching up with the top of the class. After the debacle of the ill-thought out boycott his radical fervour was moderated while he continued to be drawn to left-wing politics and Marxist ideology. But his interest now turned to writing in which he was encouraged by the school. The Principal was a poet and man of letters, while the teacher of Arabic was a covert communist. He joined with other students in getting permission to start a student weekly wall journal, a so-called editorial board was self-constituted with him as editor in chief. The Journal's aim was creative writing including short stories and articles, and translations of texts from the French and English classics. His own contribution was the occasional article dealing with a social question, plus an interview that he had with an eminent English writer and journalist who happened to be passing. Polemics were shunned and politics avoided. While the youth was respected by his peers he yet came under attack for his political belief -- from the Zionists on one side and more vociferously from the other side by members of the underground National Liberation Party, the communist party by a different name. During the period of his editorship there was one contribution by the Arabic teacher which was not openly political, and the blessing of a short poem composed by the Principal. When the young man completed his two years of study at the English school the editorship passed on to his best friend whom he later discovered to have been a member of the Zionist underground.

The young man had ambition to combine the law, writing and journalism for a career. The English school was close to the courts complex and to coffee houses nearby which were meeting places of the *literati*. A typical coffee house would have a newsvendor standing outside with all of the ten or more titles, it is remarkable how many Iraqi newspapers existed then. A lawyer after court, a teacher after school, a professional politician dreaming political dreams or anyone with literary pretensions and social ambitions would for the price of an istikan of tea spend hours going through the newspapers one after the other, lent by the newsvendor to read for the price of buying one. The young man loved to go to the courts, observe the idiosyncrasies of judges and the rhetorical tricks of the advocates using metaphors and analogies to raise the merit of a client's case to a higher level than was warranted by the bare facts. And there was the curious procedure in some of the courts in which a defendant in a criminal trial would be cross-examined with his advocate standing one pace behind him or to his side prompting him how to answer a question.

One day after perambulating in the court complex the young man walked into a coffee house nearby which was the haunt of the political activists. He saw a serious looking man walk in who was acknowledged and greeted by about half the men while the others averted their eyes. The one setting next to the young man told him in a low voice that the pallid looking new arrival was 'Abdallah Mas'ud al-Qurayni, the former head of the communist party. His history was that he was betrayed to the authorities and was given a long prison sentence. He was immediately succeeded by Yusuf Salman Yusuf (non de guerre Fahd) who seized the party press and discontinued the title of the underground newspaper *al-Sharrara* (the Spark in Arabic, the corresponding word in Russian being *Iskra* which was the title of Lenin's first periodical). The new leader Fahd replaced it with the title *al-Qa'ida* meaning 'the Base'. He explained the change by an editorial in the first number: The top of the party had been swept away, but the base remained indestructible, while alleging that his predecessor had let down the cause. There were some who suggested that the betrayal of Mas'ud to the police and his replacement as leader were intimately connected. ʿAbdallah Masʿud did not serve his full prison term and it was rumoured that he owed his early release to the intervention of the British after he had written to the ambassador pleading for his freedom. That fuelled the accusation that he had sold out which he vehemently denied. It was more likely that the British intervened to secure his release hoping thereby to embarrass the incumbent leadership of the party and to spread mischief in its ranks. The young man could now see how fractured the Iraqi left was. Outside the monolithic communist party, it consisted of many factions; theoreticians and Marxist ideologues, each seeking to recruit some disciples to validate their particular stance in the movement, but without producing a meaningful practical political effect. Several claimed to have been invested by the imprimatur of Moscow or the Comintern while there was no way to prove or disprove the claim, a situation which some wag summed up by citing a notorious saying, "Everyone claims a tryst with Layla, which Layla does not admit". It was left to the leadership of the communist party to lay more stress on organisational matters and recruitment than in theoretical debates, thus attracting and maintaining a loyal base of members in the trade unions and the professions that would be counted on to respond to the call and who together represented a significant political force nationally.

On one occasion the young man entered a coffee house and was surprised at the absence of the loud confused noises that are commonly associated with such meeting places. The radio was on and everyone was listening attentively, a few taking notes, to the eminent Iraqi poet al-Jawahiri declaiming his panegyric at the millennial celebration in Syria of the death of al Ma'arri, great medieval Arabian writer and philosopher. As the broadcast ended the hubbub returned with people debating the merits of the poem and supporting their respective contentions by citing particular verses. The young man himself was particularly struck by the passage describing the blind al-Ma'arri 'reclined on his straw mat, taking sips of water from the earthenware jug beside him, while above his head were shelves bearing his books'. The young man then got into conversation with the publisher of a daily newspaper who offered him an unpaid week's experience as a sub-editor. His task was to act as an additional proof-reader. The compositors would arrange the entries and blocks for each sheet, take a paper print which a sub-editor would go over to check for mistakes. But however many times a proof reader went over a text there always remained the risk of his missing some. That's when a second or additional proof-reader becomes useful. On one occasion, as the block was going to print. a small blank patch was noticed. It was unintended and had to be filled. He was teasingly told to think of something, so he came up with "Earthquake in Costa Rica – damage to buildings – no human casualties". That was his first shameful involvement in false news. He also had one contribution published in the newspaper, on the front page with the banner headline 'World Exclusive'. It was his translation from English of an interview with Madame Sun Yat-seen. Sun Yat-seen was the founding father of the Kumintang and of the Republic of China of which he was its first president (1911-2). When he died, he was succeeded by Chiang Kai-shek as leader of the Kumintang. At the time of the interview the Kumintang under the leadership of Chiang had been at war with the Chinese communists for more than twenty years. The significance of the interview was that Sun Yat-seen's widow, a prominent politician in her own right, was now declaring her support for the communists led by Mao Zedong. The article was well received in left-wing circles and went some way to rehabilitate the young man's standing with the communists. After that article which was the young man's first published work, he was emboldened to self-publish another, a small book entitled *Why War?* Which was a translation from English of an exchange of letters between Einstein and Freud postulating on the causes and origins of conflict. The exchange was made with the First World War and its aftermath as a backdrop and with concern for the next that was looming. The young man, having demonstrated his ability to translate from English coupled with his left-wing sympathies was then asked to vet the translation of *How to Win the Peace* authored by Harry Pollitt, General Secretary of the British Communist Party. The Arabic translation was serialised in a Baghdadi newspaper. He vetted two instalments. Then the authorities intervened and the serialisation was discontinued.

The young man made friends across the religious divide; secularists, progressives, and socialists. Two of the closest for a time were Thamir and Ali. Thamir was a Sunni, his family of landowners and merchants, his half-brother a prominent lawyer with good connections already spoken of as the Minister of Justice that he later became. They lived in a big house in Taher Street, and Baghdadi houses did not come more aristocratic or more Sunni than Taher Street. By contrast Ali was a Shi'i from Shatra city in southern Iraq, the eldest son of a grocer. At school he had come under the influence of a communist teacher. Not long after his sixteenth birthday he moved to Baghdad leaving a scandal behind. That was when he fell into a conversation with a fellow traveller who got off the Amara bus and had a few hours to kill before the evening bus that would take him to Nasiriya. Ali, extending hospitality, took him on a tour of the town, stopping for refreshments at coffee houses and soft drink stalls. In the evening, once the Nasiriya bus was well away, he went round telling everyone that his companion had been a Jew. The following day his father put him on the Baghdad bus while a good proportion of the town went carrying tumblers, plates, cups and utensils towards the river to have them cleansed. The first time that Ali told the story he added in defence of his people that they were not ignorant racists, just plain ignorant. They had no enmity towards the Jews. It was just that in the battle of Karbala in 680 the Umayyad army of Yazid prevented Imam Husain, his family and retinue from getting to the river. Even the infant great-grandson of the Prophet suffered thirst while, so it was written, unclean beasts, Jew and pig were free to drink their fill. Anticipating a place in the pantheon of twentieth century revolutionaries, Ali wanted his obituary to make clear that he was not only a Muslim and a Shi'i but more precisely of the Ja'fari faith

The young man's family had great reservations about his associating with men who were communist and Muslim. They feared for his safety as the authorities kept a vigilant eye on the activities of the Bolsheviks and resorted to drastic measures including arrest, torture and imprisonment to suppress what they regarded as subversion and treason. The family was likewise exercised by the moral hazard to which the young man was exposed as he associated with strangers, some older than him. They tried hard to persuade him to sever his relations with men who were unknown to them but whom they perceived at a distance as exerting a bad influence leading him astray and deflecting him from his studies. But those concerns were misplaced. While in his immediate family circle he was thought of as a Bolshevik, the reality was that he was only moving in the cautious fringes of the left-wing movement, at a distance from the subversive activities of the communists, members of the underground National Liberation Party in particular, which was attracting many young persons and students to its ranks. Forming a trio with Thamir and Ali the most risky enterprise that they were involved in was spending the day of 'Ashura in the holy city of Kazumiya, an annual event commemorating the battle of Karbala and the martyrdom of Imam Hussain, a Jew and a Sunni passing off as Shi'i and Ja'fari . As regards the moral hazard the prevailing position in the close circle of his friends, as indeed in the left-wing movement generally, was the observance of a strict conservative unspoken moral code in relation to sexual matters, the perception being that in a pre- revolutionary situation all thoughts, theories and feelings including normal sexual urges should be committed to the overthrow of the reactionary regime and the ushering of a pure, unadulterated socialist dream. That left no room for levity, shenanigans, laxity in social conduct and sexual exploitation. That unspoken strict moral code extended to the avoidance of bad language and the shunning of whore houses perceived as places of sexual exploitation. The young man was to wait until he was in his twenties before he lost his virginity as a university student in London. The friendly association of the trio did not endure. There was first the departure of Thamir to England to study engineering at the University of Leeds. That was followed by preparation being made for the Jewish young man to travel to France to study medicine. Ali was left feeling diminished by the loss of his friends and by the fact that, as fate had decreed, he had no formal scholastic achievements, nor any realistic hope of acquiring any. He would say defiantly, citing Lenin, that his was the university of life while he set about finding new friends and acolytes.

In his last year at school the young man yearned, like so many in his position, to travel abroad to complete his education. His family wanted him to study medicine and he wrote for details to several American universities. Eventually he settled on going to France instead. The mother had sold the last of her building plots and given the money to Sami and Salim to set up in business, and it was now their turn to support him in his studies abroad. One of his former French teachers recommended the medical school of the University of Nancy while he was more attracted to the Sorbonne. He received acceptance from both, and the family favoured Nancy. In their eyes it provided the calmer life of a big provincial city, capital of Lorraine, than the hectic atmosphere of Paris with all its distractions and political incitements. The choice was settled by Nancy adding the offer of a student accommodation. The offer accepted, the mother got down to getting the young man well provided for the journey: warm clothing for the colder climate, new tailored suits, a trunk to hold all that he would need and some French francs in addition to traveller's cheques. Then within days of his flying out, a disaster. Trouble had flared up in Palestine and an edict was now issued banning Jews from leaving the country. But as things worked out that was providential. In the meantime Salim had become addicted to gambling, lost a lot of money in card games the extent of which, and of his alleged gambling debts, were unclear. Unsavoury men would call claiming what was owed to them and intent on recovering them. The family was no longer in a position to fund the younger son's further education and could not have been able to continue to support him if he had already embarked on his medical studies in France.

The young man now remembered his winning the short story competition and what was intimated at the time about an English scholarship. He reminded the Community Board of Education of that, and it resulted in the Anglo-Jewish Association granting him a scholarship for a three-year study in England, to be taken up once the travel ban was lifted. But there was no telling when the ban would be lifted; he had to work while waiting, and so was recruited as a clerk by the Imperial Bank of Iran which was British in all but name. Founded in London in 1889 its biggest single shareholder was the eastern trading house of David Sassoon.

He was happy working at the Bank. It was a plum first job for a young man straight out of secondary school. His starting monthly salary was more than his father was earning as the headmaster of a primary school. And it was a genial working environment; a small community in which everything was ordered, every task defined as was the hierarchy without it being oppressive. At the top were three Englishmen from Britain, the rest were some forty local men half of whom were Jewish the other half Christian including four Armenians and two Assyrians. In addition, there was a few auxiliary staff employed as messenger boys, doormen, and general dog's bodies. At the very top of that hierarchy was Mr Platt, the overall director. Nobody knew what he actually did. He spent every minute of his working hours in his room. You only saw him as he walked in from the street at opening time and walked out at closing time; a tall figure, straight as a ramrod, stern, serious, not casting an eye on nor acknowledging any of his staff as they attended to their tasks; nor did he appear to invite anyone's attention or human contact. The young man was astonished to see him one evening at the Concert Hall listening to such mundane and human thing as a Chopin minuet. Mr Platt a feeling man after all. Next to Mr Platt in the bank's hierarchy was Mr Jeffries, a young man in his late thirties, always cheerful and approachable. Told that the young man, new recruit, was a writer he asked him if he would bring along some of his stuff for him to read; which the young man did not do; his English was not up to scratch and he would have been embarrassed. The third Englishman, Mr Rose, was in his twenties, probably a trainee straight after public school and national military service, He was sociable, happy to maintain an easy relationship with the non-English staff, and behave as if he was one of them. He tried his hand at writing poetry and came one day with a short poem containing a description of the 'cream cheese moon', and asked the young man what he thought of it. Of the locals, the top man was

Leon Bushara, a Christian, who was in charge of the general banking business. He ranked immediately below Mr Jeffries in the hierarchy. It was Leon Bushara who had employed the young man.

Gourdji Barmagh's place was outside that hierarchy. He had a room next to Mr Platt's, was the only one who would walk into his room without knocking. He had nothing to do with the general banking business of current accounts, the handling of cheques and the transfers of money. His position was that of commercial manager overseeing the investment in local enterprises, and lending. Over the years he had established a network of contacts in the local markets, acquired an extensive knowledge which allowed him to evaluate the risk of a proposed loan or investment. This was the most risky part of the business of banking and also the most profitable. The young man spent the first three months working in 'Current Accounts', and was then moved to work as an assistant to Barmagh, and in that capacity be in charge of the "Bills Discounted' section. That taught him a lot about the markets and brought him into contact with business people. Later still he was offered the job of second cashier with a significant increase in salary. But that was subject to his family standing as guarantors. He discussed it at home, and it was decided to decline the offer. The decision was influenced by the fact that he was judged to be disposed to daydreaming and absent mindedness.

When the young man started working for the bank, he turned his back on politics and distanced himself from political friends. But he was not deflected from his socialist beliefs. He continued to consider himself a Marxist. Then in 1946 the powers that be declared that henceforth a party political system would be allowed to operate. Licences were granted for the founding of five political parties, one of which was the National Democratic Party which soon attracted thousands of members; the young man was one of them. At that stage the nascent party had no constitution nor manifesto. Those who were joining were in effect putting their trust in and declaring their support for the three leading founding members: The top man Kamil al-Chaderchi was a romantic figure, outspoken and lively, owner and editor of *al-Ahali* newspaper; he was well-to-do living on the income of lands he inherited from his father. The next one Muhammad Hadid was a member of a leading Mosuli family; quiet and cautious he studied at the London School of Economics under Harold Laski. The third man Husain Jamil was regarded as one of the ablest court advocates in Baghdad, a scion of the Jamil family, leaders of the Qanbar Ali district of Baghdad. The Social Democratic Party had a precedent in al-Chaderchi's al-Ahali group that had a hand in the 1936 Baqr Sidqi's coup. As first step to inaugurate parliamentary democracy, the government planned a general election to take place in February 1947. A transitional election-conducting cabinet was constituted under the premiership of the perennial, pro-British Nuri al-Sa'id. The National Democrats accepted a seat in that cabinet, Hadid to be minister of finance. The party had its first meeting in April and that was followed by its first congress in November. The young man happened to go to one of the party's weekly meetings, said a few words, and was elected a delegate.

The congress was held at a big hall and attended by some four hundred delegates. It was intended to adopt the party's constitution; but that was preceded by a succession of sycophantic speeches from the hall supporting the decision to enter the cabinet. A speaker would start by saying how surprised he had been when he first heard the news, and that when people asked him for his reaction he had to confess that he did not know what to make of it; but he then looked at it more closely when it dawned on him how correct was the decision to enter the government; good for the party, boded well for the future and was in the national interest. The high table listened to the panegyrics and were suffused in self-satisfaction and the glow of self-righteousness. After those orations the gathering got down to consider the draft constitution. It consisted of rules that fixed the rights and obligations of the membership and regulated such things as admission, subscription and discipline; also the conduct of meetings. Instead of presenting the rules as one collection and getting it approved as a single item the leadership chose to deal with each rule and sub-rule separately to be approved by the raising of hands. The leadership was blessed by eminent lawyers some of whom sat at the high table, so it was surprising how badly drafted were the rules. The young man himself interjected on two occasions to point to an uncertain syntax and a contradiction. That resulted in hurried discussions, admissions and corrections on the spot, while al-Chaderchi, secretly pleased by the discomfiture of his learned friends, beamed a big smile to the young callow delegate.

Suddenly there was a dramatic intervention, and Kamil Qazanchi made his appearance on the political stage. Hardly anything was known about his background and family life, and there were other serious gaps in his biography. A member of the Baghdad society of advocates he was acknowledged as one of the best, having a vast knowledge of the law and the gifts of a good voice and mastery of words. He was believed to be a non-practising Christian from Mosul. There was talk of a shadowy brother who was an unlicensed moneylender. Kamil spoke perfect English and displayed serious knowledge of English law, the United Kingdom's political scene including the proceedings in Parliament; but nothing was known as to how he came to acquire such knowledge. He was a communist to his fingertips yet did not adhere to the communists of Fahd and joined instead the reformist, liberal, left of centre Naional Democratic Party. Qazanchi's true model and hero was D.N. Pritt, British barrister and member of the Labour Party who was a fervent supporter of the Soviet Union and whose Stalinist convictions outlasted the death of Stalin and were unshaken by the Twentieth Congress revelations of soviet abuse. Pritt was included in Orwell's list of names of writers and others who sympathised with the communists. Orwell referred to him as 'perhaps the most effective pro-soviet publicist in the country, almost certainly an underground communist'.

Qazanchi chose his dramatic interruption well. Instead of going to the front of the hall to use the microphone and face the delegates, he chose to make his address from the vacant space at the back, relying on his powerful voice and clear delivery. That meant that the delegates listening to him shuffled in their seats and half-turned to see him as they turned their backs to the high table. He started by questioning the usefulness of the proceedings. The delegates were being asked to adopt the articles of association, but where was the memorandum of association? He was making an analogy with the constitution of a typical English company which would have a memorandum of association declaring its objects or aims, and separate articles of association regulating the position between the members. He had to repeat his question twice and to clarify it before the high table responded, Husain Jamil saying irritably that everyone knew what the party stood for which was indicated in the very name. The party stood for national democracy. Qazanchi retorted that the party was not indicating where it stood in relation to a host of real issues that he went on to enumerate and which included such topics as agrarian reform, taxation and the redistribution of wealth, illiteracy and women's rights. He then criticised the leadership for accepting the invitation to be part of a cabinet led by the imperialist agent Nuri al-Sa'id. They did so, he alleged using an English political metaphor, because they were beguiled by the hand extended to them in a smooth silken glove and not feeling the iron fist under it. He concluded by saying that the conference was a waste of time, a sham. That gave Husain Jamil the opportunity to hit back: the delegates were not there to be lectured to, and if Qazanchi thought the meeting a sham, there was nothing preventing him from leaving, whereupon Qazanchi walked out followed by a dozen of others. Standing outside they soon discovered that they were not all of the same persuasion. They discussed, debated, agreed and disagreed. Soon there was only Qazanchi and five staunch followers. They went to a tearoom and agreed a broad programme for a new faction in the name of The Progressive Wing of the National Democratic Party. Qazanchi then led the way to the Post Office where he sent a telegram to D. N. Pritt giving him the good news. The young man was the sixth founding member. The leadership of the Social Democratic Party saw it as a communist demarche to seize control. They expelled five of the rebels; the sixth and youngest one was reprieved. Qazanchi's criticism of the decision to participate in the transitional cabinet was vindicated by the results of the general election that followed. With one exception all the party's candidates failed to be elected. That even included Hadid standing in Mosul. The one exception was Husain Jamil who owed his election to his being a Jamil. On the eve of the election the electors were guests at the house of the head of the Jamil clan, and were kept incommunicado until they cast their votes.

The young man continued to see the other five but gradually distanced himself from Qazanchi. There was an occasion when after diplomatic relations were established with the Soviet Union, a soviet film with Arabic subtitles was shown at an avant-garde cinema, and many sympathisers went to watch and connect with soviet culture. The young man thought it appalling and said so; a low quality, ill-judged propaganda film shamelessly patronising Arab viewers. It featured a dark man of the Caucasus with an Arabic sounding name carrying out incredible heroic feats in support of the Red Army as he operated behind German lines. Qazanchi turned on his friend; criticism of any aspect of soviet society was an unwanted criticism of the Soviet Union. That was a minor disagreement; more serious was the decision by the Soviet Union to join America and other powers in voting for the partition of Palestine; an abrupt renunciation of the Soviet Union's long held policy of supporting the establishment of an independent, dual, democratic, homogeneous Arab-Jewish state. To many on the left including the young man that reversal was a shocking decision, some saw it as opportunistic. It even caused dismay in the ranks of hardened communists. But Qazanchi like his hero Pritt could not imagine that such an important decision might not have been sanctioned by Stalin, while there was nothing on earth that would get them to see Stalin making a mistake. Qazanchi used convoluted analysis and argument to vindicate the decision. His young follower accused him of being more Stalinist than Stalin and did not waver in the belief that the decision was a historical mistake.

In the next ten years Qazanchi was at the forefront of left wing agitation, coming more and more into the open as a Marxist activist and supporter of the Soviet Union. He supported the left-leaning regime of Abd al-Karim Qasim; and he met his death in Mosul in March 1959 in the course of bloody clashes between communists and Ba'thists. That took place almost ten years after the young man had left Iraq and had severed his ties with Iraqi politics.

Then the day came when the young man's travel ban was lifted. He went and got his security clearance and passport, the Bank accepted his short notice of leaving, and he made his way to al-Ahali building where he handed his resignation from the party. No time was lost in completing the arrangement for the travel. A ban that had been imposed for no good reason, and lifted for no better, could be reimposed. The day before his departure Habiba came to his room, brought him his favourite Turkish coffee and asked him if he was really going away. Born in the Sinjar mountains, she was now a domestic girl in her fourteenth year. Her parents had given her away as a little girl to his parents; her family was too poor to look after her, and a little money changed hands. Since then she had spent her days cleaning and helping the mother in the kitchen. She was treated kindly but she did not go to school, did not learn to read or write. She rarely went out of the house on her own, and then only on errands. She never had the experience of buying anything for herself; she never had any money. She loved it when her daily chores were interrupted by the boy as a boy and then as a young man telling her to bring him a cup of Turkish coffee; she learnt just how sweet he wanted it to be. He would occasionally put his writing or reading aside and engage her in light conversation. She would ask him what he was writing about, and he would tell her about the story he was writing or the book he was reading, and about important people in far away lands. She asked him when he would be coming back, and he told her that he may never come back. She broke down, started to cry and said 'What shall I have to live for here?". As an old man recalling the occasion he would have liked to remember how he put his arms round her to comfort her, tell her that she had a whole life ahead of her, that his parents would find her a husband as they did for the maids before her, that she will get married, have children to bring up in her own home where she will have her own money. And he would have liked to recall her saying that if she had a son she would want him to have his name and be a clever writer like him…Except that none of that happened. As the teenage girl opened her heart to him, he engrossed in his own uncertain future, drained the last of the Turkish coffee and said that he will write about her. "Will you really?" she asked, "will you not forget?", "I shall not forget, that's a promise", he replied but nearly did.

The Argonot made an unscheduled stop at Beirut to pick up a very important personage, then a scheduled stop at Rome. Four Iraqi students on their way to London were directed to the airport restaurant where the waiter guided them to one side where tables were set for lunch. A serious looking man came in, had a look and made to go to the other side. The waiter stepped in front of him and directed him to the side where the students were sitting. Nuri al-Sa'id pushed him aside and went to a table at the other end. The waiter lifted his eyes to the ceiling and turned away with a latin shrug

This is it. Europe. He has arrived.

Mrs Atlas

I t was his first week in London and first experience of living in somebody else's home as a lodger. The widow Mrs Atlas was on the list of the Students Union as one who took in weekly boarders whom she called paying guests; and so he found himself in a small room in a semi-detached house at the foot of Seven Sisters Road, close to Finsbury Park and within an easy walking distance to the underground station. He happened to be the only lodger when he arrived. Mrs Atlas would cook him a breakfast then an early dinner which allowed him when the mood took him to put aside his books and go take the metro to the West End. On the first Saturday he happened to be having tea with Mrs Atlas when the house was suddenly shaken by a massive collective shout of thousands of people. Mrs Atlas looked towards him, assured him with a smile and said: "That must have been an Arsenal goal." A fortnight later he could be seen as one of thousands of men standing on the hallowed terraces of the Gunners at Highbury cheering on Lishman and Mercer, Barnes and

Roper, Jack Kelsey and Daniel, little Jimmy Logie and the fiery redhead Scotsman Alex Forbes. A love affair that lasted more than half a century before it was partly displaced by interest in Liverpool under the influence of his Northern family of sons and grandchildren.

Mrs Atlas's domestic regime was lax; you had a house key, you could come and go as you pleased, invite guests as long as they were not more than two at a time and not too loud which would annoy the neighbours. Her one strict rule was about the house telephone, there was no other type of telephone in those days. It stood proudly on a side table in 'The Room'; you could only use it with her permission. She was ever exercised by the thought that a student boarder missing his family back home might be tempted to take the opportunity of making a long distance call while she was out.

Mrs Atlas always referred to it as 'The Room' which marked her Yorkshire beginnings. She was born in Ackworth, a mining village between Pontefract and Wakefield, and was brought up in the shadow of the headgears of the colliery down the shaft of which her father, uncles and all the men in their street went to work every day. She was a bright school girl, passed the eleven-plus which got her a place at a Grammar School, after which she came down to London where she met Mr Atlas who had a desk job with the local authority.

A wedding photograph, a full-length studio one of Mr Atlas as a young man and a small black-and white of Mrs Atlas at the seaside stood on the mantelpiece next to each other. A display cabinet contained elaborately decorated plates, vases, cups, saucers, and others the bric-ā-brac of summer holidays in Herne Bay. The pride of place and focal point atop the cabinet was the framed photograph of a young man in the blue uniform of the Royal Air Force, Mrs Atlas's only son who made the ultimate sacrifice for his country as he piloted a Spitfire in the Battle of Britain.

It was a surprising encounter at the Senate House library. He had no idea that Saleh was in London. He was more than twice his age, had been one of his schoolteachers yet was now a fellow student. He never knew his full name; everyone in the school referred to him as Saleh Jaber, he taught arithmetic and *al-jabr* (the *jabr*) was the Arabic name given it by al-Khwarizmi, its progenitor, in 825 Baghdad, later to be universally known as Algebra. They left the Senate House together and found their way to an unoccupied bench in Russell Square, Saleh became agitated all the while at any mention of their home country and full of invectives against Nayil, the security chief. He said his worst experience was the first night in the dread detention centre of Abu Ghraib, not knowing what will happen to him nor the reason for his being there. All he knew was that it was the doing of the accursed Nayel. The cubicles were made of partitions that did not extend right up to the ceiling. It was a bitterly cold night, his teeth were chattering, while his misery was more than he could bear. He cried and his sobs were heard by the man in the next cubicle who called out: "Comrade, be resolute". Saleh told him he could not bear the cold and the communist passed to him his own overcoat over the partition. "You can keep it", he said, "I may not need it after tonight". Saleh was freed after three days. He had been given no formal reason for his detention; now he was told nothing as they let him go.

Saleh had now enrolled at University College in Gower Street for an undergraduate course of anthropology. The younger man was surprised to hear that and asked him if he had not thought of going for a Master's in Arithmetic to add to his Iraqi qualification. That evinced an angry outburst; he had had enough of arithmetic, of Nayel and of Nayel's moronic son; and of the persecution, injustice and suffering that he endured. There followed a discussion of their present situations and how they managed for accommodation. Saleh said he was unhappy with his lodging. His room was next to the street so he could not sleep well; that, besides the noise created by the other lodgers holding parties at all hours. He did not like the landlady and the feeling was reciprocated; they had arguments, and he was keen to find out how the younger man managed. Within a week Saleh Jaber was a second paying guest of Mrs Atlas's. He was soon followed by Karen, a Jewish woman in her twenties who came down from Manchester looking for excitement and a job.

Saleh's relationship with Mrs Atlas did not have an auspicious beginning. He had arrived with his ration book and she was upset to discover that his former landlady had removed more coupons than she was entitled to. "How am I going to feed you for the next two weeks", she asked then added "I can get the meat off ration from the butcher's, but it'll cost more; lucky you have not lost any coupons for the chocolate and sweets". He said he would not mind having fish instead of meat as long as it was not the whale meat that everyone was talking about. In any event he preferred lamb to beef. Before coming to England he had heard reports of food shortages, butter and beef in particular. Then after his first night in London he came out of the hotel in Woburn Place, and there he saw it chalked on a black board outside a butcher's shop, 'Dog Meat Sold Here'. That put him off meat altogether for a while even after he had cottoned on to the true meaning of the statement.

Sitting at the table Mrs Atlas was visibly upset at the two men talking to each other in Arabic, particularly on the occasions when it was fairly obvious from the bodily disposition that they were talking about Mrs Atlas or Karen or the food in front of them. Mrs Atlas objected, said it was rude, not the sort of thing you did in England. The men accepted the reprimand and thereafter initiated all exchanges in English while still using the occasional Arabic word as one got stuck at remembering the English equivalent. In addition there were inexcusable lapses by Saleh. Mrs Atlas was furious when she caught sight of him making an observation in Arabic as he looked with dismay at the plate that she put before him. She in turn said she was dismayed to discover that someone had used the telephone without telling her. She added pointedly that she had a way of knowing when it had been used. Karen said that as the two men spoke Arabic it would be easy for them to conceal the fact that they were Jewish. That stunned the two men. While they had been subjected to a measure of ethnic discrimination at home it had not occurred to them that anti-Semitism was rife in England, a country that for six long years had devoted all its human and material resources in the cause of defeating Nazism. Mrs Atlas said there were some misguided people who while hating Hitler and the Nazis yet blamed the Jews for the war. Karen said that she had been interviewed, as one of two applicants, for the job of secretary to a solicitor in Manchester; the job was given to the other who was far less qualified but was favoured for her Nordic looks. After the meal the young student turned to Mrs Atlas and asked her *sotto voce* if she was left-handed; she raised a finger to her lips and there was a twinkle in her eye.

Saleh's relationship with Mrs Atlas was going from bad to worse. He could not resist criticising things being done wrongly or suggesting how they could be improved. At breakfast he would point out that his soft-boiled egg on ration was to be handled with care to avoid it being too runny or closer to hard, and would suggest a way of doing it to ensure the desired level of softness; he did not want Mrs Atlas to give him a mug of tea with the milk already added; he would want to drink water from a glass and not a mug; brown bread was better than white but he would accept the rye which reminded him of the barley bread back home. It did not help that his criticisms were mostly well founded; they did not hurt any less, and may be said to be more hurtful for being true. And on occasions he would go glum as he recalled his experience in Abu Ghraib; he would say that the only food that he had in those three days was bread and onion which he had with water in a mug. He would then curse Nayel and his moronic liar of a son. One day Saleh had a furious argument with Mrs Atlas. She served mushroom on toast. Saleh ate a morsel then laid down knife and fork, looked in dismay at the plate and turned aside to tell his compatriot and former student in Arabic of his suspicion that Mrs Atlas had used the stalk and not the flesh of the mushroom. That enraged her; she told them that if they did not like her cooking, they could betake themselves to the Chinese in the next street and pay for it. Saleh also upset the two younger lodgers. He was pernickety and they kept themselves apart from his altercations with their landlady. They arranged to go on a day trip to Brighton. When Saleh learned of that he said he would go with them whereupon Karen changed her mind, said she had just heard of a job interview that she was asked to attend.

Close to the house was a district of ultra orthodox (*charedi*) Jews and the students newcomers were interested to make contact and get to know more about Jewish entities in England. Saleh was moderately observant religiously speaking, the younger student even less so. They got the dates of the High Holy Days confirmed to them. They had missed the Day of Atonement while Sukkot was in three days time. They were given the direction to the synagogue, spoken of in its Yiddish terminology of 'Shul'. On the eve of Sukkot they put on their best suit and made their way to the Shul following in the footsteps of hasidic men in their recognisable traditional dress of black coats, large brimmed hats, thick beards and curls at each side of their faces. Saleh and his younger companion were stopped at the entrance and were asked for their tickets. They said they knew nothing about tickets. "No tickets, no admission" said the verger. They explained that they were Iraqi Jews who had only recently arrived in England as students. "The rule is the rule" barked the verger, "no admission without ticket". Saleh remonstrated that surely on a night such as this, strangers should be admitted as guests. The verger's attitude softened but he had his orders. He explained that the members of the congregation paid a weekly subscription the year round in return for which they received privileges including guaranteed admission at High Holy Days. The two men left unhappy and Mrs Atlas was surprised to see them back so early. She was sympathetic and suggested that they could try another synagogue, a Sephardi not far away which she believed was for Iranian Jews.

The Sephardi synagogue was designated a *midrash* (short for *Bayt Hamidrash*, house of learning). The Sephardis descended from the Jews who lived in the Iberian Peninsula before they were expelled at the same time as the Arabs from Spain and Portugal in 1492 and 1496. It would have been more accurate to describe the congregation as *Mizrahi* (oriental). They were mostly from Iran and Iraq, and the two Iraqi newcomers were received with respect; they were seated in a place of honour next to the *bimah* (central prayer platform). After the service members of the congregation gathered round them wanting to know the latest news from Baghdad, and they were told about the then current brutal drive against the communists with allegations of imprisonment, torture and execution; and how that disquieted the Baghdadi Jewish population who feared that the political excesses might spill over to touch their community. Saleh now had the opportunity to refer to his own experience of arrest, detention and release. He had never been a communist and so assumed that he had been the victim of a false allegation made against him to the top security man Nayel, while he suspected that the informer may have been no other than Nayel's own son. On the way back to their lodging Saleh, after a probing by his companion, divulged more of the story of Nayel's son. He was fourteen years old, retarded at school and failed his mathematic tests twice in succession. His father contacted the highly-rated Shamash Jewish School looking for a private tutor; they recommended Saleh. He soon found that the boy was difficult to teach, being as dim-witted as lazy, spoiled and petulant. When he refused to do home assignments Saleh threatened to report him to his father. The next thing that happened was that Saleh was arrested and taken to Abu Ghraib. Saleh would not divulge the nature of the allegation; his companion surmised that it would have been sufficiently serious to warrant his detention but not too grave else he would not have been released after three days.

Karen got a job as a receptionist at a doctors' surgery. She also found a two- bedroom flat that she liked. She could now afford the rent if someone would share it with her. Karen and the young Iraqi student gave notice of leaving. On the last day

Mrs Atlas got out their green ration books to give to them. She confronted Saleh as she waived the third ration book in his face: "We have had enough trouble from you. You may also go as well, and take this with you." Saleh shrugged his shoulders; "I am going nowhere", he said.

The young student and Karen went their separate ways. Sharing the flat was an excuse; a white lie.

Bernstein

Mrs Bernstein was a formidable woman. She was well known to everyone in her street in Hackney Downs. She was outspoken and confident in her strong social attitudes and basic political beliefs. The men were respectful of her, many of the women admired her, the conservative party agent whose house was at the end of the street avoided her, while authority was wary of her. Once, coming out of the station, she heard an unflattering remark as she passed the ticket collector, so she rounded on him, told him how lucky he was to be earning a living at all. She said she could have employed a ten year old boy to do his job. Ida Bernstein was a big woman; she bought her clothes from The Outsize Shop near Marble Arch.

Jacob Bernstein was a spare unassuming little man. A freelance master tailor working from home he was seldom seen out in the street. He did outsource work for a top Savile Row firm and had a few clients of his own who came to the house to be measured and fitted. He had little conversation and when he spoke it was in a mixture of English, Yiddish and Moldovan. They bought their house after the Great War for 440 pounds with a 25 year mortgage. When the young student went to live with them as a weekly lodger there were two years left, after which the house will be free of mortgage and truly theirs. "It is freehold and no one would ever be able then to turn us out" Ida told Jacob.

Ida was born and brought up in the East End close to Whitechapel. One of a third generation of Russian Jewish refugees she still bore the family grudge against their German coreligionists who were less than welcoming as they saw them arrive knocking on doors seeking succour after the pogroms. The German Jews looked down on them, avoided them and felt ashamed of them. Ida will add with a morbid irony that the haughty Germans did get their comeuppance in the end.

Ida was sixteen when the Great War ended. In the course of it some 700,000 British men lost their lives causing a serious shortage of men of marriageable age. By the early 1920's there were some two million surplus women; the 1921 census documented 1,750,000. The Overseas Emigration Committee was set up in 1918 to deal with the problem. That was followed in 1919 by the foundation of the Society for the Overseas Settlement of British Women supported by a government grant. Thousands of women emigrated to different parts of the British dominions. Ida went to settle in South Africa. That lasted only a year and was more problematic than she had expected; South Africa had also sustained a big loss of young men in the war. The few relationships that Ida had did not prosper, and she was unhappy. Returning to England she blamed South Africa, its water, its food, its climate, its hectic lifestyle for her putting on weight. She claimed she had been svelte once, and was so described when she first arrived in Johannesburg.

Jacob's odyssey started with his crewing a ship in Odessa bound for London. He hoped that he might then crew another that would take him to America, or that he would earn enough in England to pay for crossing the Atlantic as a steerage passenger. His hope of going to America was dashed by the war that broke out as he landed in England. After the Bolshevik 1917 Revolution he, together with the other newly arrived Russian nationals, came under suspicion of being communists, anarchists or others generally seen as subversives. That led to many immigrants anglicizing their Jewish name or adopting a completely new English name. Jacob's Moldovan name was almost unpronounceable; he changed it to Bernstein which was the name of his first employer in England who paid him his first weekly wage. He met Ida in one of the social clubs that proliferated in the East End in the 1920's, they married, bought the house and started a family.

"My Leon is a smart boy", Ida referred to her elder son. He was an army conscript in the Second World War. Preparing for the invasion of occupied Europe his platoon was set to be among the first wave to land on the beaches. Leon sensed from what he overheard and what he saw that the invasion was to start early the following day, so he went AWOL and hitched his way back home. Ida was apoplectic. What will she tell them when they came to take him away? What will happen to him for absenting himself without official leave? He told her not to worry unduly, and that whatever punishment he received would have been worth the AWOL. The invasion started the following day, his platoon was among the first on the beaches of Normandy, he reported back to his unit with a plausible excuse and was welcomed back with a reprimand. Yes, Leon was a smart boy, and so was Ida's other son Harry who worked as a clerk in an insurance office in the City. The boys carried the lust of colonial adventure which they inherited from their mother. Leon emigrated to Canada after the war. When the young student arrived as a lodger Harry had saved close to enough for the fare that would take him to seek his fortune in Rhodesia, which he affectedly called *row-dee-sha*.

The young student was doing well in his studies but was ever discomfited by the many people he came across who would open the conversation by asking him where he had come from. That marked him as an outsider, while replying that it was Iraq meant that his interlocutor would no longer see him as he was but as an Iraqi to whom he would ascribe without more all that he knew or got to learn about the country, its people, its social conditions, technological backwardness, racial attributes, religious conflict and intolerance, as well as its political orientation. The young undergraduate set about learning all he could about English ways and social attitudes so as to smooth the edge of being an outsider. At the same time he was discomfited by the news from home, grim and unrelenting, that held his emotions tightly in its grip.

When he left Iraq as a student there were more than 130,000 Jews in Baghdad constituting one quarter of the total population. As a community they had settled in Iraq for centuries. Now, a couple of years after his arrival in England, the greater part of that community had emigrated to Israel. Some of them had been attracted by what the new Jewish state seemingly offered; others were constrained to follow after their employer had left and the business closed or after the loss of clients of one's own business, or after the loss of friends and neighbours as well as the depletion of the pool of the young persons who in normal times would be looked to as potential husbands and brides. To all of them an unavoidable impetus to leave was the official restrictions that they came under with the outbreak of the war in Palestine and the arrival of Palestinian refugees talking of what they had suffered at the hands of the Zionists, citing the massacre of Dair Yasin as a prime example of what forced them to flee.

When the demographic displacements were taking place a state of hostility existed between Iraq and Israel, there was a restriction on the movement of Iraqi Jews and what they could take out of the country. Further, there was a complete absence of postal relations between the two countries coupled with a strict Iraqi censorship. In consequence the contact between those who left and those who remained could only be safely obtained by using a third country address. The young man's family was advised to withhold his address in England from any enquirers. In the event they disclosed it to a few close relatives and before long the few became many and the young undergraduate became the conduit of letters passing between the two countries. They were mostly anxious letters which he readdressed after a cursory examination to identify the incautious ones that were written under stress in Israel. He would see that they did not contain material that, passing through Iraqi censorship, might expose the recipient to harm.

The news from Israel was truly grim; a story of high expectation and bitter disappointment. The expectation was overhyped over the years by Zionist propaganda urging the Iraqi Jews to emigrate to Israel. A leaflet would pass secretly from hand to hand in the classroom, the synagogue, the meeting place and the private party exhorting the 'captives of Babylon' to liberate themselves! That alluded to the invasion of Judea by the Assyrians under Nebuchadnazzar in the sixth century before the Christian era when a number of people from the kingdom of Judea were taken as captives to Babylon where they sat by its waters to weep in memory of Zion. It also resonated with the annual celebration of the festival of Passover when the people would recite with one voice: "This year we are here as slaves, may we be free next year in the land of Israel".

Israel as the Iraqi Jew came to believe it to be had many enticements: to the religious the allure of praying in the holy land, to the old the promise of a world class medical service, to the well-off the prospect of gainfully investing in a new state with a growing economy. The great allure to the young was an open society with a reputed big measure of sexual freedom. They all boarded the plane thinking that they were leaving a third world country to go join European society. As they landed they were received as the dark skinned proletariat that was going to be set to build the infrastructure of the new state, to populate the lands seized from the Arabs, and to inflate the numbers of the Israel Defence Force. As soon as the Iraqi Jew came down the steps of the aircraft, his feet touching the ground, he was showered with antibacterial agent then led to a tent, one of thousands, in a hastily assembled refugee camp where he was to stay until it was his turn to be processed. He was not told what will happen to him, when will he be taken out of the camp and provided with a job and proper housing for himself and his family. The facilities in the camp were basic while the authorities were under great pressure to provide for so many people at the same time. Soon there was a succession of big noisy commotions, the new arrivals close to mutiny; some wanting to go back home, all blaming the false promises that induced them to come, while there was nothing they could do about it. They had burnt the bridge and now had to put up with the hardships and the meagre food rations. The Israeli authorities dealing with them were also under immense pressure to screen and process so many. That was another shock to the new arrivals. They were now expected as part of that process to divest themselves of their 'Arab' identity and to acquire a new one. That was defined by having to learn Hebrew and to speak it with a Yiddish pronunciation, by the work that one was assigned to perform for the new state, and further defined by a change of name. One had no say on what official job one was assigned to perform, nor on the choice of town or locality in which to live. The job mostly had no reference to the type of work or profession one had carried out in Iraq. A master builder was given a shovel and told to take part in digging a trench if he wanted to feed his family. A journalist was set to work picking oranges in an orchard at harvest time. A college of law undergraduate had to work as a lumberjack. A prominent poet, headmaster of the biggest secondary Jewish school in Baghdad, became an inspector of Arab schools. A doctor with Iraqi qualifications was set to help as a hospital orderly while he retrained.

The new Iraqi Jewish refugees soon discovered that the notion of Israel as an open society was a myth. Nepotism which operated under the name 'Protexia' was rife in every walk of life. If you wanted a government job or to be allocated a place to live you had to adhere to a particular sect, a political party or a trades union that could be counted upon to intercede on your behalf. There was as yet no homogenous national Israeli personality. There was instead a multiplicity of identities brought by refugees from different parts of the world; and there existed with that a social pecking order. At its apex were the Sabra, that is members of the Jewish community who had been born in what was Palestine before the founding of the state of Israel. They were followed in a descending order by the Americans, then the German-speaking and the British, some of the latter identifying themselves as Anglo-Saxon! The East Europeans came next; they were dominant in the government and the army but that was not matched by their social standing. As regards the Jews who arrived from Arab countries, the Mizrahis who would soon constitute a very large percentage of the total population, they were all seen as inferior to the European Ashkenazis in every respect, while having their own pecking order with the Iraqis in the lead followed by the Moroccans, the Yemenis and the Ethiopians. The notion of sexual freedom was also a myth in the experience of the Mizrahis. An Ashkenazi girl would refuse to go out with an Iraqi and would face opprobrium from her family, friends and the general body of Ashkenazis were she seen to be associating with a 'black man'. It would take several generations before the disparate social and demographic strands would attract each to each so as to fuse into a single defined national identity. Humanity will always win in the end.

The Bernsteins did not belong to a political party, but Mrs Bernstein considered herself a progressive of the broad left, a supporter of the Labour Party and a doughty opponent of anti-Semitism and all forms of racism. She was a member of the Women's International Zionist Organisation (WIZO), a voluntary society dedicated to the advancement of the status of women as well as to the welfare and educational projects in Israel. Her young lodger was at the table in the kitchen when she came back from one meeting to challenge him with the reported misbehaviour of his people, the Iraqi refugees, who were seen as unruly, disruptive and ill mannered; as making excessive demands and creating mischief in Israel, a country that opened its door to them and helped them. The student wondered at her speaking in those racist terms and reminded her of the hardships that her grandparents had endured as they came out of their ghetto and passed through Germany on the way to England. She said the situations were different, that his people were offered all the help that Israel and the Jewish institutions including WIZO could offer; it was just that they were ungrateful, a matter of culture. That was the end of the conversation; you do not argue with Mrs Bernstein! He sensed that, though unspoken, he may have become personally diminished in Mrs Bernstein estimation as she got to hear about the alleged cultural deficiencies of his people. That was soon redressed in an accidental and pleasing way. As part of the general exodus of the Iraqi Jews some, the

114

better off, made their way to England directly or by way of Israel. Some of his school friends were among them. They mostly had a generous money allowance and also held as custodians moneys that belonged to their families which were spirited out of Iraq. One day Mr Bernstein returned from Savile Row looking excited which was unusual for him. He asked the lodger if he knew of a young Iraqi Jew whose name he mentioned. The lodger said he knew him well, that they were classmates in Baghdad. Mr Bernstein said that the person had just placed an order for a fifty guinea suit as he wanted it to be the very best. "And to think he is only a lad!" exclaimed Mrs Bernstein. The student lodger was now seen as deserving of more respect for having rich friends.

The almost daily volume of letters passing through the hands of the young student became so great that it became more than his financial resources and spare time from studies could possibly sustain. He got relief from that by asking everyone other than his immediate family to stop sending him letters and telling them that any that came to him henceforth will be ignored. The letters depicted an image of a new nation being born and the travails of an uprooted community struggling to dig for new roots in a foreign soil; a story of hope shining through despair, stoicism through privation, heroism through weakness, generosity through egoism – common humanity above all.

Porchester Square

After battling the-arch racists on the Continent for six long years Britain came out of the Second World War victorious yet in the grip of austerity, shortages and rationing as well as anti-Semitism and racial prejudice. During the war there were enemy aliens kept under observation or under guard in the Isle of Mann. Now there were simply aliens who came from other lands who were required to register at the Aliens Registration Office at St. James's. Resented for their apparent or presumed affluence they were generally referred to as foreigners, then more respectfully as overseas visitors while the project of the Festival of Britain got under way.

In London's East End, Jewish population in the majority, two of the biggest national breweries were notorious for their policy of not employing Jews. A provincial barristers' chambers declined to offer a tenancy to an applicant, the Head announcing the decision to his colleagues who did not demur: "I am not having a Jew boy in my chambers".

A suburban tennis club blackballed John's application for membership. When his brother Anthony, a club member, asked the reason the Secretary explained: your brother is Jewish! On every working day as the courts in a provincial city rose for lunch, judges and senior lawyers repaired to the city's traditional gentleman's club, but not Jewish judges and lawyers who had to take lunch elsewhere.

A young man looking for digs in the 1950's and scanning the many cards in street corner shop windows would find a big choice for about ten per cent of the world population. For the rest there were the regrets: regret no R.C.'s, regret no coloured, regret Europeans only. That very English word "regret!" How much of the sum total of the good work of the Foreign Office, the Colonial Office and the British Council was set to naught the moment a black, brown or yellow face saw the word on a card displayed in a shop window. To an Englishman the world beyond his shores was mostly shades of brown: darkie, coloured, half-cast, dago and wog. He will tell you proudly that "the wogs started at Calais". That did not make for social cohesion. You were stuck in your ethnic group and your place in the scale of darkness. You did not want to slip down and be damned, nor to aspire to climb and be rebuffed. You would then find ethnic minorities in clusters: the indigent Jew in the East End and the affluent in North London, the Chinese in docklands, the Cypriot in Holloway, the Caribbean in Notting Hill (before the arrival of Rachman), the mid-European in Bayswater, and the Middle Eastern in Number 13 Porchester Square.

That was one of a terrace of mansion houses, more imposing than attractive, that backed on to Porchester Square. Number 13 may have once been the residence of a merchant or a lawyer but was now a bed-and-breakfast lodging house of nine single bedrooms plus, heart of the enterprise, the basement where Mrs. Bennet ruled with the help of two Irish maids. Mrs. Bennet was proud of her lodgers; she called them her paying guests. They paid the rent once a week and were served breakfast on a tray carried to one's bedroom by the maid every morning, except on the occasions when at one's request it was replaced by a meal at teatime.

There were the students, a mix of Baghdadi Jews, Iranians, Egyptians and an Afghan. And there was the odd-one-out, a young Welshman, who kept himself apart. He missed his Valley and hated London; all that kept him was a job at the local newspaper and Donald Wolfit at the Lyric Hammersmith.

Mrs. Bennet suspected that her young gentlemen were socialists or even communists. She did not approve but was prepared to be indulgent as long as they behaved, and after all it was a rite of passage for young students. Nor could politics be avoided. At one end of Queensway was a Greek Cypriot restaurant and a covert EOKA cell. On every Sunday you would find an old woman in black selling the latest edition of a locally produced newspaper; and every Sunday she would attempt to force it on you, even as you explained that you knew no Greek. At the other end of Queensway stood Porchester Hall where ballroom dancing took place on Saturday nights on the first floor, and there would often be political rallies on a Sunday in the Hall proper. The Hall would fill to capacity to be enthralled by luminaries such as Aneurin Bevan excoriating the moves to impose charges for spectacles and dental services – dark reactionary forces seeking to impair people's vision and to rot their teeth. Then as you came out to the street you were met by the man selling *The Daily Worker* who gestured to the Hall dismissively and told you prophetically: A socialist to-day, a reactionary tomorrow! As you walked back to No. 13 you were met by Mrs. Bennet at the street door who asked you crossly if you had been to the socialist rally. She feared they might win the next election and be returned to further ruin the country, adding that the trouble was that there were just too many poor people. Yet the poor people could be counted on to be patriotic. That was demonstrated by the general fury at the "demagogue" Mosaddegh daring to challenge Britain's inalienable claims to his Iranian oil fields. The man at the barber's shop next to Royal Oak station would explain to you that but for the British the oil would have remained below the ground, undiscovered and untapped, so that "your people" would have had no benefit at all rather than what they were actually getting. He would conclude his discourse by telling you as he tapped you lightly on the head that "they" had no brains, no brains at all, even as you protested that you were an Iraqi which was not quite the same.

Mrs Bennet would not have female lodgers. She saw a moral hazard in mixing the sexes. But she had no objection to lady friends visiting as long as they left before midnight. That was a rule often broken by the Afghan to the extent that some of his lady friends left in the early hours. As Mrs. Bennet saw the situation, the young gentlemen worked hard and deserved the occasional break from their studies. They had to sow their wild oats, and it would distract them away from politics. To a lusty young man immured in a bedsitter the only distractions were the girls, coffee-house politics, the occasional visit to the cinema, and the fortnightly going to watch one's favourite football team. There were in addition the open spaces of Kensington Gardens and Hyde Park with its Speakers' Corner. That was a time when you believed in all innocence that one could say anything at Speakers' Corner, raise any challenge to the establishment or even be subversive with impunity. But on a Sunday evening the Corner was essentially a spectacle. There would be the man of religion reminding you that the end was nigh; the black man telling you to free his country from colonial rule, who will invariably be told to go home by one or more; the earnest woman of the anti-vivisection league exhorting you to sign her petition; and there would invariably be a serious man with a Karl Marx beard standing on a low box at a distance from the rest expounding to the knot of respectful listeners his views on world order. He would preface each sentence by "The point is".

Then with the setting of the sun religious man, black man, woman and bearded man would roll, fold, pack, bundle and carry away their paraphernalia, leaving that corner of Hyde Park to darkness and the thirty shilling women. Saleh did not approve; he thought it vulgar and risky, preferring a visit to Mrs. Copley's once a month after he had received his allowance. The others would tease him by asking if his loyalty might have been rewarded by a discount or green shield stamps.

There was no shortage of girls and women if you knew how to go about it. The best were the young tourists with a limited time on their hands, seeking and giving pleasure with no aftermath of painful separation, guilt or embarrassment. Reuben was particularly good at it; you would often see him return to Number 13 with a Swede or an American in tow. David's visitor for a spell was English; he proudly confided that she was a policewoman out of uniform, and was teased by being asked if it was she who walked him home after a night out. But the real wonder was the Afghan. He would have a succession of long-term relationships, that is each lasting more than a week. He was not much to look at: short, thin, bespectacled, with a small straggling beard, and so withdrawn that he hardly ever left his room. His assets were a nice friendly smile and the fact that he was completing his medical training at St. Mary's. Joseph, whose room was next to his, was green with envy. That was before he surrendered his virginity to Sally, single mother, twice his age. They met at the Hammersmith Palais, did not dance, had a chat, he, talking politics and she agreeing, one thing leading to another.

If there had been a Norman Tebbit then, and could have looked into the heart of any of the young students, the latter would at first blush have failed the test. Whenever England played against a foreign team the young man would inwardly support the foreigners, adopt them as his team, feel a glow of vicarious pride at their runs scored and a portent of personal doom at their wickets fallen. Hardly knowing anything about the West Indies he would yet in moments of quiet reflection gleefully hum the Calipso ditty to those "lovely pals of mine, Ramadin and Valentine". But at closer examination the Tebbit test was itself flawed giving rise to a misunderstanding. The young man favouring the opposition did not do so out of antipathy to the English; quite the reverse. Coming from a third world country he was dazzled by life in London: the underground railway and moving stairs, the big buildings, the statues, the stately monuments, the public parks, the public houses, the freedom, the general good manners and the orderly queue at bus stop and post office. Whenever a visitor arrived from his own country he would proudly show him round the landmarks of his London and explain the ways of his Londoners. And he adopted the ways of the host country and became progressively immersed in it to the extent that he deferred to a fellow student longer-lived in London and patronised the others shorter-lived. But however he tried there were aspects of English life that remained beyond him while he resented what he saw as the arrogance of the English, their self-assurance and their certainty of the innate superiority of their race. Sitting in the cinema waiting for the film credits to roll he is brought to attention by Pathe News triumphantly showing frames of the Test Match. As he hears his neighbours' exclamations of joy at a six by Dennis and of regret "Oh Len!" at a dropped catch, he is reminded that he is ever an outsider. It was otherwise the Saturday afternoon once a fortnight at Highbury. You would have put on your dirty raincoat and joined the packed underground train to Arsenal, emerging into a packed tunnel taking you to a mass of bodies in front of the turnstiles. Then, having paid your three shillings and six pence, you stood in a mass of bodies to feast your eyes on Jimmy Logie and Cliff Holden, the rain streaming down yours and the mass of dirty raincoats without distinction. You felt at home in a strange amorphous tribe, the name itself having no obvious geographical connotation, to which you were admitted with no questions asked. It was enough that you supported The Gunners, believed with all your heart that they were superior to the Spurs, as you felt sorry for poor old Chelsea.

Saleh who was doing a Master's was a few years older than the rest. His was a big room on the ground floor which often served as a quasi common room. They would share a pot of Turkish coffee made on the gas ring and regale each other with tales of the funny ways of the English, and of the misunderstandings. Ezra spoke of arriving for a lecture in the morning when a fellow student, Anne, came to him holding boiled sweets in a crumpled paper bag, which she extended to him with a smile: "It's my birthday", she explained. Strange it is that in this country, when it is your birthday, you are a giver of gifts and not a recipient! David spoke of his first visit to a public house with fellow students. Brian bought him a drink and insisted on paying for it, dismissing David's coy reluctance to accept that act of generosity, saying "it's our custom"; only to be followed a few minutes later by pointing a finger at David, and: "it's your turn". Saleh spoke of his mortifying experience on the first day in college. He went with others to take lunch at a café nearby. They took their seats on the first floor. The dishes were listed on a blackboard which Saleh read but did not understand. He was too embarrassed to ask for advice. He was going to see what the others were ordering before making his choice. A waiter took the orders which he shouted down a dumb waiter followed by the dishes coming up. Saleh heard someone order a thing (he did not grasp what the strange word was) with syrup. Two minutes later an enticing dish of roast beef with all the trimmings and swimming in gravy emerged from the dumb waiter. When it was his turn he told the waiter that he wanted "the something with syrup".

"Is that all you want?"

"Yes, the something with syrup."

"Do you mean the pudding with syrup?"

"Yes, just that."

The waiter bellowed the order down the dumb waiter, and within a minute or two a spotted dick with syrup was set before Saleh who looked at it with dismay while he felt that so many heads had turned to look at him. He got down to consume his lunch nonchalantly. He was not going to incur embarrassment by revealing his ignorance. There were worse things than missing a good lunch.

Things moved on. Some of the young men returned home, others ended in Canada, the Welshman fell in love with an English girl he met at the Lyric, became reconciled with life in London as he left to set up home with her. The Afghan was the last to finish his studies and depart. The last formal event before returning home was the graduation ceremony in the Royal Albert Hall. The day before, he hired the black gown from Moss Bros, which he hung on a hook behind the door. In the morning Eileen brought him breakfast on a tray with the addition of a red rose in a vase, which he thought touching. Then Eileen, excited and confused, asked: "Mr. Abdul, are you a priest?" He liked Eileen and did not want to disappoint her. But he was not going to lie. For all he knew it might be an offence to personate a priest. "Not quite", he replied.

Linden Gardens

A flat on the second floor of a modern building in Linden Gardens, close to Notting Hill underground station. Two good-size rooms and a small third. That last was to be the undergraduate's room. His first experience of sharing a flat, all the others until then had been a room in a boarding house. In reality he was now more a guest than a sharer. Meir the tenant charged him little; had persisted in asking him to make the move. That was in deference to him, two years his senior, an intellectual, a real student at a real university; and he had distinguished himself at their Shammash School back home as a writer and thinker with left-wing leanings. If there had then been a school students' union, he would have been the official leader. As it happened, he was the editor of the weekly school wall magazine, a presumed head boy representing the students in discussions with the head teacher, and he took part in the school orations on special occasions and anniversaries.

Moving to the tiny room in Linden Gardens the undergraduate was now joining a coterie of privileged Baghdadi Jewish youths, about ten in number, who had left Iraq about the time of the Jewish mass exodus of the 1950's. In each case the youth would have come to England directly or by way of Israel, his family remaining at home biding the time before they followed. That allowed the father to close down the business in an orderly manner, liquidate the stock, sell the properties and so avoid a fire sale. The moneys would then be spirited out of the country and transferred to the son in England who would be their custodian until the arrival of the family. In the meantime, he enjoyed a generous allowance to spend as he liked. That included establishing himselves in rented houses or flats in a good part of London, in some cases possessing a car, while attending a course of further education. They were all enrolled in schools and colleges, preferred subject being engineering of one sort or another. From where they came the term 'engineer' was exalted, denoting an esteemed high-ranking and earning professional. Arriving in England they were surprised to discover that in common parlance the term could be applied, as it often was, to a craftsman or a mere skilled worker. To be a student was the basis upon which they had been granted a British visa and residence permit. But their minds were on other things. They were not looking to finish their studies with the possession of professional qualifications that they would thereafter use for a career. Their minds were on finding opportunities to invest, to trade and to make money. For example, Albert opened a Middle Eastern restaurant in the square across the road from South Kensington underground station. That was surpassed by Freddie who invested in a new big high-class restaurant in Chelsea called 'Shore' with the then famous singer Sandy Shaw gracing it at the opening. David invested in 'Coq d'Or' night club in Swiss Cottage. Frank enrolled at Queen Mary College in Mile End to do dentistry; it was a five year course which he dropped out of in the second as he turned his attention to real estate. Meir came close to buying a travel agency business in Mornington Crescent then gave that up and bought a multi-story house with vacant possession in Bayswater with a view to convert it to apartments.

The undergraduate was blissfully poor, and felt it. His only income was a scholarship with an annual maintenance grant of 270 pounds. The others were sympathetic and magnanimous towards him, would express respect for his scholarship as they saw him get off the bus hugging library books, and they would do so without being deprecatory. They would invite him to the opening of a new business, be present at their poker games as an onlooker, and to accompany them on some occasions as they drove to a racecourse meeting. Left to himself, the occasional relief from his studies coupled with the call of adventure would take him to White City greyhound stadium.

He was now an undergraduate reading English at King's College London. He had already graduated at the School of Oriental & African Studies with a first class honours degree in Classical Arabic and the highest marks of any candidate after the war. His lecturer Dr Serjeant had invited him to collaborate with him in translating a medieval Arabic text *Kitāb al-Bukhalā'* which translates as The Book of Misers for which he would award him a master's degree. That took the young man by surprise and he answered, without reflection or asking for time to consider, that he had already registered to read English at King's; he suggested starting the project after he had obtained his first degree in English. Dr Sergeant saw that as an arrogant snub and withdrew the invitation in a huff. Thus it was that the young man unthinkingly forsook the chance of an academic career. The true unspoken reason for the young man's apparent snub was more to do with his emotional turmoil in the early years in England. He was confronted on a daily basis by the host country declaring the greatness of its civilisation and the richness of its culture, which declaration was vindicated by all that he saw around him. He was desperately anxious to fit in the new society as he was drawn strongly to its history, language and literature. The vista that the lecturer's offer presented to him was incompatible with that. Coming from an Arab country, steeped in Arabic language and literature, and having arrived in England after so many obstacles to surmount and political currents to navigate there was not much merit, as he saw it at the time, in getting down to develop and extend his Arabic reach and in the process miss the chance of working for an English degree. To forgo Shakespeare, Milton, Chaucer and the romantic poets would have been too high a price to pay in order to see his name on the cover of a translation of an obscure medieval Arabic text. Yet that was a mistake as he was to realise many years later, one of several blunders that he made in his lifetime. In the event the young student did get his master's degree by the conventional examination route. Professor (as he became) Robert Bertram Serjeant did complete the translation of al-Jahiz's *Bukhalā'* in his lifetime, but it took him a long time to do that. He died in 1993 and *The Book of Misers* was published posthumously in the year 2000, almost half a century after the idea of translating it into English was first mooted.

Meir was nineteen when the undergraduate went to live in his flat. He had received a limited basic education, did not hold a book in his hands after leaving school, did not read the newspapers, did not pay attention to the politics and current affairs of England as his host country while instinctively supporting the conservative party; his cultural remit did not extend beyond the cinema. But he was sociable, likeable and confident, while the trappings of wealth including having a car and a tenanted flat in a trendy part of London made it easy for him to attract the sorts of people of social weight who would not normally be expected to show condescension to a mere teenage Iraqi refugee. Whenever some came to visit, Meir was keen to show off his flat mate, and to get him involved in the conversation; thus he would gain a vicarious respect for being a flat mate of one who impressed by the good use of the English language and the display of erudition. That happened on the occasions when the cultural attaché of the Colombian embassy came visiting with his wife. He was having a hard time defending a decree that his government had promulgated placing an embargo on the activities of Protestant missionaries in the Colombian part of Amazonia. Several hostile articles appeared in the British press which the attaché countered by a letter in *The Times* saying that the Church of England had enough pagans to convert in different parts of the British empire, mostly Protestant countries, and should keep off trying to convert those who lived as part of the Colombian nation, a country with strong catholic beliefs; it was the prerogative of the Catholic Church to carry out the conversion. The letter was penned by the atheist undergraduate as a favour at the request of the attaché, which the student ghost writer did with a deliberate opaque mischief and internal merriment.

Among others who came visiting regularly were a couple, the man a barrister who had graduated from Cambridge. Meir was happy to witness the eminent guest and the flatmate debate in good humour the merits and demerits of their respective universities.

Meir also got to know a Jewish Iraqi family long established in London, head of the family a practising general medical practitioner, wife a member of a rich Jewish family. They had two children, a son and a daughter Doreen who was in her late teens. The student was introduced and became a regular visitor, went out with the children to the cinema and theatre, later with the girl on her own to concerts and musical recitals, and to visit art galleries. Doreen was attending a day course at some art school without being seriously interested in the arts or academic pursuits. She was an engaging young woman with a serene temperament and a pleasing Near Eastern Jewish physique of dark skin, chestnut hair, black eyes and a good figure. She also had an engaging sense of humour and coy mischief. There was an occasion they were at the Festival Hall on their own when she turned to him with a smile and asked mischievously if his intentions were honourable, and he responded with a smile and a nod as the recital started. Nothing more was said by anyone about that topic but there was a reasonable expectation that things would be formalised after the young man had finished his studies. There would then be the promise of a good job, Doreen's uncle was an eminent banker and entrepreneur, a traditional marriage and a calm, comfortable bourgeois life to follow.

The social horizon of the student, now an adult student, was further broadened by two new acquaintances, a few years older than him. Meir had met them by chance. Norman and Stanley were Jewish and had been contemporaries at Oxford, but the contrast between the two could not have been starker.

Norman came from a middle class family, attended the fee paying City of London School, which was followed by his gaining a place at Merton College where he read law. He was moderately left leaning politically and supported the Labour Party as did most of the Jewish people after the war. He later qualified as a solicitor, married into a rich Jewish family and set up a new law practice in one of the Bloomsbury squares then made famous, some would say notorious, by what became known as the Bloomsbury set. His chance visit to Linden Gardens and meeting the Iraqi Jewish adult student would lead in time to his acting professionally for the family of the latter and for their expanding businesses as well as several other Iraqi Jewish families and businesses.

Stanley grew up in more humble circumstances; his parents had a take-away fish and chips shop in Stamford Hill with living accommodation above. He attended state schools, excelled himself as a student, then went to Oxford to read English at Jesus College. His parents were proud of him, overjoyed to see him offered a place at Oxford and agreed to support him financially and so provide for his needs out of their modest income. He was their only child and whatever the father's reservations there was nothing the mother would not do to make him happy, to see his progress and boast it to relatives and friends. In the event Stanley arrived in Oxford handicapped by gross obesity, suppressed homosexuality, limited means and guilt for the financial burden borne by his parents. He reacted to those handicaps by creating a false aura for himself in which he wore the mantle of an intellectual who cared little for human physical shape, and of an aesthete who sought beauty with little respect for money. He bought his clothes from Cassells of Broad Street, would be the first to pay for a round of drinks at The King's Arms, and if it was agreed that he would join another student to dinner at a venue in town he would instead arrange at the last minute to hire a taxi to take them to The Trout at Godstow and to drive them back at the end of the evening. However, Stanley could not maintain that charade for long while he was shunned at the Oxford Jewish Society for being a snob. He went to pieces when a brief relationship with a student at Lady Margaret Hall turned sour and she left him for another man. He became depressed, his letters home became less frequent and his studies suffered, which was commented on by his tutor. He sought relief in T. S. Eliot and Evelyn Waugh, the latter in particular, and in joining the Conservative party. He got down to read nearly everything that Waugh wrote. At the start of the second year he followed in the footsteps of Waugh by being received into the Catholic Church. That shocked his family and surprised relatives and friends. His father threatened to disown him but was dissuaded from that course by his wife. There was nothing that would alienate the love that she had for her only son, nor anything that she would not do to see him happy. After a little more than a year at Oxford Stanley further followed the example of Waugh and went down without a degree. When he first came to Linden Gardens as a guest he was employed as the agent of an inner London constituency Conservative party, in a seat held by Labour with a massive majority.

Stanley was in the unhappy position of being a sociable man wanting of friends, an intellectual without formal recognition, an aesthete who disdained his own obese body, a self-hating Jew who turned to Rome without real conviction, a Conservative party agent tending to bohemianism, one attracted to the unconventional reaches of love while sexually inactive, and seeking out the company of some leading writers and artists of the period who were notorious for their homosexual proclivity while he excoriated the practice. He now welcomed the friendship of the younger Iraqi Jewish student. He regarded himself as his social mentor introducing him to the bohemian circles of Soho and Fitzrovia. There was at the time an inconspicuous club for the *literati* in an underground room near Shaftesbury Avenue. There they met a sombre looking man in his thirties, a poet who had just published his *A Charm Against the Toothache*. He was attracted to Stanley's young companion, said he was drawn to the mystical poetry of Hafiz and Omar Khayyam, and said that he personally knew some modern Egyptian poets and playwrights. He mentioned that he was also living in Notting Hill. As they came out Stanley told his friend that the man was the rising poet John Heath-Stubbs, and that he should be wary of him because he was a notorious homosexual predator. A week later the student was coming out of the underground when someone tapped him on the shoulder. He turned round and it was John Heath-Stubbs who asked him how he had spent his day and asked him if he would like to have coffee with him at his flat round the corner. The young man gave his excuses at which the poet lost interest and broke off with nothing more said. There were many single writers, actors and artists living in the area of Notting Hill and Bayswater, so homosexual orientation was a fact of life albeit pursued with discretion. The young student would have rubbed shoulders with it on several instances without being aware of it. He was aloof by nature and inexperienced in sexual matters, had only a vague idea about homosexuality, believed it involved an infinitesimal small number of men who did not exist in the circles in which he moved; and he was ignorant of the special words, expressions, hints, signs, nuances used for homosexual advances so became impervious to them. One day, feeling pleased with himself for having finished a weekly essay, he went down to reward himself with afternoon tea. Café Roma was small, unpretentious and there were unoccupied tables on this occasion. In fact, there was only one man sitting at a table for two. He signalled to the young student to go join him, which he did. He was a bulky middle aged man with unkempt hair and florid complexion. They exchanged their first names and the big man was enthused to learn that his companion was a student, an Iraqi with an exotic foreign name. He said his own full name was Michael Mac Liammoir, an actor. He had a plate of meat and vegetables partially consumed in front of him, and he invited the young man to have some, which he declined. The man explained that learning one's lines was the least challenging part for an actor, confirmed that he knew Peggy Ashcroft whom he admired immensely and referred to her as being at her best in the Shakespearean roles. The man then turned to the Irish cultural scene, was proud of his own Gate Theatre and urged the young man to visit if he should ever find himself in Dublin. MacLiammoir finished his meal, they exchanged good wishes, and the young man got up and left in high spirit. On another visit to Café Roma the young student made the acquaintance of a youth two years younger than him but in the swim of gay Notting Hill. He took him to the weekly parties of a notable opera singer who liked to surround himself with young men. He would emerge from the bedroom in a colourful dressing gown to cast an avuncular glance over his young followers whose admiration he rewarded with wine and savoury titbits followed by the aria *Nessum dorma* (None shall sleep) in Puccini's Turandot. The student went to only two such parties after which his younger companion went absent to have a plastic operation to flatten the tell-tale central ridge of his nose, and their acquaintance faltered and endStanley's favourite bohemian venue was another room under street level in Fitzrovia. He delighted in pointing to the walls reeking of nicotine and almost black with the innumerable tobacco and other cigarettes smoked over the years by generations of the Slade School of Fine Art students. Stanley had a catholic taste ranging from mock bohemianism to bourgeois respectability. One of his many friends was Andrew, a Jewish medical student at University College Hospital who was engaged to Monica, the daughter of a rich Jewish family living in Golders Green. She was having a 21st birthday party. Stanley was invited and he went along with his Iraqi friend. There they met two American girls who were on holiday. The Iraqi student was introduced to Doris and was smitten. A New Yorker, father a dentist, she had recently graduated from New York University and was about to start work as an occupational therapist. She had engaging looks without being particularly beautiful, the sort you would describe as a nice Jewish girl with dark hair and brown eyes. What captivated the young student was the way she looked at him when their eyes first met, the particular attention she paid to him, so important to one who was an outsider in the party in more sense than one. She turned away from everyone else as she came to stand beside him and to engage him in conversation, talking about her family and work while wanting to know all about him. Towards the end of the evening her friend Adele had to drag her away physically, they were sharing a flat in Addison Road, but not before Doris had extracted his promise to call the following day so they would go out to look at London's high spots. The following day, on the way to the British Museum, they were accosted by a gypsy woman who offered them a small bunch of 'lucky heather'. He accepted it and asked the woman for the price. She was taken aback by his guilelessness, said as he was a handsome young man with a lovely lady she would only want a token, a few pennies, which he produced, and which she accepted as she wished them good luck. He handed the bunch to Doris who was demonstrably moved by the gesture which she further showed by walking the rest of the way holding his hand with her damp, tremulous free hand. Later they stopped for tea at Russell Square, took the tube to Notting Hill, thence to Linden Gardens, his small bedroom and his bed. It was the first true sexual experience for both. He had had other sexual experiences since his arrival in London but they were transactional, their frequency depended on what he could afford. They were devoid of any emotion beyond the physical relief, the guilt and the feeling of being debased. It was so different on this occasion, clumsy in comparison, yet with full passionate embrace and tenderness given and received. The days that followed were blissful. They made a foursome with Andrew and Monica in outings to the Tate Gallery, London's South Bank and the theatre to watch Sandy Wilson's musical *The Boy Friend*. Yet the Iraqi student did not feel entirely comfortable in that foursome. Andrew, friendly and agreeable that he was, presented himself confidently as one who was conscious of his social worth as a young man training to be in the exalted profession of doctor while engaged to marry the daughter of a rich man in the City. Monica for her part let slip on occasion to show off her assets, most notably her rich family background, her being engaged to marry a doctor, and her Britishness. That last, the Britishness, irked the Iraqi student. There had very recently been the exodus of his community, the historical Babylonian Jewry, and their emigration en masse to Israel where they were being treated as culturally inferior, were actually called 'blacks', as they were set to constitute the proletariat of the new state of Israel, assigned in their inferiority to carry out the menial tasks involved in the building of the new country's infrastructure. The Iraqi student in London got the impression that the racist discrimination being practised in Israel was colouring the way Monica looked at him. He was particularly hurt when he happened to overhear the tail end of a spat between Monica and Doris in which the latter protested "What's the matter with you, he is Caucasian!" which he surmised to be a reference to him, thus a reflection of European Ashkenazis haughtily looking down on him and his people be they Sephardis or Mizrahis. That caused him not only to despise Monica but also to be resentful of Doris standing up for him in that manner and, as he saw it, diminishing him in the process. He excused himself from meeting her the following day and resolved to keep away until the end of her stay in London. But he could not keep to his resolution; he was deeply and utterly in love with Doris while he dreaded the inevitable separation at the end of her holiday. In the event it did not fall to him to resolve one way or the other. A short note from Doris told him that she and Adele were leaving England that same day, expressed deep affection for him as she will always treasure the memory of the happy times they knew each other.

He was badly affected by the end of the affair. Although there could have been no expectation it would last beyond the duration of the holiday yet he irrationally wanted it to endure, or at least not to end the way it did, which he took to be a personal rejection. He was particularly affected by the abruptness of the separation and its finality. Without any means of further communication he had to accept that, as far as Doris was concerned, the affair with all its passion was no more than a holiday fling. He did not blame her for that, nor would he have minded being used, if only it had ended with the exchange of addresses with the promise of an occasional letter or card and the chance of a transatlantic visit sometime in the indeterminate future. Afterwards he wanted to know more about Doris, to hear more about her news, which he would feel as a virtual extension of their brief affair. The only way of achieving that was to ask Stanley what if anything he heard, through his friendship with Andrew and Monica, about Doris and Adele after they had gone back to America. Stanley was dismissive: 'Why would you want to know anything about them, they are not intellectual!'

He was also badly affected by what he perceived to be a racist denigration of him by fellow Jews, European Ashkenazis of North London. Also, he was insecure about his future job prospects to the extent of feeling diminished in comparison with Andrew. It did not help that he failed in his application for a job at a leading publishing house which he attributed to his atrocious demeanour at the interview; his answer to every question was patently the wrong one, which he knew full well at the time. It was as if some inner demon was impelling him to self destruct, to ensure that he would fail to get the job in publishing while he aspired to be involved in publishing above all else. Without knowing it he was going through a crisis of the soul from which there appeared to be no escape. Then it came to him in a flash; he would turn to medicine to rehabilitate his self esteem and future career. And he turned for help to 'the Secretary". Professor Ford was the head of the Humanities hence the top academic at King's. His rooms were in the basement; he was completely blind, relied on the Secretary to deal with the day to day administration. She had occupied that position for many years, filled that role admirably, her authority acknowledged by everyone. She had a soft spot for the Iraqi student as was demonstrated the first day he came in from the street, made his way to the general office, and asked to be admitted as a student. His boldness, some thought naivety, impressed everyone in the office. The Secretary happened to be passing by, she took him down to her office in the basement, asked him a few questions then presented him to Mr Ford. Within two hours of his coming in from the street he was an undergraduate reading English at King's College London. Afterwards the Secretary gave him a wide smile every time she passed him. He now went to her saying he wanted to do medicine. He mumbled some reasons for his seeking a career change. She listened without interruption then asked him if there was a girl involved, and he averted his eyes. She thought he would not last the course but it was worth a try and to get him out of his dark mood. In the event he lasted only one term. He found the classes uncongenial, the other students among the least intellectual. He had difficulty handling the microscope and was repelled by the sight of blood and the body parts of the dog fish. Besides, the news back home were causing him anxiety. His father and most of his siblings were emigrating to Israel leaving only his elder two brothers in charge of the business, and they made it clear that with the times being uncertain they might not be able to support him in medical studies that would extend to five years or more. He just dropped out of the medical school without leave-taking and went to Oxford to do a doctorate in Arabic.

The small room in Linden Gardens was kept ready for his use at all times. That encouraged him to break away occasionally from his research in Oxford when he felt the need for a change. It also kept alive the friendship that he had with the other young Iraqi Jewish immigrants who soon became established as successful entrepreneurs. That was reflected in a general change in their sexual behaviour. At first there had been the one that emerged after leaving the repressive attitude to sex in Iraq and to suddenly enjoy the relaxed and free contact between the sexes in England. Now, a few years older in age and experience the hunger of a predator gorging himself on one-night stands had turned to a more discerning libido that led to having and maintaining a settled near exclusive relationship with a girl friend. Meir's lover now was Dodo (Dorothy), a Danish girl who had come to England as an au- pair, fell in love with Meir, gave up her job, stayed in London and was now living with him as one of a couple, an acknowledged girl friend. She was gentle, unassuming and uncomplicated. She was happy to be looked after while she, so to speak, kept a home for the two of them; which was not physically onerous since they had the money to pay for whatever was needed including a cleaner and having food delivered. And Dodo was not demanding, nor jealous. She did not object to Meir going out most evenings, sometimes not returning before the small hours. If she did feel unhappy she knew how to hide it. In fact Meir spent most of such evenings with his regular coterie of Iraqi immigrants talking business when not playing poker. Dodo compensated for her lonely evenings by playing patience and other card games with the Oxford student when he happened to be staying, her favourite game being canasta. That also responded to the student's loneliness, shortage of money in his case limiting his scope for going out. A relationship developed between the two, respectful and solicitous as of siblings. One afternoon he happened to be entirely on his own when two plain-clothes policemen came to the door asking questions about Dorothy. He confirmed that she was living there. He further explained that he was an Oxford student staying as a guest and that Dorothy was not his girlfriend but the girlfriend of his friend Meir. They were satisfied and went away to report to Dodo's family with assurance about her safety and wellbeing.

Notting Hill at the time was notorious for the number of unconventional artistic people as well as a variety of refugees who had arrived from different parts of he Continent ravaged by war and its aftermath. It was easy to think of them as secretive, notorious, and so to regard them with caution. On one occasion which was a Saturday night he was alone in the apartment when his sleep was shattered by a loud explosion. He rushed to the window and the street was empty and calm; there was no further noise, no human voices to be heard nor any new light switched on to unravel the meaning of the explosion. He rang the news desks of two Sunday papers followed by *The People* that had not yet gone to print. In the morning he had the satisfaction of seeing his short report on the first page under a bold heading "Mystery Explosion in Notting Hill"; and he had the further satisfaction of receiving a cheque for four pounds and ten shillings. That wetted his appetite and made him realise how it was possible to make a living as a free lance reporter. Things were happening all the time and there was news all round to be gathered as long as one kept one's eyes open and his hearing attuned to what was going on. The standard reward for reporting a piece of news that was accepted for publication was a cheque for two pounds and ten shillings. He got one for reporting a fracas that got out of hand outside the Irish Club in Queensway and another for a body on the Central Line at West Acton that interrupted the service and delayed his travel to work.

He was always hard up, the remittances he received from his family barely covered the basic necessities. He supplemented them by working for Mann, Crossman & Paulin, a major London brewery, which he did whenever he could take a break from his studies. There was always work for him whenever he wanted it. He worked in the accounts department which employed many men who variously took their holidays or went sick at different times. It was then a matter of concern for the department to demonstrate that any such absence left a gap which had to be filled, else it would be thought that the department was overmanned and could absorb the work of the absentee. After the first week that the Oxford student worked there, he was taken aside and told delicately to slow down and so avoid making mistakes! The times that he worked for the company marked the beginning of a commercial revolution in the British high street and with big changes to the ways that the main breweries marketed their product. MC&P was a traditional conservative company. As a major London brewery it was affiliated to The Worshipful Company of Brewers, the oldest of the City Livery companies that traced its beginning to a grant by Henry VI in 1438 with the object of promoting a friendly relations between the brewers as well as supporting charitable causes. The company maintained a muted competition with its rivals whose products were allowed for sale in its houses at cost but with an agreed handling charge. That was a practice that ran through all the main brewery companies, the only exception was Guinness which was exempt from the handling charge, the Dublin company being treated with veneration as the aristocratic head of the industry.

The affairs of the MC&P were also managed in a paternalistic way. A public limited company with shares traded on the London Stock Exchange it was yet treated by the management as a family business with George Mann as the patriarch who was often seen standing at the factory gates eyeing the men streaming in, and not hesitating to pull one aside to upbraid him for the way he was dressed or to give him a half-a-crown and tell him to go get himself a proper hair cut. The paternalism was reinforced by Mrs Mann being the Matron of the adjoining London Hospital (Mile End) where she ruled supreme. There was a general perception that she provided a special additional care for any patient who happened to be an employee of the company.

The company was also run in an old fashioned complacent way. Things were done the old way except that at the time of the arrival of the student there had taken place a big innovation which was the introduction of the IBM Computer Card system in the accountancy department; the student's holiday work was to take part in operating it. However, the company was still being run inefficiently. It was sitting on substantial assets comprising public houses occupying prominent positions in the high street, some producing little profit if at all. That did not seem to concern the management, their only concern was the sale of beer. That complacency was shaken to the roots by the city man Charles Clore amassing a big number of the company's shares then mounting a takeover bid. The management realised how desperate was its position while the mass of the brewery companies were alarmed as they realised their vulnerability, that their hold could be loosened by their shares traded in the stock market where they were regularly bought, sold, borrowed and shorted. The other brewers rallied to the defence of MC&P while its employees set up and contributed to a fighting fund to sustain their company and thwart the ambition of Clore the outsider. The bid was only defeated by MC&P merging with Watney, Combe, Reid & Co. Ltd. to form a new company Watney Mann, too big to be swallowed by Clore.

Hoping that his going to start a new chapter in Oxford would ease his anxieties the Iraqi doctoral student was soon disabused. The Arabic department in Oxford in the 1950's was not a happy place to be. At its head was (Hamilton) Alexander (Rosskeen) Gibb commonly known as H.A.R.G, Laudian Professor of Arabic . A brilliant Arabist he was also noted for his cold authoritarianism, idiosyncrasy and unpopularity in equal measures. The department was also rife with racism including anti-Semitism. The Iraqi Jewish doctoral candidate entered that milieu with a badly chosen subject in that it was not amenable to serious scholarly research; it was indicative of the deficiencies of the faculty that it was accepted as suitable for a doctorate. Also indicative was that he received no advice or help while his relationship with his supervisor was fraught. After two years in Oxford he went down before completing his thesis on the life and times of Ahmad Faris al-Shidiaq. The news of the family back home were also causing him anxiety. His eldest brother got married followed soon after by the next one. They now had their own families to support which would impact on their willingness or ability to continue to support him further. One letter after another urged him to go home where he could take his pick of eligible girls of families of good standing and the promise of a big dowry. He disdained all that and, buffeted by rough seas of disappointment, anxiety for the future and creeping self-doubt, the young man's salvation was the arrival of Helen on the scene.

Hilda

Royston is a Yorkshire village within a commuting distance of Barnsley, Wakefield and Leeds. At the dawn of the twentieth century it was a mining village dominated by Monckton Colliery and the 13th century St John the Baptist parish church. Most of the men went down the pit for work and returned after the shift to a house rented from the colliery in a street of identical houses owned by it. The house consisted of a front room referred to as 'The Room' which was only used on special occasions such as a wedding or a funeral or when an important visitor called. The rest of the ground floor was the living space consisting of the kitchen, dining room, laundry and wash room with a tin bath propped up against the wall next to the wooden mangle. Upstairs consisted of two bedrooms and a small box room. The privy was in the communal yard at the back.

Harold Caswell was born in 1903. At the age of fourteen he went down the pit to work; he then grew up to be an upstanding handsome man of a good family that was highly respected in the village. Everyone commented on his superb physique and his singing voice that he used to good effect in church and which was further appreciated at social events and in public houses. He attracted the attention of several unattached young women including Mary whose heart throbbed every time her gaze fell on him while she harboured a high expectation after their third date. Then Harold disappointed them all by marrying Annie, an outsider. It was rumoured that they had met at Barnsley Market where she worked, that her people lived in Askern near Doncaster, and there was a hint of the Irish in her ancestry. She was beautiful in an exotic way; a fine slim body, dark skin, auburn hair and blue eyes. She had a good taste in dress and food, kept a good house for Harold and was envied for the elegant touches she used in furnishing their newly rented colliery house while they waited for their first child. There were complications in the pregnancy, and Annie was referred to Leeds General Infirmary where she died as she gave birth to a girl. The child they named Hilda was taken to be cared for by grandma Caswell whose household also included her daughter Sissie and Sissie's daughter Vida who was two years older than Hilda. For the first few years Hilda and Vida were brought up as sisters and their sisterly love did not fade completely over the years, surviving separation, family disputes and the vicissitudes of life, some vestiges lasting a lifetime.

Hilda was six years old when Mary's patience and overwhelming passion for Harold were rewarded. They were married in the parish church and Hilda was moved to live with them. Mary soon bore Harold a daughter Margaret who was to be her only child. Mary did not get on well with the Caswell women who treated her as an outsider and interloper, her family the Womacks were Wakefield people, while grandma Caswell missed Hilda and was mortified to see that her favourite granddaughter, child of her old age, was now to be cared for by Mary. That said, grandma Caswell was a fair minded woman; she would tell you that Mary was not a bad woman, that she did care for Annie's daughter to the extent that social duty and church teaching dictated, but that her love in its plenitude was dedicated to Harold, anything left over she showered on her own flesh and blood.

Then there occurred the calamity of Harold falling seriously ill; he almost succumbed to the coal dust that clogged his lungs, and was close to death. Mary nursed him day and night to keep him alive. He survived but was no longer the man he was. There was no question of his returning to work in the pit; he got some support from the union and a job pushing a float in Royston to deliver milk for the Barnsley Co-op. He did frequently take Hilda along with him so she would keep an eye on the cart while he went to make the deliveries. When they came to a rise in the road Harold, out of breath, would call out to his ten year old daughter: "Push, Hilda, push!" The job was more than could be sustained and the Co-op replaced it with one that charged Harold with collecting the weekly 'subs' that the people paid towards a prospective purchase or towards repaying a loan they had for an earlier purchase. This new job was less arduous than the milk round but walking from door to door, counting the money, giving a receipt and noting the amount in a notebook was challenging enough. The Co-op came to realise that he was almost dyslexic and retired him.

Thereafter Harold was nearly housebound. The family survived on unemployment benefit and the frugality of Mary. She would walk every Friday to the Post Office to collect the money. If there was little food in the larder on a Thursday she would make sure that Harold had enough while on many Thursdays Hilda's 'tea' as she came back from a long day at school was a plate of baked beans on toast. Mary was a good cook and housekeeper, her scones reputed to be the best in the street. She attributed her skill to her years in service for the better classes and learning their ways. She would talk with pride of the years she did for the Grays and would produce the letter of appreciation and recommendation Mrs Gray gave her as she left. That was the only area of dissent between Mary and Harold, which turned on politics. Almost everyone in the village voted labour, and Mary was no different. But she admired the rich for their appreciation of the good things in life; the fine food, the smart dresses, the beautiful adornments, the general good order and the way they spoke. Harold for his part was a true labour man whose excellent voice led the singing of 'The Red Flag' at party and union meetings, and at miners' parades. Due to his physical frailty he had to reduce his appearances at such events but there was compensation to be had in the expressions of sympathy, friendship and show of solidarity he received from the union as from socialist members of the party. Don Betts and Arthur Farmer were friends who lived in the village and called on him frequently, often together. They would then sit round the table in the kitchen to discuss politics, and to debate it. Both were socialists but there were differences. Don was a parish councillor who believed in representative democracy; Arthur was dismissive of that kind of socialism, he accused Don of being a reformist while asserting that nothing but a world revolution and the dictatorship of the proletariat will bring along the socialist utopia that they both aspired. They were then joined by Brian Davy, a Sheffield academic and an administrator of the Workers Educational Association. He was introduced by Arthur who had attended some of his reading classes. Forewarned of his arrival Mary would bring out the best of the china which she set on a table in the Room next to a plate of her special scones. After that first meeting Davy insisted that they held the following ones in the kitchen, the men at the table, Mary fussing about nervously while Hilda sat on a pile of cushions in the corner avidly listening to the conversation. Mr Davy was a historian and he expounded on Marxist philosophy and Leninist ideology, ran through the history of modern activist socialism starting with Shelly's "Ode to Anarchy", then the cooperation of Karl Marx and Friedrich Engels in publishing *The Communist Manifesto* in 1848 followed by the brave but doomed experience of the 1871 Paris Commune. He would then talk about the rise of popular socialism marked by the successive socialist Internationals. Hilda listened to all that with rapt attention; she was particularly impressed by the theory posited by the academic that the resources of the earth were inexhaustible so there was enough for everyone, and that the reason for poverty and privation was an unfair distribution in which the strong took more than their just portion; and she was captivated by the communist dream of a paradise on earth which could be summed up as 'from each according to his ability, to each according to his needs.' Later, she was to carry some of those ideas to the grammar school; a particular teacher voiced concern at what she saw as the radicalisation of a section of the students; but the management turned a blind eye, most of them being crypto-socialists themselves. As for Harold Caswell his socialism was rooted in the Co-operative Movement and the Labour Party, in working people standing shoulder to shoulder owning the business and keeping the profit, none going to some bosses or city slickers but being paid to the members as 'divis'. When the labour leader Hugh Gaitskell died and it became known that he had left an estate of thirty thousand pounds Harold was aghast: How can a labour party leader be worth that much!

Hilda was a smart girl. She passed her eleven-plus and got a place at Normanton Grammar School where she shined. She passed what was the then equivalent of the GSE examination and did so well that she was marked as a university hopeful. She was also a good tennis player and they entered her for the Barnsley and District Ladies Tennis Cup. She was at a disadvantage in the changing room and abashed to see the smart expensive white underwear and skirts that the others pulled out of expensive leather bags while all she had was a rough and ill-fitting white pair of shorts that Mary had got for her from a stall in Barnsley Market. She sensed the haughtiness of the other girls as they stood in a knot talking animatedly in whispers and casting furtive, contemptuous looks in her direction as she stood alone in a corner. But she withstood that stoically; it brought out the socialist defiance that her father had inculcated in her and his contempt of the bourgeois assumption of superiority, and she walked to the court, head held high and with added resolve. She beat one competitor after another and got on the Royston bus at the end of the day proudly carrying the cup to go present to her father. She became a celebrity in the village and in the school when her picture appeared in the Barnsley Chronicle with a report of the competition in which she was referred to as "Little Mo" with allusion to the American singles champion Maureen Connolly.

The school, having advised her to apply for a university place, Harold and Mary dismissed that notion as fanciful, saying that a university education was not for their sorts of people. And there was no way they could provide any financial support. They stuck to that position adamantly to the extent that the deputy head teacher herself came to their house to tell them that the school would support Hilda's application to a certain Cambridge college with which the school had a good connection, and to reassure them that with the tuition fees paid by the government with a maintenance grant added there would be little if any financial burden falling on them. They were unmoved, Mary confiding to Harold and Hilda that she could not see how she could even fill a suitcase for Hilda with the sorts of dresses that she would need at a Cambridge college. Hilda lost the chance of a university education, a loss she would regret for the rest of her life. She now felt trapped in a hopeless life in Royston. The only jobs for girls in Royston were at the shirt factory, the Co-op and the pawn shop, while going to find work in Leeds was no easier than going to London. She felt trapped in an arid life from which there appeared to be no escape. Escape came with Vida, also desperate to get away. Vida was a rebel, she stood out in Royston as a supporter of the Tory party and for her hostility to the miners' trades union and all that it stood for, as well as deep aversion to the ways of the mining community. She now suggested to Hilda going to look for better opportunities and a better life in London.

Hilda got on the train at Leeds City Station as the Yorkshire lass Hilda Caswell and arrived at London Kings Cross three hours later full of hope and trepidation, soon to be the metropolitan Helen Caswell.

Hampstead Garden Suburb

The 1950's were to the British woman an age of respectability and conformity. Few women went out to work while the ideal as depicted and promoted in the media including the newly invented television was of the woman staying at home to look after the children and to keep house for the man who was the bread winner and head of the household. But there were already to be seen the stirrings of the transformative changes that would follow; attempts to depart from the norm initiated by some who were privileged enough to dare it; King's Road and Chelsea anticipating the Rock and Roll, the youthful fashion of Mary Quant, the mini skirt, the hot pants and the sexual liberation. And there was the attempt to break the mould of the sedate self-satisfied life of the Metropolis with some early exemplars of the Sloane Ranger girls opening bijou coffee houses in trendy parts of London. One such was "The Coffee Pot" in Notting Hill, a small shop with a few old bare tables and hard chairs, posters on the walls, *The Stage* newspaper next to *The Telegraph*, espresso machine on the counter next to a pile of copies of the latest poem of Anne Louise, the owner. A copy was seen by a local Mary Whitehouse-type woman who made her way to The Coffee Pot to confront the owner and to shame her for the immoral alliterative 'pen, penis, penicillin', and was told by the Honourable Anne Louise to piss off. That was followed by a police officer coming to investigate and leaving with a smile.

The shop had only one employee. When Helen had applied for the job she impressed by her good looks, graceful body, good deportment and good speech spiced by just a hint of Yorkshire. It was her fourth job in London. She had arrived from Yorkshire the year before with her cousin Vida and they soon separated, Vida meeting Roy and going to live with him in Norwich. Helen applied to be a nurse, did a spell as a trainee at the Maudsley Hospital, did not like it and left to take a temporary job as a teacher's assistant at Mill Hill School. That was followed by her working as a sales assistant in a general store in Kilburn before going to work as assistant manageress of The Coffee Pot, a high-sounding job description of what in reality was no better than being a waitress. Yet, it was a genteel sort of job catering for the generally genteel customers. She liked it, was prepared to put up with the poverty rate wage with tips added that just covered the rent of her bedsit in Bayswater and the basic essentials while she waited for her soul mate, and ever the optimist and at heart a conformist, the husband and father of her future children.

She recognised him as the one she had been waiting for as soon as he came in, ordered a tea, sat down and opened the *New Statesman*. She brought him a pot of tea with a scone and butter. He said he had only wanted a mug of tea; she said the rest was on the house. She asked him if there was anything interesting in *The Statesman*, adding that back home some of her father's friends often carried it when they came visiting. He told her that he was a PhD student at Oxford and she asked him if he had met or heard of a Dr Davy who taught history at Sheffield University. He said he would like to know more about her coal mining community in Yorkshire. The following day he waited for her to close the shop, and they went for a long walk and an engrossing conversation in Kensington Gardens followed by his walking her back to the street door of the building in Leinster Place where she lived. The following day they went to the Lyric at Hammersmith, took seats in 'the Gods' to watch a lively performance by Donald Wolfit after which they made their way to Leinster Place; she invited him in and he stayed the night.

The days that followed were blissful while they spent all their free time together. She gave him all her love with nothing held back, while all she wanted was his love in return. She invested her present and future happiness in him without reservation or demands. In the light of her love she saw him as the best man in the world, and told him so. She would start her day by singing or humming 'What is life to me without you', a song in Orfeo ed Euridici popularised by Kathleen Ferrier who had tragically died of cancer not long before. He, in his turn, was captivated by her incomparable beauty, serenity, generosity, innocence; added to which were the words of admiration and encouragement that restored his self-esteem. When they found themselves with not enough money for food, on two occasions he had to take his watch to the pawn shop in Praed Street, she reassured him that he will be rich one day. When he felt depressed for making no headway in his career she told him that with his innate talent and energy there will be nothing to stop him achieving great things, that in time he will be writing books that people will read and admire. But what captivated him most of all was her vulnerability. She was in London with no money or formal qualifications, no family or friends to turn to for help. He wanted to protect her, and as she needed his protection he could not bring himself to shake the bond that held them together. There were many reasons to doubt the wisdom and durability of the relationship. They grew up in different countries, cultures, backgrounds and religions. The relationship was maintained against the hopes and expectations of his family and would alienate him from his community. Those factors weighed heavily on him to the extent that at times he wished that Helen would redirect her love, be responsive to the several approaches made to her by men admirers, so that he could break free from the bond that held them together. But Helen's love of him was unshakable and excluded anything that would come between them. Nor would he have really wanted anything to come between them. The perceived burden of wanting to protect her was in reality the truest expressions of true love. She now lost interest in The Coffee Pot and got a job with the BBC as a clerk in the Audience Research Department. When he went back to Oxford to resume his work on his doctoral thesis she would buy a day-return ticket every Sunday to spend it with him. She would arrive early and leave late; they used the time walking in Christ Church Meadow, the University Parks, the bustling streets, but mostly his room in Iffley Road.

He left Oxford without completing his thesis and got a job in Covent Garden as an accountant to a Catalan group of growers that paid him ten pounds a week. Helen was very excited when he broke the news. It would have occurred to her that back in Royston a man could bring up a family for less than that, but she was cautious not to reveal her thought. He now made a break with Linden Gardens and went to live in a bedsit in Temple Fortune, while Helen gave up her room in Leinster Place and went to live in Brunner Close, Hampstead Garden Suburb, as a paying guest of the Weinbergs. They were a young Jewish family, Geert a Dutch importer of cigars, Sheila an American who stayed at home to look after Judith, their two-year old daughter. They were secular and left wing, Sheila more so than Geert. She liked Helen and her man friend and was thrilled to witness the romance blossoming under her roof.

Those were halcyon days, they were happy at work and had more time to spend together. Helen would from time to time get tickets to some BBC entertainment which they would attend, while she took the underground on each working day to Covent Garden to take lunch with him at The Mason's Arms or, on pay day, an Italian restaurant nearby. Helen's boss was Miss Williams who knew how important it was for Helen to go meet the man she was mad about, and she turned a blind eye to the occasions that Helen came back late after the lunch break. One day they sauntered about after lunch and happened to stop outside a jeweler's. It was a beautiful Spring's day when everything in nature was enchanting, and it was his pay day. She pointed to a small ring in the window, he asked her if she liked it, and she nodded. It was a plain gold wedding ring which Helen would wear on the third finger of her left hand to her dying day. To her it signified a formal engagement. He had not at the time thought of it as other than a present to the woman he loved, but then accepted on reflection that it meant more to him than a non-committal gift; he was happy to see Helen happy with the ring and to accept her interpretation of the event. That evening they went to the cinema in Golders Green to watch 'Love is a Many Splendored Thing' featuring William Holden and Jennifer Jones. The film was based on a mostly autobiographical romantic novel of Han Suyin that dealt with the doomed love that spanned two different cultures. Helen found the story almost unbearably moving, and it had similarities with her own situation. She broke down in tears at the sad ending.

Their social life was extended by the arrival of Joyce and Haron on the scene. Joyce was a cousin of Helen, her family in Wakefield. She graduated from Durham University with an English degree and now came to London to put a distance between her and her Yorkshire family while she looked for better opportunities. Haron was the man's best friend from their school days in Baghdad. He had emigrated to Israel, worked in the government and has now arrived to pursue an Oxford course of anthropology. In the meantime Helen told Sheila the circumstances of getting the ring on her finger. Sheila thought it wrong to let religious differences stand in the way of true love and suggested a non-religious marriage ceremony at the registry office. A date was set for the wedding, but the news got back to the man's family in Baghdad, so his eldest brother Sami flew over, stated the family's objection in no uncertain terms, and only returned after extracting a promise that the wedding would not take place. Back in Royston the rumor of an impending marriage of their Hilda to an unknown and unseen foreigner was received with surprise and some dismay. They would tell the inquisitive neighbours that Hilda's man was an Iraqi, a Jew but, so he was described to them, 'as white as you and me!' Joyce and Haron were not surprised that the wedding was called off; Sheila was dismayed and surprised that the young couple, the man in particular, had so much regard for the wishes of their families. Helen was submissive. However great the disappointment and the sense of betrayal she made sure of keeping those feelings to herself; not a word of protest or reproach was heard from her. More important to her was to ease the pressure on the man she loved and to maintain the relationship. She did not want it to end the way it ended in 'Love is a Many Splendored Thing'.

They were married in the Hendon Registry six months later with Joyce and Haron as witnesses. No one else was told. They started married life with fifteen pounds, which was all that was left of her monthly salary and his weekly wage after paying the Registry fee and the deposit for the double room in Alma Square. They took their witnesses to dinner at 'Mon Plaisir' a small French restaurant in Monmouth Street, Seven Dials. They celebrated their new state with their first taste of Beaujolais wine.

Alma Square

Their first home as a married couple was a rented furnished bedsit in a Victorian house in Alma Square, St John's Wood. The name invoked the Battle of Alma which marked the climax of the Crimea War in which the combined armies of Britain, France, Turkey and Sardinia defeated the Russians in 1854. The room was on the first floor, had a wide window that overlooked the private communal garden square. The furniture was scanty and shabby: It consisted of a double bed, a wardrobe, two dining chairs, an old threadbare easy chair, hooks on the door for coat hanging; a wash basin on a stand by the window with another small table next to it, and a coin operated gas ring. On the third day they had their first spat. He came back from work to find that the furniture was rearranged, every piece moved around. She was to repeat that process almost every week giving vent, as he saw it, to her suppressed housekeeping instinct by rearranging the few items of other people's furniture for want of their own. A month later there was an additional piece; a cold storage box for fruit and vegetable in the shape of an eighteen inch cube, top sheet thinner than the rest with a depression in the centre into which you poured a little water that cooled as it evaporated. She meant to surprise him. After a little discussion whether it was worth the four pounds that she had saved at the rate of one pound a week out of her weekly wage they went out to The Warwick Castle to celebrate their first married acquisition.

There's little privacy to be had in a house of multiple occupation. You compensate for that by creating virtual screens separating you from the others. As you happen to pass another lodger you would exchange the conventional formal greetings while averting direct eye contact. You may feel lonely and claustrophobic in a small bedsit, you may even wish to have social contact with the serious looking man across the landing or the attractive young girl on the ground floor that you would pass as you go out to work. But you are held back by the thought that once you become really friendly you surrender thereby your right to be on your own, of not having to put up with people coming to knock on your door at times of their choosing and staying for a coffee and a chat. There were several bedsit lodgers at the rooming house. He never got round to work out the number or to know much about them, or at all about some of them, But there was no avoiding a closer view of two of them.

Sinhini's room was the one closest to the top of the stairs so he would pass it on the way out and on his return from work. A Kashmiri woman, he judged her to be in her early forties, fresh-faced, tall and full-bodied, body attractive in its fullness. She carried herself with dignity and the self-assurance of one who was conscious of her innate superiority without using it to challenge or oppress. She would wish you a 'Good Morning' in a high pitched voice as though she really meant it, and would look you straight in the face. She occasionally left her door open so the room would be suffused by the rays of the sun flowing from the window across the landing to where she sat at the table with an open book. He got to know more about her when she was indisposed, sofa converted to bed, and three men who appeared to have come to offer their good wishes. As the door was opened letting in two, the third left standing self-consciously outside waiting for his turn, they were heard to address her as 'Doctor Sinhini' and with some mention of Kashmir. Was she a medical practitioner, and were they work colleagues come to cheer her up in her illness? He dismissed that notion. Medics commonly went about dressed casually smart whereas these visitors were strictly formal in appearance; plain dark grey suit, jacket fastened over a discreet tie. He conjectured that the woman may have held the doctorate in a discipline other than medicine, was perhaps a social activist with political aspiration holding court for would-be followers and acolytes.

It was well past midnight when the air of Alma Square was rent by the bloodcurdling scream of a woman. That was followed by the sound of moaning coming from the direction of the room at the end of the corridor where Mr and Mrs Williams lived. It was then followed by further beatings and Mrs Williams screaming with every blow. The whole house froze, nothing and nobody stirred. The newly married young wife slid closer to her husband and he instinctively put his arms round her shoulders for reassurance. The atmosphere then dramatically unfroze with heavy banging on the Williams' door and Dr Sinhini calling out loudly: "Mr Williams, stop beating up your wife" The beating stopped, a little moaning was heard, then a further shout by Sinhini, telling Mr Williams with all the peremptoriness that she possessed: "Stop it, stop beating your poor wife!" Everything went deadly quiet after that; come the morning nothing was heard to stir in the room at the end of the corridor. Mrs Bennett who lived on the ground floor was the oldest resident and over the years had seen and heard everything. She now told anyone who asked that Mr Williams left the house very soon after Dr Sinhini's intervention, and that Mrs Williams was too embarrassed to come out of her room before the others had left for work. She would confide further that Mrs Williams had a good job managing a dress shop in Swiss Cottage, that Mr Williams was a nasty man who preyed on her. He was an inveterate gambler and frittered all that she earned. If, as it happened on this occasion, he lost all his money in gambling he would return to force his wife to give him more to take back to the card table hoping to recoup his losses. A week later Mrs Williams invited the young married wife to her room, showed her a nice designer dress that she would let her have for one-third the price. The wife liked the dress, discussed the offer with her husband; they revisited their budget and concluded that they could not afford it

There was in those days a big building in Euston Road run by Westminster Council for evening classes for adults. They covered over a dozen subjects including English for foreigners, foreign languages, social sciences, martial arts and fencing. The young wife arranged for them to go to investigate at the beginning of the academic year, and they decided to subscribe for a course of French for those already with elementary knowledge of the language, and a course of Spanish for rank beginners; classes held on Tuesdays and Thursdays respectively. The wife was thrilled with the venture which had several attractive features. The signing up fees were modest; they would be spending two evenings a week together in a clean, warm building with nothing to spend; attractive courses which were not challenging while opening one's mind to different cultures and new expressions as well as dreams of the warm continental south.

The French classes were well attended and Mr Dando knew how to hold the attention of every one. A portly middle aged man he was always neatly turned out: hair neatly dressed with a parting in the middle; tie of a minor public school held in place by a mother-of-pearl clip; three-piece grey suit; trousers freshly ironed and creased descending to a pair of highly polished black shoes. The husband conjectured with nothing to support it that Mr Dando had a good woman at home, probably a doting mother who looked after him and was proud of him. He was not diminished by self-doubt nor would he miss an opportunity for self-aggrandisement. As he smugly surveyed his full first class of eager adults he felt pleased to tell them that they had come to the right teacher, one whose mastery of the romance languages, French in particular, would not bend the knee to that of an Oxbridge don. On the third Tuesday he arrived to see the class diminished by a few leavers; he said that it was to be expected, part time evening classes were always thus. He picked a chalk and went straight to the blackboard where he wrote *ave sum iam onet*, turned round and asked the class what they thought of it. "That's Latin" one called out; the teacher asked the others if they agreed. No one said otherwise and there were a few signs of assent. The teacher looked around, then turned back towards the blackboard, pointed a finger to the words and pronounced triumphantly 'Have some jam on it' followed by a barely suppressed giggle.

The Spanish teacher Garcia had one thing in common with Dando. While the latter was an Englishman teaching French the former taught Spanish while at heart a fervent

Basque separatist. But otherwise the two men were different in character. Garcia was always intense; full of self-doubt and seared by the experiences of the Spanish civil war, the wounds still raw. He clearly needed the job and the money that came with it. He approached it very seriously and conscientiously; would go out of his way and often in unpaid overtime to help any of the students who were seen to be in difficulty. He started the course by getting the students to learn the forms of conventional greetings and the numbers, things which would come handy to anyone visiting the country He would start each lesson by pointing a finger to one of the students and ask 'Que hora est?' as he looked at his wrist watch for confirmation. Then he came one evening looking distraught. He missed the usual opening and got straightaway to unburden himself of the unwelcome news that this was to be the last lesson, the last of the evening Spanish course for beginners. Of the students who signed up for the course several had dropped out and the Council decided that the number that remained no longer justified the cost. Garcia thought it shameful that the fate of education and culture is left in the hands of accountants, and railed against a cruel and short-sighted political system that for the sake of saving a little money was prepared to deprive hard-working people the opportunity of studying in the evening to improve their knowledge. He concluded his bitter discourse by urging everyone to write to the Council to claim a refund of the subscription. Finally, by way of adieu, he pointed to the young wife and called out for the last time, voice quivering with emotion: 'Senora, que hora est?', and she cried.

A summer's day as bright as the sun's rays shining on Alma Square and streaming through the window next to the top of stairs to fall on Dr Sinhini lying stretched on the sofa, back propped by cushions against the wall. She was leafing through a notebook as he emerged from the stairs. He saw the open door, had a quick furtive glance and softly said "Good afternoon" as he averted his eyes. "And such a lovely afternoon", she called back, "come in, come in." He stepped into the room shyly. "Take a seat and tell me a little about yourself", she added. As he stepped further into the room hesitantly his wife appeared and took him by the hand, and "Your tea is at the table, it'll get cold", as she led him away. On the Friday of the following week he came back from work and saw their suitcases packed ready to be taken to West Hampstead, "It's a lovely big room with only two others on the same floor, close to Finchley Road Station", she explained, "and only fifteen shillings a week more."

Compayne Gardens

ondon is a collection of neighbourhoods each having
its own identity with a focal point such as a church,
a public house, a stadium, a notable store or market; and
each having its own peculiar ambience. To leave the bedsit
in Alma Square and move to Compayne Gardens was to go
from the mature and sedate surroundings of Lord's cricket
ground, the legendary Abbey Road recording studio, and the
proud and dignified villas of Hamilton Terrace, to then go
join the hustle and bustle of the area surrounding the West
Hampstead railway stations, the boutiques of Swiss Cottage,
the shops and bakeries of Finchley Road and the boisterous
informality and bonhomie of the several 'Gardens' between
Finchley Road to the east, Edgware Road and Kilburn to
the west. The room was also on the first floor, bigger than
the one they had left at Alma Square, similarly furnished but
shabbier; you could discern the bare wooden floor through
patches of the threadbare carpet. A good feature of the room
was a big window that overlooked the street where several

similar houses took in weekly lodgers. Phil, a young man in his thirties, was then the only lodger in occupation on their floor. He happened to be in as they arrived. After the conventional exchange of greetings, he told them his name, said he worked at the local public library, wished them well, then went to his room and closed he door. Then as she busied herself unpacking the suitcases and sorting out the contents her husband went to have a look out of the window. Across the street a young woman, he thought she was a student, was watering the flowerpot on her windowsill with a used milk bottle. She lifted her eyes, saw him looking at her, and she smiled. The wife's last concern was to find a suitable place for the cold box. The following day the husband came back from his new job with a hand of bananas. She was minded to put them in the box and he stopped her. They were still green. So he had them fully wrapped up in newspapers then placed in a drawer under a pile of clothing where they will ripen themselves gradually with the ethylene that they will naturally exude. The man was now in the banana ripening business.

The woman opens the letter and screams with excitement. Her cousin Joyce was coming down to London to start a job at the Priory Community School and would be looking for a bedsit nearby. It was to be a temporary stopgap while she completed a year of teacher training then looked around for a full-time appointment as a graduate teacher. Joyce added that her coming down to London was against the wishes of her mother but with the muted support of her father. That last bit of information went down well with the young married woman; she could never get on with Clarissa and, truth to be told, not many people did in Wakefield. Within a month Joyce was living with Eric in a bedsit in Acol Lane. They had been together at Durham; Eric was working at Zarnicos, commodity traders in Mincing Lane, and dreaming of being promoted to a dealer. Another letter, one with an Iraq postal stamp, informed the young married man that Ephraim Shammash was touring in Europe with his wife Gladys. They were married six months before and this was a sort of delayed honeymoon. Ephraim had a store in Baghdad for the sale of general goods including imported electrical appliances, and he had the Iraq sole agency of the British company Morphy Richards.

Joyce and Eric called one afternoon and the young married woman turned the occasion into a tea party, the first of her married life, by inviting Phil. It turned out to be a lively encounter of opposites. Eric was full of confidence, bubbling with ambition and hope for the future. Phil by contrast was taciturn and generally morose. He had little small talk but a store of politics which was uncorked at mention of the prime minister's address to the nation. Harold McMillan's speech was a celebration of the end of the years of rationing and austerity after the war, coupled with near full employment, increases in production and revenues with a general improvement in the standard of living; "You have never had it so good", he told the nation. Phil was dismissive, said it was typical of the Tories, tapping the hard-working man on the back with one hand while picking his pocket with the other. Eric took umbrage at that talk, called it divisive, the sort of language using the class warfare trope to further the aims of the socialists and so destabilise the national cohesion. He said he himself had never had it so good. The librarian said he made no apology for being a socialist while respecting the political system of representative democracy. He had read Marx and had great respect for him as a political thinker and economist. The would-be commodities trader retorted that the man truly fit for respect was not the bearded German immured in the British Library but the one who got two-and- a- half tonnes of wheat from one acre of land when only two had been got out before. That moved the argument to another more refined level. Phil posited that the fault for famine and human misery did not lie in the scarcity of resources, the world was full of them and they belonged to everyone as a natural bounty. Rather the social ills resulted from an immoral distribution of those resources. He backed that argument by statistics of which the most striking was that five per cent of the inhabitants of the United Kingdom owned ninety-five per cent of its total wealth. He quoted a famous saying of Bernard Shaw: "The world economy is between my beard and my pate; abundant production but bad distribution." Eric's thrust went to the very heart of Marxist theory and dogma: The entrepreneurs, so-called capitalists, innovate, create jobs and produce wealth that goes to the workers apart from a small part that is retained as profit without which there would be no investment, no industrial renewal and no innovation. At this stage the hostess, alarmed as to where the discussion was likely to lead, asked Joyce how she was getting on at school; and the latter asked disingenuously if someone would explain to her, she had never had a satisfactory explanation, who precisely was to be classed as capitalist and who as worker. Were the Arnolds, the landlords living on the ground level, capitalists? Phil said they were petty bourgeois capitalists charging him three pounds a week, almost half his wage, and what do they give him in return? Before Eric could reply to that the hostess intervened hoping to prevent the argument becoming a dispute. She said that what was required in general was moderation, a fair exploitation of resources and a moral distribution of wealth. She added that the one she admired most was Leo Tolstoy who gave away his estates to the farmers. Phil said that Tolstoy's saintly image was tarnished by his freemasonry which everyone knew was of a secret society for the rich and influential. There was then an argument as to whether Tolstoy was a true adherent or a mere observer of the craft. The banana ripening man disengaged himself from that erudite discussion, moved to the window, and his wife asked him who he was waving to. He said he was returning the friendly gesture to a neighbour at the window across the street. At the end everyone said how much they enjoyed the party and the discussion. Eric said he would look forward to a return match at Acol Lane.

The Shammashes arrived from Baghdad and were staying at The Cumberland Hotel. On the way they had stopped in Switzerland where Ephraim called at the Tissot watch makers company, placed an order and put out feelers for an exclusive Iraq distribution agency. Calling on the son of their friends back home they had not expected to see him with a woman companion but were now curious to know more. The young couple took time off work to meet them and be their guides. First, there were the never to be missed consultations at Harley Street, Ephraim complaining of back pain, Gladys of women's troubles. The following day the young man accompanied Ephraim on a visit to the offices of Morphy Richards while the women went out shopping. They all ended up at Compayne Gardens in the evening, and Ephraim observed with no malice implied that it was time the carpet was replaced. That was followed by a late supper at the local public house; the young couple disclosed that they were married, had done so without telling their Baghdadi or Yorkshire families. Gladys complimented them and said she could be envious of the beautiful children that they would be bound to have.

The two men spent one evening in a night club while the women were not unhappy to be left on their own. Ephraim had dealings over a number of years with AEG Domestic Appliances, he now called on them for discussion, accompanied by the younger man in case he was needed in the translation. They were expecting Ephraim and had made arrangements to take him to a select night club for a night out. In the course of the evening, and with the drinks flowing, the AEG executives disclosed that they looked forward to the arrival of an overseas client. They would then be able to enjoy the personal benefits of extending hospitality, which would be treated as a tax allowable business expense. In the meantime, the two women were happy to be sitting in the hotel lounge talking about marriage, children and men, the hesitancy of the conversation due to language difficulty covered up by the soft music and having sight of other women in their assortment of evening dresses. When the young newly married woman returned home she put on the light and went across to draw the curtain; the light came on in the building across the street and the face of a young woman appeared at the window.

Eric got his promotion with an increase in his salary and the prospect of an annual bonus. If he had never had it so good before, it was now even better. He went about using his full name, Eric Brunton-Speake, with emphasis on the hyphen, Bachelor of Arts. There were then new housing estates rising almost by the day in Essex within a commuting distance to the City; Eric and Joyce went to have a look in Billericay. They talked of marriage but Joyce confided to her cousin that she was not quite sure. Not that there was anything not to love about Eric. He was passionately in love with her and ever willing to carry out domestic chores to please her. They were thinking of acquiring one of the several brands of washing machines that suddenly proliferated, and which were offered on hire purchase. Until then Eric would take the washing to the laundrette on Saturday and bring it back for him to iron. Joyce further confided that he would even iron her smalls. The woman said that she had no hope that her husband would ever do the same.

The Shammashes, with their visit to England coming to an end, wished to invite the young married couple to a farewell dinner. They made enquiries, and with Gladys being partial to spicy food, booked a table for four at Veeraswamy, a top Indian restaurant in Regent Street. The restaurant had a strict 'smart/elegant' dress code which gave concern to the young married woman; she did not think she had a smart enough evening dress, nor did she have the time and money to buy one. Cousin Joyce came to the rescue, lending her a smart evening black dress that fitted. During dinner Ephraim gave the young husband a Tissot alarm wristwatch and told him that his brothers Sami and Salim were planning to move to England with their business. Gladys got out a silver bangle and a pair of earrings which she gave to the young wife. Afterwards the young couple were exercised by how the news of their marriage will be received in Baghdad now that their secret was out. With a view to propitiate her husband's family the young wife made some tentative approaches and then confided to him that she was thinking of converting to his religion. "Don't be daft" was all he said.

One day the young wife returned home early, went to close the curtain and found the 'student' at her window looking in her direction. She was cross and motioned to her, using an 'impolite' gesture, to go away, leaving her in no doubt that her interest across the street was not welcome. The other disappeared then reappeared at the window, stark naked from the waist upwards and as far down as could be seen.

It was time for the young couple to go look for another bedsit.

Wedderburn Road

A tiny room in an undistinguished house in Wedderburn Road, Belsize Park; a charmed world beyond the street door; close to where Haverstock Hill became Rosslyn Hill, at a short walking distance to Hampstead village with its shops, restaurants, cinema and the corner café where they would stop for a break from the weekly shopping for groceries, be served mugs of tea with scones, would watch the two men at the chess table, the same two elderly men there every time, before they would get up to wheel the wicker basket to the laundrette then back to the bed-sit to hang the damp clothes, snatch a quick snack, and go out again for an afternoon stroll.

The district was dominated by the Royal Free Hospital, halfway down Pond Street. As one got to the bottom of the street and turned left one passed Hampstead Heath railway station then Keats Grove where the romantic poet composed the bulk of his oeuvre while writing love letters to Fanny Brawne, his muse, fiancée and neighbour at Wentworth

Place. Continuing along East Heath Road one reached Willow Road and Pilgrim's Lane where Michael Foot lived; he was often seen walking his constant companion, the terrier Dizzy, across the road to the Heath. Continuing along Willow Road one came to Hampstead underground station at the top of the rise with the coffee house Andalus close by where one could for the price of a coffee spend an hour or more to read that week's edition of *The New Statesman* and *Nation*. Proceeding along Heath Street in the direction of Highgate one would pass the former mortuary of the New End Hospital where Karl Marx's body was laid prior to its removal for burial in Highgate. One came next to the Whitestone Pond where grown men would be seen standing side by side on Sunday afternoons to watch the remote-control-operated toy boats. That was followed by walking the length of Spaniards Road to Kenwood House where open air concerts were held in the summer. Highgate lay beyond with the cemetery holding the remains of many notable personages, one in particular venerated by millions worldwide.

A big amenity of the area where they now lived was Hampstead Heath railway station. They would get up early on a Sunday then take the train across London to Richmond and the river which the man loved in particular as he had been brought up on the banks of the Tigris and now sought beauty and happiness in the sight of running water. They would climb towards the Park, stopping on the terrace to take in the iconic view from Richmond Hill up the river that was painted by Joshua Reynolds and by many other artists who like generations of people were enraptured by the panorama of the Thames snaking in a bend through meadow and common land with the small Glover's Island in the middle. That was the only view in Britain specifically preserved by an act of Parliament being the Richmond, Ham and Petersham Open Spaces Act of 1902. The view and the island reminded the man of the happy days of his youth when they would swim the Tigris to the island that appeared in the summer. The couple would then go into the Park and stop at Pembroke Lodge for a light meal that on a sunny day they would carry outside to one of the benches on the slope that allowed a distant view across Petersham Common to Ham House and Teddington beyond. On some other occasion, after enjoying the view from Richmond Hill, they gave a miss to the Park and went down the steep Nightingale Lane to Petersham Road and the meadow where they sat to have the picnic that she had prepared for the occasion. Later, as the shadows began to lengthen while they lay on the cool grass to gaze on the wisps of clouds floating down Petersham common towards the river he got up to carve their initials on the old sycamore to celebrate her birthday. She turned towards him and looked at him look at her look of happiness and pride celebrating his manhood.

That was the time when the young couple could be said to be carefree. She was doing well at the BBC's Audience

Research Department and was promoted from typist to clerk. He was now working for an Italian called Antonio Spolti in the banana business earning eighteen pounds a week; that replaced the twelve that he had earned working in potatoes for the Spanish firm of Luis Matutanu. But the new position of ssistant was fraught with hard work, anxiety and insecurity. Antonio Spolti was mean, overbearing, choleric and unforgiving of any mistake however small. And there was no way of avoiding his close attention. He owned the first floor of a building in Erlham Street. The office was one room with a long table filling most of it. The boss would sit at one end, his assistant at the other. Antonio Spolti had a strict work ethos; everything had a place and every function had a way of being done, which he insisted on. The ledgers and notebooks had to be stacked neatly and placed at a strict right angle to the table edge; no writing was allowed to be made in a shade other than unrelieved black; a chair once vacated had to be pushed right back into the table cavity. He would feel pain which would be etched on his face at any infringement of those and similar strict requirements.

Antonio Spolti's was a small operation in a market dominated by Fyffes and Geest. He could not hope to compete with them, so he found himself a niche of friendly small suppliers and small friendly wholesalers, the lot overlooked by the big two operators. That allowed him to have a fringe presence in the market. He sourced the bananas mostly from Tenerife where he had established good relations with owners of small plantations near Orotava. He also sourced the fruit from Madeira but in a more modest way. The bananas would be brought by the Norwegian Fred Olsen and the Spanish Aznar lines to Canary Wharf and to a small dock by London Bridge. The green bananas would then be taken to a 'go down' warehouse in Covent Garden that Antonio called 'the Baby' where they would be hung in bunches to be self-ripened by exposure to the natural ethylene that they exuded as they ripened. A bunch would next be stripped of the rows of hands that are cut off and put in boxes to be marketed. Antonio maintained another ripening room in Ilford. It served as an additional facility with the added advantage of it being outside Covent Garden which was held by the trades union in an iron grip. Ilford was an insurance against the hazard of the operation in the Baby getting hampered or blocked altogether during industrial disputes; and they were frequent. Over time Antonio got to realise the hopelessness of challenging the union's authority. He would have a conciliatory meeting in the office which he would open by saying that he was on the side of the workers, had always voted Labour; that he had been a committed socialist in Italy and had come to England to get away from the fascists. He would qualify that by stressing that he was a Menshevic, never a Bolshevic! A declaration that the crude market porters found hilarious and did nothing to deflect them from their demands. In the course of his working for Antonio Spolti, the assistant witnessed two particular manifestations of Antonio the republican, socialist, rebel, iconoclast. The first was quite outrageous. It was prompted by the news of the demise of Pope Pius XII in 1958. Antonio picked up the telephone and called the office of the papal nuncio to introduce himself and offer his condolence. He started in Italian interspersed with English spoken in a soft doleful tone referring to the departed saintly holy father and what he had to put up with in his lifetime, what with accusations of being a reactionary, a consort of racists and fascists, a friend of the Nazis who tolerated the deportation of the Jews to the death camps, also the suppression of the nationalist movements and the brutal extermination of true socialists. Antonio ran through the list of accusations starting with a low voice rising with every accusation. He then concluded by shouting that Pope Pius XII, a crude reference made to his mother, was all those things and more besides, slammed down the receiver, rushed to the bathroom and pulled the chain. The second manifestation of Antonio's socialist pretensions occurred at about the same time. A tall, spare, dignified gentleman came visiting, disturbed by the news of Charles de Gaulle assuming wide powers as President of France under a new constitution. The visitor spoke mostly in Italian but it was clear that he was alarmed by the news; he could be heard to say 'El Deuce' and 'Fascismo' with deep concern while Antonio reassured him that de Gaulle was unlikely to go the way of Mussolini; he then went to the kitchen and came back with a bottle of wine that he shared with the guest in memory of their past political adventures. They left to consult Madame Lena.

Madame Lena was the doyenne of the many Italian traders in Soho and of the few in Covent Garden by extension. A successful woman, she had a high-class delicatessen, the best known store in Soho. Antonio Spolti was in awe of her and of her success; he would frequently say on leaving the office that he was going to see Madame Lena, never just Lena. She had a significant presence in his English history. When the war broke out he was interned in the Isle of Man as an enemy alien. He convinced his interrogator, one Major Nathan, a real English gentleman, that he was anti-fascist and on the side of the Allies in the war and was set free. He then worked for a spell as a commis waiter before becoming an associate of Madame Lena in the making of spaghetti as a contribution to the war effort. As Madame Lena got to know of Antonio's assistant, she said that she would like to make his acquaintance and would be happy for him and his wife to visit her store. Significantly that invitation was made after an outburst by Antonio which his assistant took very badly to the extent of his threatening to leave. Madame Lena was a good hostess, she commented on the good looks of the young couple, served coffee with vienoiseries in her private quarters and gave the wife a parting present of an Italian cheese in an elegant box and a decorative carrier bag, and with a jar of olives added. Throughout the visit Antonio was fussing over Madame Lena, showing his respect, admiration and deference to his 'cara' in all that was discussed. On their way back to Wedderburn Road the young couple speculated what was the true relationship between Antonio and Madame Lena. The assistant thought they were lovers; his wife was not persuaded, thought that a close physical intimacy was incompatible with the respect and adulation displayed by Antonio in the course of the visit.

A fundamental weakness of Antonio Spolti's business was that it relied on a single commodity, the supply of the bananas. Hence the price could suddenly be impacted by political events far off such as a cargo ship company making changes to its schedules so as to reduce the calls to a certain port or to discontinue making calls to it altogether, or by adding a new island to its schedule. The price of bananas in the shops in the United Kingdom would also be subject to the vagaries of the weather and its effect on the crop of strawberries, a rival commodity. Alive to that weakness Antonio considered expanding the business by the addition of tomatoes. He gave a trial order for tomatoes to a grower in Tenerife. The tomatoes were marketed in Covent Garden and that was how Antonio's assistant got to know the grower's son Manolo. That was followed by the grower, Manolo's father, coming over to explore the possibility of a long-term joint venture. He wanted Antonio to join him in a partnership whereby Antonio would provide the funds to expand the plantation and to take charge of the marketing of the produce in commercial volumes in England. Antonio's assistant was present throughout the discussion but without being involved. One detail that particularly caught his attention was that Manolo's father did not pay his workers in pesetas but in company scrip that the worker would exchange for purchases from the company's store. There was a law against that practice which was circumvented by the employee being seemingly allowed to exchange the scrip or part of it for pesetas in the store; but, as Manolo's father added with a mischievous smile, there were ways of discouraging people from doing that. After a full consideration Antonio turned down the proposal saying that he knew what he got to know about bananas and did not want to stray to other fields. The assistant made a mental note of the proposal and discussion. His brothers back home were coming over to Europe and would be looking for new business opportunities.

For love of her husband and exercised by thoughts of his family coming over to England when she will be seen and be judged it occurred to her to convert to their religion. Her husband dismissed the idea and said he would not want to hear more about it. She made discreet enquiries that led her to Lily Montagu. The Honourable Lily Montagu was the woman who played a major role in the rise of Progressive Judaism in England. She was one of ten children of Samuel Montagu, First Baron Swaythling. As one of the most eminent Jewish families in England in the early part of the twentieth century the Montagu family was above all else rooted in the upper reaches of English society and politics. It was implacable in its hostility to anything that would tend to distinguish it as a family of Jews practising their religion from the English society of which it formed an indissoluble part; it was staunchly anti-Zionist. Lily's brother Edwin was a member of the cabinet holding the portfolio of Secretary of State for India during the period 1917-22. He was the author of a Memorandum addressed to the British Government in which he vigorously opposed the Balfour declaration of 1917 which he considered to be anti-Semitic in that it would prove to be "a rallying ground for Anti-Semitism in every country in the world"; and as for its effect on the inhabitants of Palestine Edwin perceived that the declaration "meant that Mohamedans (Muslims) and Christians are to make way to the Jews and that the Jews should be put in the position of preference and should be peculiarly associated with Palestine".

Lily saw no impediment to the conversion in principle provided the wife resolved of her free will to do so after a period of instruction, and further provided it was not actuated by an ulterior motive. There were two factors in this case that were favourable for conversion. The applicant was already married to her Jewish husband and she had lived with the Weinbergs so became cognisant of Jewish culture and beliefs. That offered some explanation for her wish to convert and held out the promise that, once converted she would adhere seamlessly to the Jewish faith and practices and become integrated in the wider Jewish community. Lily suggested that prior to the commencement of the instructions it would be a good idea if the applicant would attend at least two services at the West Central Liberal Synagogue, preferably with her husband. Lily would then entrust the instruction to Miss Lazarus, a colleague rabbi and member of the congregation. The wife broke the news to her husband who raised no objection, in fact he was secretly pleased as it would smooth the way for his reintegration in his family, and he said nothing to discourage her.

The wife got on well with Miss Lazarus who lived in Chalk Farm, an easy walking distance from Wedderburn Road. The instructions were not challenging, and the wife would tell her husband that she enjoyed them. They covered elements of ordinary conduct such as the place of the wife or mother in a Jewish home, the Friday evening family reunion, and the rituals of Jewish festivals. The instructions did not extend to matters of dogma and serious religious discourse. It was enough that one believed in God and placed one's trust in Him. To the questions of heaven, hell, retribution and the hereafter there was only one comprehensive answer; Miss Lazarus knew that she will be taken care of by Providence. Over the following twelve months the wife walked to Chalk Farm two evenings a week to meet Miss Lazarus, while the couple attended Lily Montagu's Saturday's services regularly. Then the day came when they were married in the synagogue, Lily Montagu conducting the ceremony in person. One of the witnesses of the civil marriage Haron was now a witness of the Jewish wedding with another Iraqi Jewish man also named Haron.

It is a Sunday in late summer and they took the train to Richmond then went walking along the river. They had been married for two years in which time they lived in a succession of furnished bed-sit rooms rented by the week. They wondered when if ever they would be able to have a place all their own. They dreamed as they surveyed the unattainable splendour of the big houses along Petersham Road, Sands Lane, Ham and Ham Gate leading to the Park. Then they found it, a modest modern flat to rent in New Road off the Common, and they wished for no other.

Ham Common

Maranda Court was a small development on a small site in a quiet residential street on the periphery of Ham Common. The development consisted of two blocks, each with a flat at street level and another above it, a total of four identical flats.

It was a Sunday afternoon, the couple happened to be passing, saw the 'To Let' sign and knocked on the door of a neighbour who was holding the keys. They viewed the unoccupied and empty flat on the upper level, and they were smitten. The flat comprised two bedrooms, a reception room and a kitchen that ran along the whole of the west side. The kitchen was gleaming modern with a double sink, work tops, drawers and cupboards. It was suffused in the light and warmth of an August afternoon, afforded a partial view of Gordon House among the trees, and a glimpse of the Common. The modernity was further self-asserted by the tiled floors and the electric under-floor heating.

The prospect of moving to Maranda Court presented the couple with several disadvantages. For a start the weekly rent was double that of their last bed-sit in Belsize Park, while the flat was way out in Surrey, beyond the underground railway network. In order to get to one's place of work in town one would have to walk across the Common to the corner by the public house in Petersham Road, take the bus to Richmond station, thence the underground or overland train to central London. Apart from the inconvenience and more time spent in commuting to work there was the additional cost involved. While one would feel privileged to enjoy the modernity of an under-floor electric heating, the neighbour confided that it came with monstrous monthly bills since it operated with only one setting. The couple pondered those matters as they came out, walked to the Common where all negative calculations and considerations melted away at the sight of the Georgian splendour of Gordon House, the serene duck pond with two swans paddling nonchalantly, and the men in white at their Sunday cricket nearby. They went straight back to Richmond and left a note in the mail box of the estate agents, Chancellors, intimating a serious interest.

After a succession of rented furnished rooms in St John's Wood, West Hampstead and Belsize Park, life in a self-contained flat close to the open spaces of Ham Common, Richmond Park and the Thames was felt as an unalloyed idyll. Whenever the days were long and the weather forgiving they would ignore the bus and walk all the way back from Richmond station to Maranda Court, exhilarated and buoyed by the exercise, the fresh air, the magnificent views and the unspoken hopes for the future. On Sunday afternoons they would stroll down to the river holding hands to feast their eyes on the swans, the ducks, the proud motorboats and the BBC sailboats and boathouse on the opposite bank. They could now entertain and make friends, added to which was the pleasure of buying items of furniture, objects of everyday use and, when their tight budget allowed, going to Bentalls to buy modestly priced pictures and posters to brighten the bare walls

It was a Sunday in Spring, a stroll like any other. She stopped suddenly, let go his hand and raised hers to her abdomen. He looked at her quizzically and she was euphoric, "That was a kick; I felt it!" Thus it was that Rebecca first announced her presence. Five months later she was delivered at Kingston Hospital then taken to Maranda Court where the second bedroom had been made ready to receive her.

He made up for the loss of the wife's wages by teaming up with some of his Jewish Baghdadi contemporaries who were in pursuit of gainful ventures. It was left to him to research and identify business deals that would be funded by the others and at their own risk, while he would receive a share of the gain. It started with a shipment of Cypriot potatoes. At the time, the largest imports of potatoes in volume and value were from Spain and the Canaries. They would be landed free of customs duty until a certain set date in the year when they became subject to a 30% charge. The date was set to coincide with the assumed start of the harvest of the local produce, duty meant to guard against competing foreign imports. The man was now in the discrete business of importing, ripening and marketing bananas, but was alive to what was going on in the rest of the market. He became aware that on that particular year the start of the English potato season was going to be inordinately late which meant that the period from the date when the duty came into effect to the actual start of the domestic potato season would be one in which the supply would be tight and with the import duty adding to the price in the shops. He saw an opportunity of benefiting from that set of circumstances. It was to import potatoes from Cyprus to be landed duty free during that charmed period. He presented his proposal to his friends and three of them agreed to provide the money. The Bank of Cyprus put him in touch with an exporter in Limassol and a letter of credit was opened for the shipment subject to a strict stipulation as to the date of loading. The project did not proceed entirely to plan. A wildcat strike by the dock workers in London necessitated an urgent diversion of the ship to Liverpool. The strike then spread to Liverpool but not before the cargo was discharged and the potatoes already in the markets. Thus, the strikes were fortuitous, ramping up the price. The profit exceeded the most optimistic expectation. The man, initiator of the project, received his

25% share of the profit and now faced the clamour of so many others wanting to be involved in his next project. He followed that by importing Cyprus watermelons. That resulted in a break-even position; the project was impaired by poor packing and insufficient allowance made for the ripening process on the way. Watermelons for sale were a rarity in England at the time, while their exportation was a novelty for the Cypriot growers and exporters. The commercial disappointment was mitigated by the man seeing some of *his* watermelons displayed on the pavement outside a shop in Charlotte Street.

Another profitable deal related to a distressed shipment of ladies' blouses from Hong Kong. A company had placed an order for 1000 dozens to be paid for by a letter of credit provided by Chartered Bank (later to be known as Standard Chartered as it merged with Standard Bank). The business effect of the letter of credit was an undertaking by the Bank to pay the value of the order upon its receipt of a bill of lading giving it ownership of the goods as they were loaded on the ship. The Bank's arrangement with the client was that the latter would pay the Bank 40% of the value upon the opening of the letter of credit and pay the balance on the arrival of the goods. In this particular case the shipment was said to have become distressed in that the client was no longer able to pay the balance and take possession of the goods. The Bank clerk handling the matter was one Peter Jenkinson who had worked for the Banco Espanol in Covent

MATTHEW CASWELL

Garden and got to know the young Peter who at the time was working for the Catalan firm of Luis Matutano. Peter now asked him if he would take up the blouses upon paying the Bank the 60% balance that it was out of. That was an enticing proposition since it meant acquiring the blouses at 40% below cost. The young man and part-time entrepreneur found a man, Zelkha, an Iraqi Jewish businessman, longer established in London, who had connections and was prepared to try find him a buyer or buyers in return of a share of the profit. They called unannounced on Leslie Porter, a textile merchant. It was a hot summer's day and they found him sprawled on a deck chair in the middle of the warehouse in an unbuttoned floral shirt, beach shorts and sandals. After a ferocious hour of shouting, swearing, gesticulating and threatening to come to blows the whole shipment changed hands at a price that left a good profit to share. The young man was a mere bystander in the course of that haggling. He was astonished at the manner in which it was conducted, and was struck most of all by the common barrow boy demeanour of this Leslie Porter, later Sir Leslie, husband of Dame Shirley, daughter and heiress of Jack Cohen founder of Tesco Dame Shirley was to attract a great deal of controversy and notoriety as leader of Westminster City Council. The distressed shipment of ladies' blouses became the first item of personal wear that was ever sold in a Tesco supermarket.

Fouad, henceforth to refer to him by his first name, gave up his job at Spolti's after he received four thousand pounds from Baghdad. He was to set up a business in readiness for the arrival of an older brother Salim. He used part of the money in entering into a joint venture with Zelkha for the importation of tomatoes from Tenerife. That lasted one season and Fouad looked around for another venture. He acquired a ready-made company Granex Limited, bought a small van, rented a small shop in the East End, filled it with shirts, jeans and other items of personal clothing, and employed a retired man to assist him as well as to mind the shop while he was out in the van calling on customers. A big question was how to secure a visa for Salim as he applied to the British Consulate in Baghdad. Fouad made contact with a small engineering company run by two partners with a workshop in Willesden. They were receptive to his suggestion and provided a letter evidencing an offer to employ Salim as their export manager. With the visa granted the two directors were invited to dinner at Maranda Court. In the course of the evening Fouad confided to them his reservation about employing his brother whose command of English was limited. It was then agreed that Salim would not take up his employment on arrival. To compensate the two directors for their disappointment and for all the trouble they had gone through, as well as to maintain their goodwill, the sum of three hundred pounds was offered and accepted.

The day came when Salim and Doris arrived with their two children, Diana who was seven and David five. Their first impression was one of dismay. In the course of their journey they fell into conversation with an English couple who gave them a glowing report of Ham and the Common as an attractive and good class outer London suburb. That raised an expectation that was now belied by the reality of a small living space, part of a modest building in an undistinguished street. Anticipating their arrival Helen had moved Rebecca's cot out of the nursery which she then made ready together with the sitting room for the use of the new arrivals, retaining the only other room for herself, husband and baby. That was a temporary arrangement and after a few weeks the flat below became available, Salim rented it and it became for the time being the London home of his family with the benefit of continuing to be close to his younger brother's family.

The two brothers set out to work together every morning, Salim would be in the shop all day which allowed Fouad to go out in the van looking for business. Helen had the new arrivals registered at the local doctors' surgery and got the children enrolled in the local primary school; and she took Doris around the village introducing her to the local shops, the cooperative in particular which was home from home to the woman who had been brought up within sight of the winding gear of Monkton Colliery and who had helped her father push the co-op milk float in Royston.

The children settled well in their new surroundings. They were sufficiently exotic to receive a special attention from the teacher and the good natured interest of the other children. They were full of excitement as they came home every day to describe their experiences. They would tell their mother about the things they did that day. They would then go up to show off to their aunt Helen the new words that they had learned at lessons and at play. She was like another teacher, encouraging them, correcting them gently as she expanded their vocabulary. Diana loved the baby and was allowed to carry her gently in her arms as she recited a popular Baghdadi nursery rhyme greeting the rising sun smiling over the cot of Layla.

Doris was unhappy. The confined space that she now had was a poor substitute to the villa with daily help that she had in Baghdad, and she felt isolated. She missed her family and friends back home and the weekly tea parties that were held at each other's houses in turn. Ham was quintessentially English and she stood out as a foreigner. She was treated correctly and politely, but she hated being asked repeatedly where she had come from while she struggled with the language. But most of all she was uncomfortable because her husband was unhappy.

Salim had for many years been the dominant partner in a business in a Baghdad market with the eldest brother Sami. Now he found himself having to defer to a younger brother. Fouad was the face of the new business; he was the director of the company, handled the money, dealt with the bank, the suppliers and the customers. Salim resented that situation but was incapable of doing much about it while he was trying to improve his knowledge of English and find his way in English society. The resentment was manifested in openly criticising Fouad's easy and pliant way of dealing with the Bank, of giving, as he saw it, too much ground in bargaining, and for being so trusting of people as to tend at times to gullibility. He criticised the payment to the men who had provided the letter of engagement to secure his visa. It was too much, could Fouad not have persuaded them to accept less given that it was a pure bonus, the letter of engagement costing them nothing? The shop was not doing well; he was thinking of leaving and then go find a better opportunity in some other country, or back home. In any of those scenarios that payment to secure his British visa would have been wasted; could his brother not have got them to agree to defer the payment until after he had arrived in England and decided to stay? Fouad was in effect accused of being free with his older brother's money. They had a real spat one morning on their way to work. Salim had been thinking of booking a coach tour of Europe with his family before settling down. He asked his brother to let him have the money for a deposit. Fouad said he could not do that there and then because the money they had in the Bank was required to meet a bill that would fall due to be paid the following day. Salim was very upset, accused Fouad of behaving unnaturally by denying his own brother whose money it was. Fouad would not relent, the priority as he saw it was to avoid a dishonour of the bill. The payment of a deposit to book a tour would have to wait. The relationship was even more sour the following day by which time Salim had pondered the situation and worked himself into a frenzy for what he took to demonstrate his younger brother's dominance. "We are not staying; give me my money and we will go". Fouad said that the money was in the van, the shop tenancy and the goods on the shelves; they belonged to Salim while he had no money of his own. If Salim was truly determined to leave the answer was to wait for someone to buy the business or otherwise have it wound up, with a serious loss in each case. Helen intervened, took Salim aside and persuaded him to bide his time, make no decision until after their trip. In the event that trip was paid for, as Fouad had surmised, out of the moneys that Salim had got out of Iraq and which far exceeded the money that had been provided to set up the new English venture.

The tour lasted one month in the course of which Salim met up with other Iraqi Jews who had left Iraq and settled in different parts of Europe. A close acquaintance was now trading in textiles in Milan, another had opened a restaurant in Paris, and the tour was extended to Tenerife where Salim discussed business opportunities with the tomato grower, Manolo's father, who Fouad had met at Spolti's. In the meantime changes were taking place in the East End. Fouad moved the business to a more prominent shop in Commercial Street, a wide thoroughfare, and filled it with a fresh stock he obtained on a 'sell-or-return' basis from a company that dealt in articles of personal clothing it imported from the Far East. There was also another distressed shipment that Chartered Bank reserved for him. It was a big order and the arrangement was that the Bank would release parts of the shipment on a revolving monthly basis; Fouad would have one lot released to him on credit, and would draw the next lot after paying for the last one. That was a shipment of ladies woollen jumpers which were presented in an attractive style, a variety of colours, and at a moderate price. They attracted a big interest; flew out of the shop! A typical customer, other than a market trader, was one working in a factory or office; she would buy several and sell to work colleagues. A customer calling for one item in particular would be likely to be attracted to other goods at the same time. "We are going to be rich", said Salim as he first came and saw them queuing to be served. "You'll see our friends come with open cheque books wanting a piece of the action" he told his younger brother exultingly. Theirs was a predominantly cash and carry business with a big and growing turnover. Every morning Fouad would go to Barclays Bank to deposit the takings of the day before. Emboldened by the success of the business they extended the lease of the shop in the name of Granex with the personal guarantee of Fouad as the company director. By then Fouad and Helen had become friends with the manager of Barclays

Bank and his family. The Overins were Yorkshire people, Helen and Anne Overin became quite close.

Shalom was a business man trading in agricultural produce in Iraq. He was a brother of Haron, school friend of Fouad and best man at his wedding. Through that friendship their families became close and led to another brother of Fouad marrying a sister of Haron. Now Shalom who had run down then liquidated his business came out of Iraq and arrived in London looking for new business opportunities. He came to Commercial Street as a friend and relative, formed a favourable view of the business and introduced into Granex a sum of money that gave him an equal share of the capital with Salim and an equal share of the profit with Salim and Fouad. That injection of new capital allowed the company to take the lease of an adjoining shop, and a new arrangement was put in place whereby Salim and Shalom would mind the new second shop on a daily basis while Fouad continued to look after the first while retaining the overall management of the company, its finances and external relations. As was to be hoped the business expanded further; but that success and the separate allocations of the business of the shops created unwittingly a fault line that as yet was imperceptible. Sunday was the busiest day of the week; the takings of *their* second shop would be handed to Fouad to add to those of *his* shop. That was an occasion to compare the two while the lot would be taken to the bank the following day to pay into the account of Granex,

Shalom had arrived in the United Kingdom under a visitor's visa and now sought a right of residence. In furtherance of that Fouad set up a new company in the name Jackson Fell Limited. Fell and Jackson were two employees of Granex who had been recruited by Fouad; Cecil Fell, nominally the Chairman of the new company, was Fouad's assistant and answerable to him personally. The new company never traded, its sole function was providing a formal letter evidencing the engagement of Shalom as export manager.

The lease of a four-storey building close by in Commercial Street was next acquired as a warehouse to answer to the increased turnover and extended remit of Granex. The building, a converted house, comprised the basement used for storage, the ground floor and the first floor as sales areas while the top floor was converted to an office for the use of Fouad and a secretary. Fouad had now established contact with manufacturers in the Far East and was importing goods directly in the name of the company and its brand 'Cutty Sark'; and he was dealing with banks, the customs, forwarding agents and other importers. He now had less time to be engaged in selling which was left to Salim and Shalom in the two shops and to employees in the warehouse. The fault line was getting wider by the day without anyone noticing it.

A major Far East supplier was a shirt-making factory in Kowloon, and it agreed to dispense with letters of credit.

It shipped the goods against bills 'for collection', presented through Hong Kong and Shanghai Banking Corporation (later HSBC) the net effect and benefit of which was that Granex was not required to provide the purchase price or any part of it with the order but to do so after taking delivery of the goods upon their arrival. Granex continued to be favoured by Chartered and Barclays in relation to distressed orders and ordinary banking business respectively. After it had been the conduit of a succession of the 'For Collection' bills the HSBC invited Granex to open an account. But the biggest gain was securing the backing of Knowles and Foster. That was a British merchant bank that was founded in the early part of the 19th century with a prominent presence in South America. Curiously and exceptionally, it was started as an unincorporated partnership and so remained throughout its long history. A young man related to one of the partners and now working in the Bank had been an acquaintance of Fouad at Oxford. Knowles and Foster extended a big line of credit to Granex, releasing funds against time promissory notes signed by Fouad as director and additionally as personal guarantor. Knowles and Foster would, as was the case of nearly all banks, raise money when needed by having the promissory notes discounted. There were at the time six discount houses whose remit and standing in the City was but one rung below that of the Bank of England. There was one memorable occasion when a Knowles and Foster partner called at one of them for afternoon tea and to discuss a particular matter; he took Fouad along. The afternoon tea turned out to be gin and tonic offered amiably as one reclined on a chintz sofa.

Those were halcyon days for Granex. It was successful in its own way as a small business that was well regarded in financial circles, and given a higher rating by the credit agencies than could have been objectively warranted by the capital employed, the annual turnover and the profit. Granex owed its high standing to the perception of Fouad as an interesting young man and entrepreneur of promise, and the general perception that he was Granex. Yet the reality was different. He had no capital of his own in the business, but an equal share of the profit. Under the loose, informal arrangement that he had with Salim and Shalom, the three of them would each draw the same amount of money on account of the assumed profits. Upon cessation of Granex to trade for whatever reason the initial capital would be returned to Salim and Shalom respectively; anything left over would be shared equally by the three of them. But for the moment no one was contemplating the cessation of the business. Shalom was living in a house in Finchley Road, Salim gave up the tenancy of the Maranda Court flat, and moved with the family to a house in Golders Green that was quite close to Shalom's. That was followed by Fouad purchasing a house in Teddington, the money provided by Barclays on a 100% mortgage. The future looked rosy and trouble-free as far as one could see.

King Edward's Grove

It was a small detached house close to Teddington's riverside. It had once been the coach house of Broom House and has since been tastefully converted to two bedrooms and an open plan ground floor of sitting room, dining room and kitchen; a pretty box in a moderate-size garden. The young couple, romantic by nature, fell for the charm of the old weathervane, the majestic old Scots pine that could be seen as a landmark from as far away as the top of Richmond Park, and the house's exotic history and the reference to it as a coach house. It was their first house which marked the improvement in their finances and their prospects; and they could now think of adding to the family. They had very little capital but Granex was doing well and Fouad's one-third share of the profits was adequate for their needs. The amount of the drawings out of the profits was fixed by Fouad himself who kept it as low as was tolerated by his two partners. He wanted a good part to be retained in the company as a reserve. Granex to him was a child that he was proud to have begat, and which he would now assiduously nurse, provide for and see grow.

As the business continued to grow so its structural weaknesses became apparent. Outwardly a limited company that had its own constitution, objects and regulations, the reality was that it was a partnership of three men who were closely related, and who never had the time nor saw the need to put in place a set of procedures to deal with problems and differences as they arose. There were no regular meetings, focused discussions, periodical reviews or collective plans for the future. At the end of a working day Salim and Shalom would go in one car to North London while Fouad would drive himself to Teddington. The following day Salim and Shalom would arrive together to question Fouad's ways of doing things, to advance criticism in the form of stock questions beginning with "Why did you? Why didn't you? Could you not have?" Salim missed no opportunity to make a snide remark to undermine Fouad's self-confidence while he waited for the opportune time to wrest the leadership.

They had different outlooks on the business. Fouad would want to promote Granex as an English company with an expanding remit and good reputation. That was a time when two enterprising young men were making waves in the City. Jim Slater and Peter Walker started with little money, bought a small dormant company H. Lotery that had a property in Houndsditch, not far from where Granex operated. They soon had a big following as they renamed and refloated the company on the London Stock Exchange. Fouad was dreaming of emulating them and one day see Granex become as successful as the company that became Slater Walker Securities. That was an unarticulated dream which would have been anathema to Salim and Shalom to hear. They lacked the most rudimentary knowledge of company law, had no idea about the company being a corporate body with a life of its own separate from those of its participators. They would be horrified at the mere suggestion of Granex becoming a public company with its management, governance and finances under constant public scrutiny. All that Salim dreamt of was a business along the same lines as the one he had with brother Sami in the Shorjah market in Baghdad, but hopefully many times bigger. Shalom was neither a thinker nor a dreamer. He followed Salim.

Life was good at King Edward's Grove. There were young families in the vicinity and Helen made friends easily. Some became regular visitors, and she got together with Deirdre nearly every day. Deirdre was from Ulster married to Max who worked for an advertising agency in the West End. Fouad got on well with Max; they would leave their wives to their natter while they went for a drink at the Tide End Cottage Public House by the Lock. The Overins called almost every Sunday, the women exchanging reminiscences of life in Yorkshire; Anne would speak of the back-to-back houses in Leeds and Helen would talk of growing up in the mining village of Royston. James Overin would talk of the misunderstandings and hilarious episodes that can occur behind the solemn façade of a bank. Ken James, the manager of Knowles and Foster, lived with his young family in Wimbledon; they would often drop in on a weekend. They had a six year old boy they wanted to send to Ampleforth and wondered if they would ever find the money. Fouad's and Helen's social life set them apart from their relatives in Finchley Road and Golders Green. When Helen had John, her second child, Doris and Salim came over with presents and good wishes for mother and child. That was their only visit to King Edward's Grove.

The crunch time came with twenty thousand pounds received from Sami and credited to the bank account of Granex. For upwards of thirty years Sami and Salim had traded from a shop in the Shorjah bazaar selling household goods. Sami was the eldest of five sons but Salim the next in years was the brains behind the business, the market man. He had left school at the age of fourteen and went to work in the market as a travelling agent selling boxes of Swedish safety matches on commission. He never held a book or other newsprint in his hands after he left school. Sami's first job was as a meter reader employed by the Baghdad electricity company. He gave that up and teamed up with Salim when the latter had the tenancy of a shop in Shorjah. When the mass exodus of the Iraqi Jews occurred in the fifties the two brothers stayed on to run down the business and gradually convert the assets to money they would take out to start a business outside Iraq, favourite destination being England where Fouad lived. They planned for Salim to leave first taking out part of the money. Sami was to follow with the rest once Salim had established a new business which would be a substitute for the one that they had in Shorjah.

The introduction of the new money into the company's account coupled with the arrival of Sami necessitated radical changes. There would have been discussions in North London to which Fouad was not privy. A scheme was hatched up and proposed to him. It provided for Granex to continue to be accountable to Sami, Salim and Shalom for the sums introduced by them respectively, and for the profits to belong to the four participants in equal shares. The proposed new arrangement was not much different in principle from the one that preceded it, but it presented two significant consequences as far as Fouad was concerned. His share of the profits would be reduced to a quarter, while Salim now made it clear that it was time for him to take control of the finances. For a start he would have the cheque book in his hand, and he wanted Fouad to introduce him to the banks. Until then Fouad's was the only face of Granex that was recognised by banks, discount houses and public bodies generally, while Fouad was concerned, a case of inverted racism, at what impression Salim and Shalom would project given their language and social limitations coupled with their alien ways of doing business. From the very beginning

Fouad had regarded Granex as his company while he prided himself in the belief that he was the progenitor of the business and the leader that had brought it forward a long way. Now it dawned on him that his position all along had been no better than that of an employee, that he had been used to start and promote the business as the only one who was available to do it at the time, and to do it for a share of the profits while he waited for Salim to catch up.

Fouad rejected the proposal and gave notice of his intention to leave. He would resign the directorship of Granex, dissociate himself from the business on condition that they procured his release from any personal guarantee that he had given or personal liability he had assumed as the company's director. He gave the notice with a heavy heart. He had become attached to the company that was Granex, he would hate to surrender it to one he considered less able to direct it. And there were the needs of his own family including the new baby to think of. Yet he was confident that with his ability and connections he would be able to start a business that will be entirely his own.

They came back with a compromise. Salim would withdraw from Granex, take out his share of the business together with the tenancies of the two shops in Commercial Street, and would accept so much of the existing stock at valuation as would satisfy his entitlement; Sami would withdraw his twenty thousand pounds and go join Salim in the two shops; Fouad and Shalom would remain in

Granex to hold the rest of its assets including the warehouse. Fouad turned to Shalom and asked him if he did not also want to come out of Granex? "Why would I want to do that?" he replied, "I am going nowhere!" When it came to the valuation an issue arose whether Salim was entitled not only to his share of the capital, but also to one-third of the retained profits. Fouad left it to Shalom to determine that, and he determined that Salim would receive an addition of one tenth of the basic sum. It is of historical interest that the agreement was implemented and the split completed the evening the news was received of the assassination of President Kennedy in Texas.

The split was favourable to Salim. He walked out with all that he had invested in the company and more besides. He would no longer be concerned, let alone be liable, for the company's debts, its exposure to the orders, letters of credit and shipments on the way that had to be paid for; nor for the legal and moral obligations towards the employees. That he got his entitlement in the form of the stock was also favourable; it allowed him and Sami to have the edge in competing with Granex. They were holding the same goods, trading in the same street while Salim had full knowledge of how much the articles had cost and what Granex was selling them for. There was also the expectation that Granex's regular customers or some of them would continue to tread a path to the familiar shops. Fouad was alive to all those matters but felt able to put them aside. He was full of self- confidence, had been successful in all he undertook and thought in his arrogance that he would never fail to overcome any obstacle calculated to impede his progress. In the meantime, he continued to import goods from the Far East to which were added hosiery, stockings and superior quality shirts from Austria, Lancashire and Yorkshire. Granex had started its life selling items of personal clothing to market traders and casual individual dealers; now the business was focused as much on the importation of goods as on its wholesale side. Cecil Fell managed the warehouse business with three employees and there was Harvey Jackson in addition as the company's travelling agent. They were supervised by Shalom who now had the use of a back room to himself on the first floor which was fully equipped as an office with a telephone. He seldom went up to the top floor where Fouad had his office assisted by a secretary.

Cecil Fell was the first to sound the alarm. He confided to Fouad that Shalom was having regular discussions with Salim. He would receive and make several telephone calls a day. They conversed in Arabic so Fell could not tell what they were talking about but gathered from the few words that he understood that they were discussing business, prices and finance. Fouad dismissed Fell's concern; Salim and Shalom were friends, neighbours and relatives so it was quite natural that they conversed with each other. Fell turned away, face clouded over, muttering 'let's wait and see!'

They didn't have long to wait. Shalom suddenly said he wanted to get out of the business and required Fouad to pay him what was owed to him. He said he now had a change of heart and mind; not for him spending the rest of his days in the warehouse selling articles of personal clothing. After so many years in business and the traumatic experiences in Iraq he needed a respite. He said: "Give me my money and I'll go". Fouad remembered hearing those very same words before. He pointed out that he had no money of his own, nor had he ever had. He offered to pull out himself and leave everything to Shalom. That was to no avail. Shalom protested that he did not have the capability of running the business to include ordering and importing goods, nor the ability to deal with the complex financial transactions. He said that with the moneys at Fouad's disposal he would have no difficulty raising what was required to pay him off. He concluded with a brazen piece of moral blackmail: You bought out your brother, why would you treat me differently?

The argument went on and on for two weeks, getting worse all the time causing alarm to the employees and affecting the business. Fouad enlisted the help of Bob Leffe, the company's accountant, but Lefffe's advice fell upon barren ground. It was arguable that Shalom was not competent to assume control of Granex with the several aspects of its operations and their ramifications. But Fouad could not agree to pay off Shalom with borrowed money while it was far from certain that Granex was solvent after the split with Salim. Shalom then took advice from a local solicitor and came back with the argument and implied threat that he had been neither a shareholder nor an office holder in Granex. The position was that he had advanced moneys to Granex which were recorded throughout as owed to him. If the dispute led to litigation it would take the form of a claim by him against Granex for the repayment of his money.

The only option left to Fouad was to liquidate Granex, but that would have been ruinous. He had a word with Ken James of Knowles and Foster and got more money to pay off Shalom who then shamelessly asked for his share of the presumed retained profits in addition, pointing to the settlement with Salim as a precedent. Bob Leffe urged Fouad to dismiss that additional unreasonable demand. But Fouad by that stage was anxious to put an end to the argument and moral blackmail and to clear the road ahead. He agreed to the addition of one-tenth, the same as had been the case with Salim.

Once he received the money Shalom moved to the two ex- Granex shops in Commercial Street to become associated with Sami and Salim That was the final business involvement of Fouad with Shalom. But there was a sequel, a matter which had been overlooked in the course of the discussions and negotiations. Shalom was purported to be Jackson Fell's export manager, and that was the basis upon which he had been granted a British residence permit. Fouad had set up the company Jackson Fell Limited for the sole purpose of providing Shalom a pretend letter of engagement as export manager to accompany his application to the Home Office. Jackson Fell Limited was and remained throughout a shell company that never traded. As Shalom now applied for the annual renewal of the permit the Home Office required confirmation that he was still holding the same position with the company. He came across, presented the document to Cecil Fell to sign. The latter was taken aback; he hesitated, looked across and Fouad nodded.

In later years Salim would be heard to reminisce about the time when he, an Iraqi refugee, managed to successfully find his way in English society. He would also talk of Granex, his involvement in its beginnings and the superior skill he displayed in the way of his leaving it. That vindicated his long held belief that formal education was not a pre-requisite to progress in business, and can even be a hindrance. He tried with some success to dissuade his children from studying for and acquiring professional qualifications. As he saw it, a life of book reading and university education puts 'ideas' in one's head that would take the edge off one's determination and competitiveness in the market place, and would be liable to cloud one's vision as it held one back. For his part Fouad was gnawed over the years with regret for how badly he had played his association with Salim and Shalom, and as he recalled the manner and circumstances of its ending in particular. Could he have, should he have played it better, and what was it that stopped him?

Granex was now wilting under the competition. Salim would stand outside his shop, greet Granex's regular customers and would invite them to look at his new stock. With the unlocking and withdrawal of the moneys that Salim, Shalom and Sami had in Granex they were able to extend the range of the goods they had on sale; and they made up for the loss of the direct importation of goods by buying from other importers. That was a situation that required Fouad to make cost savings by terminating the employment of some of the workers, but he did not have the heart to do that. They had all been recruited by him, they were to a man loyal to him, while he hoped that things would so work out as to obviate the need to dispense with the services of any. He was now the sole owner of Granex, it had a good credit rating, enjoyed the support of the banks, principally Knowles and Foster, as well as the support of manufacturers and shippers in the Far East.

The calamity came like a bolt from the blue. Knowles and Foster that had an illustrious place in the City going back to 1828 collapsed suddenly. It gave notice on the 9th of December 1964 that it was going into liquidation. Overnight Granex lost its principal supporter and bank. And overnight Granex's rating was reduced drastically by the credit rating agencies.

What's more, those happenings coincided with a general credit squeeze and the imposition of a fifteen per cent import surcharge adding to the financial difficulty that Granex was labouring under. Seen in hindsight that was an occasion when Fouad should have put Granex into a members' voluntary liquidation which would have led to an inevitable destruction of value yet in a fairly orderly winding-up. But he could not bear the thought of that, the admission of defeat, the obloquy he would get from the creditors and the derision in Commercial Street. He continued to try to retrieve the situation, and in so trying Granex was caught in the clutches of secondary banks and predatory money lenders. Two would feature dramatically in the history of Granex and Fouad.

Zelkha was a Baghdadi Jew who had a general business in Baghdad that he ran right up to the time of the big Iraqi Jewish exodus in the early 1950's. When that happened he came over to London where he started a new business in the name of Luso Limited, rented a small room in a building in the City, had it furnished with a desk, a telephone, three chairs and nothing else. He worked entirely on his own. He did not deal in any commodity or merchandise or real estate or in any activity that would be associated with any particular trade or profession. He was an entrepreneur who kept his powder dry until he espied a special situation that was overlooked by others but which he thought he could turn to advantage; he will then pounce. He would come to his office every morning, make a telephone call to his stockbroker followed by calling a few contacts. The contacts were his eyes and ears informing on what was happening in the business world, what trader was in difficulty, what company struggling, what stock in distress, what enterprise on the brink. He would go home to lunch and then stay the rest of the day. Zelkha seldom went out looking for deals. He would sit back and wait for them to come his way; a predator lurking in the shadows, a patient spider waiting for an unwary victim to fall in his web. In the recent past Fouad had introduced two deals to him on a profit sharing basis. He now brought him another. Granex's regular Far East supplier was The Hong Kong Manufacturing Company. That company now asked Granex if it would help dispose of a large quantity of mackintoshes that were lying distressed in London docks. The mackintoshes had been ordered by a chain store that had gone bankrupt. Granex had the opportunity of buying the goods at a very substantial discount to cost. To Zelkha it was an opportunity to make money by financing the deal rather than participating in the purchase and the marketing. As Luso Limited he had an account with the City branch of The Eastern Bank and had the benefit of a big line of credit that he was not utilising. He agreed to lend the money to Granex on a weekly basis, interest to be paid separately at a rate agreed verbally. There soon followed a succession of loans which were not self-contained but ran into each other. That clouded the account, particularly since

Zelkha missed no opportunity to inflate the rate of interest, sometimes retrospectively, in line with the heightened state of panic and urgency displayed by Fouad as he asked for another advance. It was after six months that as Fouad asked for a new loan, that Zelkha produced what he claimed to be an up-to-date statement showing a balance of twelve thousand pounds allegedly owed by Granex to Luso. That was seven thousand pounds more than the corresponding figure in Granex's books. An explanation for the discrepancy was that Luso's statement was based on an arbitrary rate of interest exceeding what had been agreed at the outset, and further inflated by using the formula of a weekly compound rate as against the simple rate that was assumed by Fouad. There was a big fall out: Zelkha will no longer support Granex with loans; Fouad made an alternative financing arrangement with Jerry Truman, got the money and paid Luso what he admitted and be owed, and refused to pay any more. Zelkha was furious for not getting what he alleged was due and that was aggravated by his losing the Granex milk cow to Truman. His threat to sue was dismissed by Fouad. Zelkha swore retribution, and it would seem that in July 1965 one Mr. Hann, manager of The Eastern Bank, may have put Zelkha in touch with Detective Sergeant Isaacs.

Truman traded in textiles and got to know Fouad as a fellow trader, and they were both clients of the Palestine-British Bank. Truman came to Fouad in the first place on his own initiative. It was to do a swap. He had a lot of jersey wool while Granex had a lot of twin sets, and they made a bargain whereby a part of the jersey was exchanged for a part of the stock of twin sets. Granex at the time had a credit facility of thirty thousand pounds provided by the Palestine-British Bank which was fully utilised, while the Bank was beginning to apply a squeeze to reduce it. Truman then said that he also had a credit facility with the same bank which he was not using to the full; he would put it at the disposal of Granex charging it interest at a higher rate than he had to pay the bank. The arrangement that they put in place was that Granex would on the face of it sell a parcel of goods to Truman, the latter would send the invoice to Mr White of the Palestine-British Bank with an instruction to pay the amount to Granex. That would take the form of White crediting the amount to Granex's account and debiting Truman's account for the same amount. A few days later Truman would issue an invoice showing the same goods being sold back to Granex for a higher sale price payable after thirty days. The net effect of the transaction was to give Granex a thirty days credit in return for the difference between the two invoices representing the interest or benefit received by Truman. The transaction was purely one of financing, the goods themselves did not need to change hands. In fact it was immaterial what particular parcel of goods was chosen to be used in the transaction or whether it existed at all. It is likely that White at least had an inkling of the true nature of the transaction and chose to turn a blind eye. There were several such transactions with variations that became involved and complex, one running into another, thus liable to fall into irregularity and error. Such did arise with dramatic consequences. Consistent with the financing arrangement Fouad sent Granex's invoices to Truman for parcels of goods held by Granex's forwarding agents Translloyd. Truman passed the invoices to the Palestine--British Bank and the amounts of the invoices were debited to Truman's account and credited to Granex's. At about the same time and consistent with the agreed arrangement Truman raised invoices against Granex for the same parcels of goods and received from the latter thirty-day post-dated cheques with delivery orders addressed to Translloyd. When the cheques were presented to Palestine-British Bank for payment on their due dates they were dishonoured because they would have exceeded the overdraft limit that the Bank had now imposed. When Truman then presented the delivery orders to Translloyd he was told that the goods were under a lien to Knowles and Foster. Therefore, and it so appeared on the face of the documents, Truman had paid moneys to Granex for goods that Granex did not have the right to sell; a prima facie case of Granex obtaining money by false pretences. Truman confronted Fouad and the latter admitted the irregularity which he explained was due to a genuine mistake. There followed an argument as to the total amount of money that was due to Truman, the Bank got involved in the discussion, a figure of £2,600 was ascertained and agreed, and the matter was settled on that basis after which Truman continued to trade with Granex. In the meantime D. S. Isaacs was pursuing his investigations relating to Zelkha's complaint. In the course of those investigations he came across Translloyds's dealings with Granex, and so had knowledge of the bare facts of the 'spurious' delivery orders that featured in the financing arrangement with Truman.

It was the 30th of November 1965, Fouad was at his desk when two policemen in plain clothes came up the stairs to arrest him. D. S. Isaacs showed him the arrest warrant and told him that the warrant was not endorsed with bail which meant that he would be incarcerated until he appeared before a magistrate and was allowed bail. Until then Fouad had no inkling of the criminal investigation. No one had come to him with a complaint, no policeman had been to see him to ask him questions or take a statement. He now asked what he was being arrested for and D. S. Isaacs said it was for false pretensions and fraud but would not give any details, nor explain the reason for the withholding of the bail. It passed through Fouad's mind that what was happening to him was more to do with wanting to humiliate and damage him than carry out a proper investigation of a serious complaint. He was taken to the police station and put in a cell. The two detectives left without any questions asked or details provided, nor was he told how long he would be kept in the cell or what was to follow. After they had gone and the station warder had taken away his shoes he racked his brain for an explanation and could only get one answer. It had to be the malicious doing of his erstwhile partner Zelkha.

The cell at Bishopsgate police station was brightly lit. A metal bedstead and a toilet bowl took up the whole of one side. As he lay down in his city suit and stockinged feet, his outstretched arm touched the iron bars which extended the length of the other side, floor to ceiling, providing neither privacy nor shield from the strip light in the passage. He craved another cigarette.

He heard the heavy footsteps of the warder as he came down to make his round. He got up and shook the cell door to attract attention. "You'll kill yourself", said the warder as he lit his cigarette. "Is there a reason why I can't have my shoes back without the lace", he asked? The shoes were returned on the warder's next round. He put them on and paced forward and back until he finished the cigarette, threw the butt in the bowl then checked that he still had four left. Just as well they wouldn't let him keep the lighter, he mused.

He was woken up at half past two. Two policemen in lounge suits stood in the cell blocking the light. They were not the ones who had arrested him. The warder stood above him holding the shoelaces. As he was lacing up the shoes the two new arrivals stood stock still, silent with steadfast gaze; the warder eyed them cautiously. As he climbed into the police car the warder came hurriedly down the steps and told them sternly, voice raised, "I want him back the same as he is." He was driven to another building where he was photographed and fingerprinted, after which he was driven back. Not a word was spoken from the moment they had left the police station to the moment he was returned to be met by the warder who led him back to the cell, lit another cigarette, "you'll kill yourself smoking", he said, then locked the barred door. In the morning the warder brought him English breakfast on a metal tray. He accepted the mug of tea and declined the rest. Then it was time to step into the black police van that was to take him to the Guildhall building to appear before The Mayor's and City of London Magistrate Court.

The moment he stepped inside the door was shut, the motor started and the car lurched forward. He groped his way to a bench. As his eyes got used to the dark he realised he was not alone. The other was surveying him and taking in the city suit, silk tie, polished shoes, a twenty-four hour growth of beard and dishevelled hair. 'Would you be going to the stipe?' The voice was Irish and he recalled that another name for the Black Maria was the Paddy Wagon.

"What do they have you for?"

"Forgery; and you?"

"It's my partner" he started but could go no further. This is ridiculous, he told himself.

"I understand", said the other.

In the Magistrate court he was met by his counsel whom Cecil Fell had instructed to represent him. It was a brief hearing, he was remanded on bail for trial at The Old Bailey.

Then something curious happened. He received an invitation to a solicitor's party. He had never had any dealings with the city solicitor's firm of Harry Goodrich. He left it as late as good manners permitted to get to the office party. He was not in the mood, had a lot on his mind; but had felt he should not refuse. It was the solicitor's annual party, and the formal invitation was followed by the solicitor telephoning in person to make sure he would attend.

An as yet restrained party, reception by the host with a drink on arrival, an exchange of good wishes, seasonal decorations tastefully arranged, soft dance music from a record player. One of the office girls led him to the space in the middle of the staff room that had been cleared. "We have this every year," she explained, "but I had not seen you before." They bumped into another couple. "I come to this party every year," said D.S. Isaacs. The music stopped and he said he had some business to attend to. As he was leaving he went across to thank his host. 'Merry Christmas' was exchanged. "If he came back they will crucify him again" said the policeman enigmatically.

Granex was doomed. With the news of his arrest those who were owed money came hurriedly wanting to be paid; some of those who had sold Granex goods on credit came to reclaim them, while those who owed money were delaying payment. He used the last free resources of his company and all of his own to meet the demands. But when those resources were exhausted and no money was left he went with a very heavy heart to a solicitor and put Granex into liquidation to ensure that whatever was left would go to all the general body of its creditors.

The family at King Edward's Grove was now destitute. The house in mortgage to Barclays Bank had to be sold; the Overins stopped visiting. The car was sold to raise money for the food and household essentials. The prosecution bundle of documents contained a statement by Ken James referencing the dealings with Knowles and Foster. Helen's asthma that had been in remission now flared up. John had a fracture of a shoulder blade sustained while Rebecca was playing with him; the hospital identified it as a hairline fracture which they immobilised with a sling, and which was expected to heal within two weeks. Helen took the children back to her Yorkshire family for a respite and returned back with them after one week to be with her husband. He terminated his instructions to the solicitor; he could no longer afford the fees. There was a lot to read in the prosecution witness statements, and he now pored over them as he prepared his defence. Apart from the vituperative statements of Zelkha and his banker the rest were mostly factual with hardly a malicious content. They were mostly of men he knew well and did business with on an almost daily basis. They must have been questioned by D.S. Isaacs and formal statements would have been signed during the period July to November, yet no hint of any of that was given to him by any of them. But there may have been a reason for their cautious reticence. They were not told the purpose of the inquiry, nor of the questions that were put to them, nor of the intended use of their answers which were noted on the spot then turned to typed statements which they solemnly signed as required. One had to allow that they were mostly the owners of small businesses in what was commonly referred to as 'the rag trade'. They would have been vulnerable to questions by the police and to having to produce their books, if such they had, for inspection.

He was very nervous on the first day of the trial. He had no experience of appearing in a court of law other than the brief attendance at the magistrate court that dealt with procedural matters. He now found himself in the dock of court number eight of The Old Bailey where the most serious criminal cases were tried. He had surrendered to his bail and so was in custody and will remain so until the trial judge granted him bail again. That was of particular importance since he was to conduct his own defence. The judge noted that he had been represented by counsel at the earlier hearing and wanted to know why he was now to conduct his own defence unaided. In reply he mentioned the change in his financial circumstances. He declined the offer of the services of a barrister on legal aid, 'a poor man's brief' nominated by the court. He had come intending to defend himself in person and was going to do just that. After a few questions, the judge granted him bail for the duration of the trial. He now was bold to ask if a table could be added to the dock as he had many documents to cope with. The judge directed that rather than conducting his defence from the dock he may be seated at the long side bench in the body of the courtroom with the warder sitting next to him. That was an important concession. He will now be facing the jury, separated from them by a few paces across the court room, with the judge's raised bench to his left and the witness stand next to it at an angle. The seating arrangement was reflected in another concession. Now and for the duration of the trial he will be addressed and referred to as 'Mr. Zelouf' and not by the customary 'the defendant' and 'the accused'.

There were six counts in the indictment, the first three related to the complaints of Zelkha's company Luso, the others to the dealings between Granex and Truman. The prosecution led evidence relating to the Luso counts first; it consisted of the testimony of Zelkha followed by that of his banker Hann. It was Zelouf's baptism of fire. There was the frontal assault of Zelkha accusing him of betraying his trust and cheating him of twenty thousand pounds. When he put it to Zelkha that his claim was disputed, that Luso had brought an action then outstanding in the County Court claiming less than half that amount, and that Granex had filed a full defence with a counterclaim, Zelkha lost his cool, said Granex's defence was a sham as he launched a tirade against Zelouf whom he claimed to have trusted and helped as a partner only to see him repay favours with ingratitude and running away with 'my money'. That riled Zelouf who accused Zelkha in turn of being an unconscionable and ruthless moneylender who sought retrospectively through the application of financial pressure to wrongly extract more than fifty per cent interest.

Mr Hann who followed was arrogant, preening himself as an experienced banker with so many years in the City. He asserted that in all his years as a banker he had never come across as blatant a case of fraud. But he admitted in cross-examination that he had never had any dealings with Granex or the defendant, that the first time ever that he and the accused cast eyes on each other was at that very moment in court. He accepted that whatever arrangement he had with Zelkha and Luso was one of which and of the terms of which the defendant had no means of knowing.

At the conclusion of that testimony and with Mr Self, counsel for the prosecution, indicating that he had no other evidence to adduce concerning the first three counts the judge ordered them to be struck out. He said that on the totality of the evidence it was a case of a money dispute with no element of criminality present; that even were one to accept the testimonies of Zelkha and Hann in full, that would not amount to fraud.

That was a big turn in the trial, and a great relief to Fouad Zelouf. All he had to concentrate on now was the charges relating to his dealings with Truman. It was not even certain that Truman would appear in court as the complainant given the settlement concluded with him already.

That the trial extended to a third week was due to the prosecution calling more than a dozen witnesses to establish facts which were not disputed. They ranged over the involvement of three banks, a finance house, a transport and holding company and several importers and merchants. It was a case of following the movement of each particular bundle of goods to which each of the counts related; which in turn required its examination as a part of a complex line of shipments dovetailing with each other. That was gone over to establish concerning each of the counts that the delivery order was spurious in the sense that although it related to existing goods, those goods were not free to be delivered because they were already held under a lien to Knowles and Foster. That was not disputed as a fact. The only issue in contention was whether in raising money against any of the three delivery orders Zelouf was aware that they related to goods under lien or whether it was a case of a muddle and mistake. Accordingly, there was little challenge by Zelouf of the majority of those witness statements. He successfully turned any statement that could be construed as hostile to make it supportive of his defence while he extracted affirmations from the witnesses that the way he and Granex dealt with each of them over a period of time was above reproach.

Throughout every moment of the trial Zelouf was entirely on his own. He had no legal representative, no witness to call, nor anyone turning up to lend him support. He did receive moral support from an unlikely quarter. The warder was an old man who had spent years at the Old Bailey and witnessed many trials. He sat on the bench next to Zelouf throughout the trial. He warmed up to him to the extent that at the end of some days, as they were left alone, he would tell him cautiously that he was doing well.

There were two highlights that emerged in the cross-examination of the prosecution witnesses. Truman looked uncomfortable as he took the oath to tell the truth. He looked even more uncomfortable as he weighed up every question put to him in chief by Mr Self. He hesitated before he responded and then in monosyllables. He averted his eyes away from Zelouf. He gave the impression of being a troubled man who wished to be elsewhere. When it was his turn Zelouf looked straight at Truman and asked "Mr Truman, are you alleging that I defrauded you?" Truman was taken aback, hesitated and looked towards Mr Self. The latter rose to object to the question and was cut short by the judge who said: I want to hear what he says. Truman said after hesitation: "I don't think Mr. Zelouf would do it if he can help it". Zelouf could have followed that up by asking Truman if he had any claim against him, and whether he was asking the jury to convict him. But Zelouf was wary of Truman and unsure what his answers would be, and left it at that. There followed a long cross examination of Truman's evidence in the course of which Zelouf managed to turn it mostly against the prosecution.

The other highlight involved D. S. Isaacs. As the arresting police officer he would be called to give evidence as the last prosecution witness. Before it was time for him to give his evidence D. S. Isaacs sought out Zelouf during the lunch break and asked him with ashen face and in a low conspiratorial voice if he was going to refer to Mr Goodrich. Zelouf said he will not. D.S. Isaacs was a bag of nerves as he came up to give evidence. He admitted in cross-examination that he never interviewed Zelouf, nor asked him questions, nor sought to obtain a statement before he arrested him. He next admitted that after the arrest Zelouf contacted him offering to go to see him to be interviewed and to make a statement in writing, and D. S. Isaacs further admitted that he refused to see him. With a red face, shaking hands and in a tremulous voice the detective attempted an explanation to an astonished jury and an incredulous judge. He said he did not think it proper to interview Mr Zelouf because he had a solicitor at the time.

With the prosecution evidence closed it was the turn of Zelouf, and he had the option of either going to the witness stand to give his own evidence and submit to be cross-examined, or to offer no evidence and proceed forthwith to making his final address. He chose the risky option of going to the witness stand, taking the oath to tell the truth, giving his evidence and exposing himself to be cross-examined. Having criticised D. S. Isaacs for not accepting his offer to state his case, he felt he could not withhold it from the jury. That exposed him to a whole day's cross-examination which included a break to bring along Granex's books which were by then in the possession of the Official Receiver at Inveresk House.

At the conclusion of the cross-examination, and after the court had risen leaving him alone with the warder, the latter could not contain his feelings. He chided him for making the tactical mistake of electing to give evidence, and to do such a rash thing after all the unerring decisions that he had made until then. Seeing Zelouf's face cloud over the warder hastened to reassure him that nevertheless 'he had done all right', then added words that lifted Zelouf's spirits to a new level. The old warder told him that on that very same day there were barristers at the Old Bailey whose job was to conduct criminal cases day in, day out, but he doubted that any of them could have done a better job in his defence. Zelouf was cheered up; those words planted the seeds in his consciousness of what profession he would pursue if he walked out of the Old Bailey with a stainless character. But before that he had to think of his final address to judge and jury that he was to deliver in the morning.

After days of listening to dry, boring, complex details of accounts, delivery orders, bills of exchange, consignments and shipping schedules the jury were now focussed on hearing Zelouf laying down his explanation, anxiety and plea before them directly. There was an eerie silence as Zelouf rose to deliver his final address.

"Members of the Jury. It would have been ridiculous if it were not so tragic. Since my arrest on the 30th November I have had my business placed in the hands of a liquidator; I have had my house put in the hands of estate agents; I have had my name emblazoned all over the local newspapers; my wife's heath in ruin; and this now, the greatest indignity any man may suffer, of having to stand in court to defend his good name and his liberty; and all for what? You have heard all the facts and seen all the witnesses, and the first basic fact you have to consider is that nobody was done out of any money and nobody is claiming that he was done out pf any money. These counts which remain now are, in respect of dealings with Mr. Truman, and again I want to stress the basic fact that Mr. Truman does not owe me anything and that I do not owe him anything. I have got no claim on him and he has no claim on me, and that is not in dispute. What is in dispute is that the prosecution suggest that I sold him goods or gave him goods in January/February of last year, delivery orders of goods, to which I had no title, against which he lent me money. It is also suggested by the prosecution that when I gave him those delivery orders I knew I had no title to the goods, and even though I settled with him afterwards, if I knew I had no title to the good and passed them on to him I was doing a fraudulent act. That is the only point which is in dispute."

"What does this last point boil down to? It boils down to my state of mind at the material time. The prosecution have not produced any evidence or any witness who said "Yes, we knew that the man was going to pass these off fraudulently". What they are saying is that I should have known and would have known; and what I say is that I did not know. How can I prove my state of mind at that time? Neither the prosecution can prove it, nor I myself can prove what my state of mind was at any particular moment in time. I know, but how can I put it in a clear enough way to convince everybody? The only thing I could bring to substantiate my innocence is the circumstances of the case, the circumstances leading up to it and the circumstances afterwards, to find out if they are in accordance with someone who did it as an honest man making an honest error, or a man doing something fraudulently with fraudulent intent."

"What are the facts leading up to this? It is not in dispute that in the last half of 1964 I was under pressure in my business, facing pressure on top of the pressure of having to run a business. It is not in dispute that after December 1964 the pressure became very intense, principally through no fault of mine. The credit squeeze, the surcharge, our main banker going into liquidation and being involved with all sorts of headaches from day to day. That is not in dispute. At the best of times I am a hardworking man, and I was working very hard in my business, a one-man business in those times. I was working extremely hard. I was not going home for days on end. The prosecution would say that this is the state of mind in which one would do a fraudulent thing. My contention is that this is the state of mind in which an honest error would be committed by an honest man. Again, what are the circumstances of all this pressure? I did not panic, I did not run away, I did not try to defraud and then go away. I stayed at my post. You heard all the evidence of the witnesses, you heard the bankers – Davies, Translloyd, everybody, I stayed on there and tried to sort out my affairs, to try to sort out my financial affairs, to reduce my liabilities to all and sundry, and I have done that to a great extent, until the whole thing was put a stop to by the prosecution bringing this case in November last year. Is this the act or behaviour of a dishonest man, in January, February December or even after? Nor is there evidence that after I did something with Truman, that I could not pay him and settle with him. I stated there and I state again, that at that time I had a quarter of a million pounds' liabilities. All those were paid off during the year. There was no need for me to try and defraud Truman of even £2000 and pay him later. It is suggested that I am a businessman and as a businessman I should know when I make a slip or an error. Errors do happen from time to time, they inevitably happen. Normally, an error happens, you go and see the man and you sort it out, and that is the end of the matter. Once in a while you come upon a nasty character or a nasty situation where it would not for some reason or another, you cannot settle the following day. I am not saying I am a bad businessman, but also I am not stupid. What does this amount to? This is not a clever trick, it is the most stupid one in the world. I go along and give somebody a cheque or delivery order – a telephone call and he will find out the goods were not all there. He sends the delivery order and back comes the reply "the goods are not there". What happens to me in the meantime? I do not leave the country; I do not close down the shop. I was still here meeting everybody. Then what do I do? After I discovered the error, the honest error? I do not know what is in dispute there. You have heard my evidence and you have heard the evidence of Truman, and Truman's evidence on that point is distinctly vague; not quite so vague last Monday when he was recalled, but then what does he say ? "Yes, there were a lot of telephone conversations between Mr. Zelouf's office and my office. Yes, we did meet, I cannot remember when and I cannot remember the date". I suggest if he was a man who had just been defrauded he would not be so vague on that point. He would come to me and say "Mr. Zelouf, what is this nonsense? You have tried to defraud me. Give me back my money". He would not leave it to me to telephone his office. What happens immediately afterwards? What did the records tell? Mr. Truman's memory is vague on that point; my memory is considerably clearer than his on that point. What happens afterwards? The following points are not in dispute. Immediately after the error was discovered a cheque for £3,100 given to Truman dated the 3rd February, that was met. A few days later a cheque for £900 given to Truman, that was met. A few days later another cheque for £1200 given to Mr. Truman, that was met. Exhibit 15, the delivery order of those 50,000, 500 dozen, was met and delivered to Mr. Truman. On the 13th March a Bill of Exchange for goods I had bought three months earlier for £1,640, presented, that was met. On the 20th March, another Bill for £1,640 and that was met. What is the evidence? The written evidence we have of Mr. Truman's records? He had an adjustment in his books in February. He sent me debit notes on the 26th February, He made adjustments regarding the jeans in February."

"The other evidence, two post-dated cheques were given to him for £1,300, as the tail end of a series of post-dated cheques he has in his hands, and those two cheques for £1,300 each come to £2,600 – more than covered the amount which is outstanding between

Mr. Truman and myself. Those two cheques were dated the last week in March and the other in April. Those cheques were not met. I will deal with that in a moment."

"What I suggest is that in the evidence in February, the written evidence suggests that far from anybody defrauding Truman or Truman thinking I defrauded him, it is completely the opposite. I went along straight to him, sorted out the whole thing, he had post-dated cheques in his hands. He cannot remember chasing me, he cannot remember complaining. Are these the actions of a man who had just been trying to defraud Mr. Truman? By the same token, are they the actions on Mr. Truman's part of a man who had just been defrauded?"

"Again, let us look at a small point following on to that. He had collected 500 dozen shirts. I suggested to Mr. Truman, and he does not deny it, that he telephoned complaining that his customers in Nottingham, who he sent the shirts to, were short of fifteen and a half size shirts, so six dozen shirts were sent from my shop to Nottingham. Is this the action of a dishonest man? We were still talking to each other and meeting each other as friends. He accepted it was a genuine error, just as I suggest to you it was a genuine error."

"Let us look at the evidence again. Was there any hint of guilty conscience on my part? I suggest there cannot be. If I was feeling guilty about the delivery orders I would redeem them first of all. I would say: Mr. Truman, give me back the delivery orders and I will pay you the cheques. I will pay these two cheques of £1,300 and stop the Bills of Exchange. I will not pay the Palestine-British Bank and Wintex, let them wait a little, and let Mr. Truman be paid first. The evidence suggests there that this was a genuine error, agreed between us, two cheques of £1,300 given to him, two post-dated cheques he has in his hands with the intention of clearing up the whole account. The two cheques were re-presented at the end of March and the first week of April. The cheques were not met. Barclays Bank had foreclosed on us by then, through no fault of our own. Knowles and Foster had dishonoured some of their Bills of Exchange and we were trying to sort it out in the discount market. It so happened it appeared later on Barclays Bank knew of all this; they were worried about us. Even then it is not suggested that after Barclays Bank foreclosed our account that we stopped trading. We still had other banks. The Bill of Exchange for Truman for £1,640 was returned by Barclays and we gave a banker's draft by another bank, and we still kept on trading and paying our way. When the two cheques were not paid there was another meeting with Mr. Truman. "Mr. Truman, sort out the account, how much do we owe you?" as had been the basis between us all along, but by then other considerations came in to the matter."

"You have heard Mr. Truman last Monday saying he claimed £5,000. Why £5,000? I have asked him for a statement of account. I went over to his office, wanting to reconcile my account with his. You have heard him admitting he would not give a statement. In his hand by that time he had two cheques of £1,300 each, he had delivery orders of £4,500 or £5,000, securities, on the face of it, in his hand of £7,000. Was he trying to pressure me into pay him £7,000 or £5,000? In his own words he said £5,000. Or was he under pressure by the bank, if he had submitted the statement to me, if I had paid him £2,464 then he would not be able to stall the bank? We know he went to the bank; the bank pressured him and very likely he said to the bank "I cannot pay you £10,000, Mr Zelouf owes me ten". No delay in payment of Mr. Truman was there? No fault of mine, it was entirely due to him."

"I said to him on Monday, is this the action of an honest trader who is a creditor? You come along to your debtors and say "Look, this is the amount; you owe me this, you pay me this and settle". Mr. Truman said "no", he would not give the statement. Eventually he had to give the statement to the Palestine-British

Bank. They then telephoned me. The evidence is I went along straightaway to Mr. White. "Let us get one of your colleagues to work them out, compare the two, and then we will settle", as eventually we did."

"Where does Mr. Truman come into these proceedings? Did Truman go to the police and complain? I am sure he did not. The police went to Truman. This case here is not concerning the Truman counts, it is concerning the first three counts relating to Luso. There was a complaint; somebody went to the police and said "This fellow has defrauded me". You are not concerned now with the first three counts. There is not even a prima facie case there. What happens is, I do not know when the police first started or when Luso went to them. Mr Davies said they called at their office in July. So they go to Davies, they go to Sale and company, they go to Translloyd. Do they tell them what they were after? Mr. Davies said they did not tell him. At Translloyd Overseas, likely going through all the files of the year's trading to find out any other irregularities regarding G. Truman and they go along to G. Truman and what could the poor fellow say? He had already claimed £5,000, £10,000. In his own words he said 5,000. "Yes, these are the delivery orders, Mr. Zelouf owes me that," and that is good enough for the police. Mr. Truman is brought as a witness. As for my part, silence, absolute silence, on all sides. If they started their investigations in May, June, July, August, nobody told me anything. The police did not come to me and say "What are your records? Show us your records, what was your state of mind at the particular date?" Nobody says anything and the witnesses; my bankers, my forwarding agent, my suppliers, every one of them silent as the grave. What sort of statement they got out of them I do not know, but it might explain their peculiar behaviour in this court."

"So one day, on the 30th November, Detective Sergeant Isaacs and somebody else come to me, visit me at my office "Mr. Zelouf, you are under arrest".

"What for?" "False pretences and fraud". I make no reply. I was asked no questions, taken to Cloak Street Police Station, the charge is read to me formally. I make no reply. Nobody asks me any questions. Detective Sergeant Isaacs says to me "I am sorry Mr. Zelouf, the warrant is not endorsed for bail". I said "Why is that?" There is no reply. After that, still silence, until we come here and when I have to cross-examine the witnesses and until we get some sort of pattern and sense out of the thing. Whom have I defrauded? Whom have I cheated?"

"Members of the Jury, at the beginning of this trial prosecution Counsel said to you that a man is innocent the first principle of law is that a man is innocent, until proved guilty, and that is an excellent point to repeat to you. It does not tell the full story though. A man could be ruined before he could prove his innocence. I do not come here pleading for mercy. I have come here as an innocent man with a good character and I want to go out as an innocent man with a good character.

I am not concerned whether count 6 is valid or not, whether Mr. Truman gave me money for that or not. I am not concerned whether the counts are for fraud or attempted fraud. Nothing but a complete exoneration of my name would be an unmitigated disaster. I have got no business. I have to go out in the world and build up a career for myself. I have to follow a certain profession. I have a family to raise, any slur on my name would be the absolute finish."

"I am not here asking for mercy, I come here asking for justice. Yet when I left home this morning I left a wife bed-ridden with anxiety and two young children, blissfully unaware that their father's and their future are today being decided. On that last point I leave the matter in your hands."

There was then a lull, the judge, Mr. Commissioner Marnan, fixing Zelouf with a long reflective look of barely concealed admiration, before embarking on the summing up.

The Judge was a meticulous note maker in the course of the trial, and he was now to go over them, setting out the evidence in full while pointing out several times, and so concluding, that most of the facts were not in dispute because the defendant Mr. Zelouf admitted the majority of the evidence adduced by the prosecution. In the event the summing up lasted more than two hours and covered fifty pages of court reporter's typescript. An experienced lawyer would have characterised it as a summary for acquittal.

As the judge directed the jury to judge the facts on the evidence they heard in court and nothing else he went on to add

> "Of course, you will give to the speech you have heard a few moments ago and the points Mr. Zelouf raised close attention and such weight as you yourself think right. I have little doubt that you have all admired the courage and ability with which Mr. Zelouf has conducted his defence in person."

And later, as a further appreciation of Mr. Zelouf's speech

> "You have heard his speech this morning. If I may say so, he made his speech this morning with admirable conciseness; he made it point by point.

I have no doubt you will bear them in mind, but I will remind you of the points he made when I deal with his evidence. I am able to do it because he made it so clear and concise; and it is only right that you should give him full credit for what his points were so you appreciate what they are."

Referring to the fact that Mr. Zelouf knew nothing about the investigation that extended over several months and involved interviewing and taking statements from several witnesses, the judge observed

"It would almost look as if for some extraordinary reason there has been a conspiracy of silence to keep Mr. Zelouf in the dark Mr. Zelouf never really had an opportunity of presenting his explanation of all these matters until he came before you in point of fact, he did offer to make a statement and Sergeant Isaacs agrees 'You offered a statement, but I refused'. Detective Sergeant Isaac agreed he had not visited Mr. Zelouf or made any enquiry of him before he went and arrested him."

Dealing with the gravity of the alleged offence the judge harked back to Mr. Zelouf's stressing throughout his speech that no one had been done out of any money.

> "So far as Mr. Truman is concerned, as Mr. Zelouf has pointed out to you this morning, all this matter has been settled. Eventually accounts were submitted and eventually the balance, £2,400 odd, was paid and, as he said, in the end Mr. Truman has not lost anything at all. So, looking at the case at the very worst and assuming that Mr. Zelouf, assuming against him for the moment, just for the purpose of argument, assuming he was dishonest in relation to this transaction, it is not as bad as the type of case in which a man by fraud, by false pretences, manages to relieve somebody of £3,000 and disappears with the money. It is not that case at all, and nobody suggests it is. It is nothing like such a serious case, looking at it at its very worst. But you are not concerned with the question of seriousness, you are concerned with the question of honesty and dishonesty."

That was the part of the summing up that caused Mr. Zelouf a great deal of anxiety. The judge was making it clear that in the event of a conviction the penalty or sentence which was within the remit of the judge and his alone would not be severe. Listening to those words Mr. Zelouf hoped that the jury would not be induced to make a finding of 'guilty' in the knowledge and expectation that it would be followed by a mild sentence such as a fine or conditional discharge. Hence, Mr. Zelouf sought to pre-empt that in the concluding passage of his speech which was very unusual coming from an accused addressing a jury in a criminal trial. It was the strongest plea to the jury to think beyond their verdict as to the facts to the extent of allowing their judgment to be influenced by their expectation of the possible sentence. That was outside their function and remit as a jury and would fly in the face of the judge's direction that it was none of their concern. Mr. Zelouf's plea in those concluding words of his address to the jury was such as would be thought impertinent in all but an exceptional context: "I am not concerned whether count 6 is valid or not, whether Mr. Truman gave me money or that or not. I am not concerned whether the counts are for fraud or attempted fraud. Anything but a complete exoneration of my name would be an unmitigated disaster".

But there was also the irony of the situation. An alleged offence at the lowest scale of seriousness, the sort that would normally be disposed off in a magistrate court was actually set to be tried over a period of more than two weeks at The Old Bailey no less.

Dealing with the Truman counts generally the judge referred to the admissions made by Mr. Truman when he was being cross-examined by Mr. Zelouf.

> "Mr. Truman, when he was being cross-examined said our transactions were involved and complex, and one ran into another. No single transaction was self-contained, we were in close contact and I certainly did not expect that you would defraud me. I believe that Mr. Zelouf was under pressure and I do not believe that if it had been within his power he would have deliberately defrauded me. When he said 'within his power in relation to pressure, it is a matter for you, but I understood him to imply he thought unless there had been some exceptional pressure and Mr. Zelouf was in some terrible difficulty, that he would not have done anything deliberately dishonest, and it is common ground that in the long run Mr. Truman was paid back."

The jury retired and returned to court 90 minutes later with a unanimous verdict acquitting the defendant on all counts of the indictment. He softly thanked the jury. The judge's voice rang out

"M. Zelouf you are discharged".

Mr. Zelouf thanked the judge. He turned to get his holdall containing his papers. He had it placed throughout the trial on the side bench between him and the warder. The warder now got up and with all eyes fixed on them shook Mr. Zelouf warmly by the hand, picked up the bag and presented it to him reverentially. Mr. Zelouf walked out looking for a public call box to tell his wife that all was well, that he would be home soon.

Outside the public callbooth he stood still, seized by a sudden emptiness. For the first time in his life he felt aimless. He looked about him but everything was changed. Nothing will ever be the same again. Looking towards a featureless future the signposts of his past life flooded his consciousness. He will let himself be carried along by the tide. That much he learned from his experiences of the last few months. He will walk until physical exhaustion had exorcised the demons in his head. He imagined himself drawn towards the river, along Mincing Lane and the Baltic Exchange, the Monument, Lower Thames Street, the wharf by London Bridge where ships of the Aznar Line brought the produce of the Canaries and Madeira, on to Tower Bridge where at lunch time a small knot of men would listen to Lord Soper addressing them from atop a soap box, on to Wapping with a halt at the Prospect of Whitby where the river, sensual as a well used woman, opened up to receive the tide, on to Canary Wharf, past Albert Docks, sailing with the Bajamar and the Orotava, down towards Creekermouth, Tilbury and out into the Channel, the wide open sea where one was free to sail to distant shores with no frontier posts or warders in the way. But before that he will go home to comfort his wife, indulge his children, later to call at the police station to collect his property and see that his fingerprints and photograph are destroyed, now that he would be walking the streets of London a free man with no stain on his character.

The end of the trial brought a great relief to King Edward's Grove, but no jubilation. The future looked bleak as far as one could see. Fouad had no job nor the near-term prospect of a good one that would ease their financial problems. He had now enrolled as a student member of the Middle Temple, but it would take several years before he will have qualified and started to earn money as a barrister. In the meantime the house belonged to the bank and the family was allowed to continue living in it on sufferance pending its sale, the estate agent having advised marketing it occupied rather than empty. They no longer had a bank account. The car was sold for cash that was being used to pay for necessities. Granex was in the course of liquidation, and Fouad was in trepidation at the ordeal of having to be present at the first meeting of creditors to face criticism, obloquy and disgrace. Helen's asthma was getting worse and when it was the school holiday she went to Royston with the children for a respite.

But it was not all unrelieved gloom. The Hong Kong Manufacturing Company, Granex's main Far East supplier, sent him a letter of support. They wanted him to start a new business and they will supply him with goods on credit to sell for his own account or as their agent. He declined the offer. As a businessman he was broken; nor did he have the mental reserve and moral fortitude to start again. The liquidator of Knowles and Foster indicated that there was no claim against him personally. The sale of the house would leave a balance owed to Barclays Bank. His friend Haron who also had an account with the bank came to an arrangement that cleared it. After two years of unremitting struggle to save Granex he could now get up in the morning burdened by his business failure yet without the anxiety of his erstwhile state of managing Granex and wondering if he could somehow raise enough to cover its financial obligations that would have fallen due that day. He felt happy to be a student again, immersing himself in Roman Law, the English constitution and legal history. In the meantime things were happening in Royston that will have a lasting impact.

Royston

Number 17 North Road was one in a row of rented houses in the mining village of Royston. Each of the houses had a privy in the yard and a tin bathtub in the kitchen. Most of the houses belonged to Monckton Main colliery which dominated the village, its pit at one end with its winding gear nodding to the parish church's spire at the other. Monckton Main was opened in 1878 and that attracted many families that came looking for work and swelled the population of what had been a small rural community between Barnsley and Wakefield. The Anglican Church of St. John the Baptist was ever the spiritual heart of the village. It was Norman, constructed in 1234, one of a very few churches in England that boasted an Oriel window. The people of Royston were a religious folk, the churches were well attended, and there would be a march every Sunday headed by the band of the Salvation Army followed by a meeting at the Wells. That was the space at the main crossroad in the centre of Royston. There was also a Methodist chapel and a small community of Roman Catholics who kept themselves apart, religiously speaking. One was not aware of any Jews living in Royston; a pawn shop in a side street was run by Barry who was local and it was rumoured that the owner was a Jew from Leeds. No foreign faces could be seen in the village and absent were such things as Chinese and Indian takeaways. The people of Royston did the weekly shopping by taking the bus to Barnsley market; there was one convenient store in Royston that belonged to the co-op.

There had existed actual wells at the crossroad sometime in the past which were later culverted. The Wells was the place for holding public events and assemblies, political meetings and hustings. People would talk grimly of the soup kitchens that were held there during the general and miners strikes. They would then point to the big tree in the field nearby which was reduced to a bare stump by the end of the long strike of 1932.

There were many public houses, two just across the road from the parish church. They were in addition to the Working Men's Club which was always well stocked and well attended. It organised a trip to the seaside once a year. You paid a weekly subscription to the holiday fund, and that paid for your weekend in Blackpool. There was always a place on the coach for Jonah. He was the village idiot who was indulged by the others. They would take pleasure to tell you of his oddities and the good natured japes played on him. Every time the coach was about to depart friends and relatives would come to wish the lucky ones a fabulous holiday and to tell them what mementoes and keepsakes they hoped they would bring back. On one such occasion an old woman came along, handed an empty milk bottle to Jonah with a shilling and asked him to bring her back a bottle of Blackpool water. After they had got to their destination Jonah dutifully walked down to the beach and saw a man in a boat. He gave him the shilling piece and carried the full bottle of Blackpool water back to the boarding house where he stopped for a nap. When he got up later and went down to the beach he saw the same man in the same boat that was now quite further away. He called out to the boat man: "Ee Bah Gum, you hadn't half made your fortune whilst I were away."

When news of Helen in London got back to Royston many were surprised, and some young men dismayed, that 'our Hilda' was going out with a foreigner in London. But after Fouad had come and stayed two nights at 17 North Road Mrs Shaw of number 15 felt it necessary to go about correcting a general misconception, telling everyone that Hilda's young man was from Iraq but was not foreign because he was as white as you and me. She would then lower her voice to add that he was Jewish and in business.

Number 17 North Road was cheered on by the news of Hilda's progress in London. Harold Caswell went about telling everyone, spreading no little envy in the process, how well 'our Hilda' was doing in London; getting married to a clever businessman, becoming rich, having two lovely children being raised in a beautiful house all their own on its own plot of land. Then there was the change in the young family's fortunes, one piece of grim news following another with visits by Hilda arriving with the children when she would talk of Fouad's falling out with his brothers and relatives, the failure of his business, the trial, the loss of their home, the penury. There was nothing her parents could do about her woes, while some of her contemporaries at Normanton High School, on hearing the news, felt a glow of self- satisfaction for not having been seduced by the lure of London but stayed in Royston, married good local men, did well on the new post-nationalisation miners' wages and deputies' salaries, and were now living and raising families in the desirable neighbouring villages of Notton and Woolley. Harold was left to inveigh against Fouad's brothers who came over from Iraq, were well received and helped by Fouad and Hilda, only to see them turn against them. Why did we have them, he exclaimed; what were they doing in our country? It did not escape attention that nearly all the individuals involved in the troubles that Hilda described were Jewish. Harold called them traitors; Mary referred to them as Judases; a neighbour who was in the Salvation Army invoked the blood of Christ shed on the cross; the Gospel narratives of the Passion were recalled ascribing to the Jews the torment and death of the Son of God. Those historical references were taken up by several of the women neighbours as by the men at the Working Men's Club. In the midst of the expressions of racism and anti-Semitism Hilda defended her husband; she would not allow anything to come between them, and she was very cross when she learned that her father contacted a councillor he knew to enquire whether a house could be found in the village for 'our Hilda' and the kids. Racism including anti-Semitism was never far below the surface of the working class. Weakened by the ordeals of the past months she had the notion that the whole of North Road, Royston, Yorkshire and the world were against the Jews. She looked at her two children and became anxious for their safety and well being. When her husband came to take her and the children back to Teddington she told him that she had made up her mind to have the children baptised. He was stunned and asked her why she would want to do that, and she was adamant. She will do anything to protect the children and give them a good start in life. After what the family had gone through in the last two years culminating in the trial, the loss of all they had including the house she was determined to have the children brought up like all other ordinary children, English and Anglican. Fouad did not feel able to raise much objection. He had failed her. She had tried to please him and his family to the extent of converting to his religion, and what was her reward? They walked to the parish church with the children. Atheist and socialist that he was he felt it as a grievous loss, the giving away of his children. The vicar looked bored as he mechanically went through the proceeding. Fouad was in a daze not quite taking in what was happening. Two things stuck in his mind for ever afterwards; the man tracing with a wet finger the sign of the cross on the foreheads of his children; and Helen at the end telling him to reward the man of religion for taking away his children. He had only three pound coins in his pocket which he gave to the vicar. They looked like three pieces of silver.

Chiswick

A damp, dark, dismal basement flat in Chiswick. It marked the lowest point in the family's financial situation and social standing. He knew nothing about it until his wife took him along to see it. They got off at Gunnersbury underground station, walked out to the main road, turned along the side of a house, down narrow, dark steps, then she announced, "That's our new home". Yet another assertion that she was now in charge. Nor could he complain. Traumatised by the failure of his company, the loss of the Jaguar and the forced sale of the house, on top of the searing experience of the trial at the Old Bailey and the ordeal of Granex's creditors meeting the husband was beyond being able to search, consider, discuss, negotiate or make a decision. With the little money they had she paid the deposit and premium for the monthly tenancy and paid the removal people. There was then the incongruity of a small, low-class living space covered by a Persian Kashan and filled by Heal's trendy Danish furniture. But why Chiswick? He never got to know. After registering at the doctors' surgery and introducing the children to their new Church of England school the wife got hold of a pot of paint and a brush, and added a little cheer to the facing wall of the dim stairs. Up those stairs was the garden, a big neglected garden overgrown by weeds. The children loved the garden when they were allowed to roam on their own. Rebecca would pick the puny flowers struggling among the weeds to make a daisy chain to take to her mother.

The way to the primary school was along busy streets of tenements that housed a diverse humanity of many colours, Somali black dominant, that spilled out of doors to lounge on the steps, take in the cool air, discuss the prices in the shops and the last episode involving the school as they waited for their kids to come home. Miss Davies was the head teacher. She was very strict. Everyone was wary of her, and she was very religious. As she surveyed at assembly the progeny of diverse humanity in her charge she felt the urge as of a missionary to bring people together, have them treated equally, fairly and with respect as they were led to the true faith that engendered happiness out of suffering, enlightenment out of darkness and eternal life out of death. Rebecca and John had been just one week at school when they came home with Rebecca singing Miss Davies's favourite hymn:

There is a green field far away

Without a city wall
Where the dear Lord was cru-ci-fied
He died to save us all

John asked what crucified meant and wanted his
mother to take him up to the garden to chase the birds.
That was how they met Danny who lived with his father on
the ground floor. He had come down to clear a blockage in a
drain under the manhole at the far end of the garden. There
were also people living on the top floors but were barely seen
or heard. When there was the same blockage again some
time later Danny came down with his father this time. They
lifted the manhole, had a look then replaced it, the older
man heard to say, "Leave it Danny, that's landlord's". The
problem was reported to the solicitor's clerk as he came at
the end of the month to collect the rent. Until the blockage
problem was sorted out Helen told the children to keep out
of the garden, which made them unhappy. But John was
pleased that he had made friends with William at the school
playground. William lived on the other side of the railway
truck; he came with his mother every morning over the high,
grey metal bridge, holding hands; sometimes they heard the
swish and rumble of the train passing underneath. William's
people were on the way up, father working in an office, their
house two streets away from Strand-on-the-Green and the
river.

The daily struggle to put food on the table. No, that was not simply a literary metaphor or a political cliché. It was a brutal reality when you had children to feed and no money in your pocket. He had worked continuously in the last ten years, and paid income tax and national insurance contributions yet was diffident as he stepped across the entrance of the local labour exchange and social security offices. He would feel the shame of going across to the counter of an official to own up to his job loss, his penury, desperation, the needs of wife and children, and to plead for help. To his surprise the official was friendly, did not pry deep into the facts and history of the matter; nor did she ask for proof of identity and verification of the facts that he stated. She made a quick calculation, and he walked out with six pounds, seventeen shillings and six pence. That was the amount of the unemployment benefit that he would be calling to collect each week until he had found a job. Later that day the family took the bus to the Chiswick street market. They left it till late in the afternoon. That was when the market would be about to close and the prices of fruits and vegetables got slashed. The talk on the way was of the money they had to spend, what to spend it on, and of the prices going up all the time. Rebecca who was listening intently said she will grow up to be the Prime Minister and will then order "All prices down!" Fouad said the help they received from the state reinforced his socialist beliefs; of a community in which everyone contributed to the general welfare, and which came to the aid of one who stumbled and fell on hard times. Helen's socialism was of a more robust, combative stuff. She picked the paper and wielded the pen:

> I dreamt of you last night
> You were on my side of the counter
> And you had a twinkle in your eye
> Now I am out of bed on the wrong side
> And we are in line of the dish out
> You looked quite jarred this morning
> Are you thinking I'm not deserving?
> Yeah, I'm in a right old stew
> Jinxed to the eyeballs
> Except I've got no side-kick
> I'm busted and I'm strapped
> Just an out of work hack
> With not much backbone
> But give us what's our due
> Because it's not charity, lady
> It's your security too!

He called to collect the money on five consecutive weeks and then stopped.

That was after he was engaged by a correspondence school of creative writing to act as a reviewer. A student client would submit an original piece of work, be it a short story, article or poem which will then be sent to him to review, assess and comment on and have it returned to the client with helpful suggestions added to smarten it up. In reality he was employed to further the interests of his employer, a commercial enterprise, so he was expected to flatter the piece by attributing to it such pleasing attributes as engaging, perceptive, innovative, sensitive of feeling, robust of message, modernist of outlook with post-modern style of writing. The flattery would be laced with suggestions for minor improvements. That job lasted two months. He was dismissed after the management had received a letter of complaint. It was from a regular client who delighted in cruelty, violence and the wallowing in blood and gore. The reviewer dutifully returned the short story, commented on the lurid but robust description of the bayonet in contact with the enemy's entrails, and suggested that the piece might benefit from some toning down. The client's next contribution salivated over a still greater violence. The reviewer again counselled some moderation and added as an observation that the violence on top of the pornography was so outré that it would have caused the Marquis de Sade to blush. The client looked up the word in the dictionary and took its use to be an insult. He sat down with pen and paper to give vent to his outrage.

Fouad received the sacking with equanimity while regretting the loss of income. The effect of that was mitigated by his getting himself on the list of a tutorial agency that allocated to him some paid work which was to help students to pass their examinations. In the meantime Helen got a place at Acton College to read for an English degree; that came with a maintenance grant of £290 a year. The children had settled well at school while Fouad was admitted to the Middle Temple to train to be a barrister. Little by little things were looking up for the family. They were now on the way up.

The days that followed were uplifting notwithstanding the deprivation and daily struggle to make ends met. A thrill went through the wife every time she set out to attend the evening classes while the husband stayed at home to look after the children. That made up for her the disappointment of missing a university education after grammar school while still living at home in Royston. She would now come back to talk excitedly of Sylvia Plath's Daddy and of Manley Hopkins's Margaret as she grieved over Golden grove unleaving. He, for his part, would have spent the evening poring over his law books, and he would now find pleasure expounding over some strange concepts in Roman Law: How to determine the ownership of a colony of bees that swarmed and was pursued by its owner; and what of a part of a riverbank that broke off and, carried by the current, went to adhere to another bank? He was an instinctive lawyer. Other students would start by reading the reported cases from which they would extrapolate the principle and the resolution of a problem; he would instinctively visualise the problem and the answer, then go to the reported cases for confirmation and authority.

In order to embark on the road of becoming a practising barrister one had to start with eating so many dinners in Hall and passing the examination of a set number of subjects. It was a permissive regime. One was not required to take the dinners successively, and it was likewise as regards getting credits for the subjects. Examinations were held twice a year; a candidate could enter his name for any one or more of the papers and pay the fee for each. One was free to take or retake an examination as often as one wanted until one passed them all; and there was no time limit on how long that took. There were some who spent several years making one attempt after another. You would come across Bill who would tell you sardonically that if he had saved up all he had wasted on examination fees he would have had enough to open a shop in his native St. Vincent. And there was Ursula who had not sat a single examination since she joined the inn. She was married to a successful businessman operating in the industrial tools, cranes in particular, business. They had a sumptuous apartment in Chelsea and no children. Being a member of the Honourable Society of the Middle Temple was a social cachet that Ursula used with pride. After a visit to Coutts in the Strand it was agreeable to drop in for a bit of socialising at the inn's junior common room. She was older than the average and became friendly with Fouad. She was convinced he was mad and so told him to his face. She once confided to him that she would not have been admitted to the inn if the powers that be had wind of her antecedents. She hailed from Limerick which was noted for horse racing, and she was the most popular girl in town because she worked at the pharmacy! After imparting that confession she leaned back in her chair and let out a hearty Irish guffaw of laughter.

The inns of court had set up a school for beginners located as an annexe to Gray's Inn. The classes were held in the late afternoons and evenings, the teachers were junior practising members of the Bar. Consistent with the general permissive regime the students were left to organise their own studies and were not mandated to attend classes regularly if at all. In consequence, at any time of the day, the inn's junior common room would be well attended. It was an engaging meeting place of bright young people from different parts of the world; future advocates, administrators, politicians and leaders. You would see them reading the newspapers, playing chess, discussing legal questions or just socialising.

The Bar's permissive regime suited Fouad well, allowing him to complete and obtain credit for all the prescribed subjects in a short period of time. He attended very few lessons and lectures at the Bar school. He raced through the textbooks and law reports at his own rapid pace and hungry desire to learn. After the dark days of being in business, of having to deal with the demands and criticisms of brothers, relatives and partners; of being beset by debts and creditors as he dealt with bankers and financiers there was now the freedom of being a student again in charge of his own destiny. His brain absorbed the law with the avidity of a dry soil absorbing the rain. He got credits for all the prescribed subjects in three examination sittings over eighteen months. He came top in the combined contract and tort paper, passed first class in constitutional law and conveyancing, and missed a first in land law by a few marks. He acquired a reputation in the junior common room of being a 'legal eagle' as he gained the respect of a coterie of amiable youths and budding lawyers. The majority were English, two from Cambridge, most of the rest had come straight from the public schools. And there were overseas students who had come from past and present British colonies where the English common law had continued to be practised.

But passing the written examinations was as to nothing compared with the next stage of the odyssey, which was to be accepted in some chambers as a pupil. The requirement was to spend a year as a pupil of a practising barrister to whom one paid a pupillage fee set at £100 for the year. That was a considerable expense in those days to be added to the cost of the accoutrement of horse-hair wig, black robe and wing collar. In cases of real and admitted hardship one's inn might step in with a grant to cover the pupillage fee. Nearly every one of the students was related to the judiciary or had a connection with a practising barrister or with a solicitor who instructed barristers' chambers, so it was not too difficult to be admitted as a pupil. Fouad had no such connection and did not know how to go about finding a pupil master.

Ursula encouraged him to go take his problem up to Master Arnold, a Middle Temple master of the bench and eminent chancery silk with chambers in Lincoln's Inn. John Arnold did not disappoint. He fixed him up with a pupillage in two parts, the first six months to be with Martin Nourse to be followed by one with Alan Heyman.

Martin Nourse was a brilliant chancery lawyer. When Fouad went to be his pupil Martin was in his early thirties, well connected, ambitious and a rising star as a member of chambers at 2 New Square, Lincoln's Inn. That was a prestigious set of chambers specialising in trust law and taxation. It catered for the English aristocracy as they sought to preserve their wealth and, in particular, avoid the ravages of inheritance tax. It was the object of envy by other practitioners who would allege metaphorically that 2 New Square had a copy of Debrett's Peerage and Baronetcy in every room. The leaders of the chambers were John Brightman as head followed by Sydney Templeman (they both ended up in the House of Lords), and Maurice Price. Every member had a big room to themself, his pupil would have a smaller desk to the side. There were strict rules of behaviour; you do not intrude on another unless for a serious purpose; you do not knock on the door nor announce your presence as you stealthily entered another's room to pick a book from the shelf or, as the office boy, to return it. There was not the jollity that one would expect of men working at close proximity to each other. The members got together in the afternoon for a tea break in the room of the head of chambers or, in his absence, that of the most senior member. The pupils took their tea separately in the room of the most senior pupil, that is the one whose pupil master was senior to the other pupil master or masters. A pupil would speak to his pupil master with deference and not at all to the others unless spoken too. There were no female tenants or pupils. Margaret Thatcher left Somerville College, Oxford with a degree in chemistry, dipped her toe in 2 New Square to learn about the setting up of trusts and their reconstitution and about the tax implication. She left to go into politics. The day after Fouad started his pupillage he was asked by Martin Nourse if he was in receipt of a grant to cover the fee, £50 for the six months. Fouad said he had not thought of applying and came up with Helen's £50 in banknotes the following day, which Martin pocketed with nothing said.

Brilliant that he was as a lawyer Martin may not have been the ideal pupil master for one who came straight from the inns of court school. Martin had a very busy and highly specialist practice; he dealt at the time almost exclusively with the convoluted intricacies and applications of the newly enacted Variation of Trusts Act; that mostly passed over the head of the pupil. There were only a few breaks when Martin could lay aside the particular case he was dealing with and use the time to instruct and explain. Fouad would walk with him to court, sit behind him to listen to him making submissions without fully comprehending the salient points. The same thing happened when Martin advised in chambers. He would brilliantly expound upon the matter in hand to the obvious satisfaction and admiration of client and solicitor while Fouad, at his desk, listened intently without fully understanding what the case was about. At the end of the six months Fouad felt that he was marginally better fitted to be a chancery lawyer. Yet he derived a lasting benefit from those months. He got to know and to become lifelong friends with another pupil at 2 New Square. Jeffrey Hackney was at the time a tutorial fellow in law at St Edmund's Hall, Oxford. He considered becoming a barrister, then gave up the idea and went back to Oxford to pursue a long and distinguished academic career as Fellow at law of Wadham College. Once, during his brief spell as a pupil Jeffrey was heard to rail incautiously against a capitalist system in which 5% of the population owned 95% of the national wealth. When that became known Martin Nourse reacted mockingly: If that's how he feels, what's he doing here! In time, Martin as Sir Martin Nourse rose to be a Lord Justice of Appeal of England and Wales; he served as Vice-President of the Civil Division of the Court of Appeal, and for a brief spell, as Master of the Rolls. He died of undisclosed causes on 28 November 2017, aged 86.

Alan Heyman specialised in company law and insolvency. By birth, a scion of the Danish royal family and by marriage an associate of Europe's aristocracy he possessed a well-built Nordic frame and spoke with strong, confident and cultured English without a trace of an accent. Free of racism and xenophobia he held the presidency of the International Tennis Federation. He welcomed his new pupil warmly, found out that he was an Iraqi by origin and did not want to know anymore. He waived the £50 pupillage fee. A man of wide amiability and broad sympathies his door was always open to anyone who came to seek his views on a troubling legal question or to discuss a matter of chambers administration or just to take a pinch out of his snuff box which he always carried in his breast pocket.

On Fouad's first day as pupil Alan came across and asked him to look at a set of instructions from a Manchester solicitor seeking advice. Fouad returned the instruction with a written opinion which he placed on Alan's desk. When Alan returned after lunch he picked up the papers, took a pinch of snuff, relaxed and sat back to read the opinion. He generously complimented his pupil: "This is good", he said, "really good." That was followed by several others, and it got to the stage that on the receipt of a new instruction Alan would discuss it with his pupil then leave it to the latter to pen the advice and settle the draft proceedings. Alan would look at the typed end result and except for the odd rare case allow it to be returned in his name without alteration.

Alan had a big family house with acres in Suffolk where he spent the weekend and all other non-working days. He also had a flat in Knightsbridge which he used on weekdays. They may also have had a place on the island of Elba; that was where the family's festive holidays were spent. Alan took a three week holiday the summer that Fouad was his pupil. In his absence Fouad dealt with all the instructions that Alan had left behind and the ones that arrived while he was away. On his return Alan brightened up to see up to twenty separate instructions and briefs covering several areas of the law that were fully dealt with in his absence, and in good order. The highlight of the pupillage was Fouad's involvement in the case of Introductions Limited. That was a statutory company whose memorandum of association defined its objects as introducing tourists to places of entertainment plus a clutch of other objects with the proviso that other events could be included if agreed. In fact, the only activity that the company undertook was to rear pigs as a commercial enterprise, and to invite the public to subscribe as an investment. The project failed and many subscribers lost their investments and were looking for an explanation if not a meaningful remedy. Alan was to appear in the Companies Court at 10:30 on Monday morning. He was travelling from Suffolk and was held up on the way. He arrived in chambers with a few minutes to spare. He picked up the brief and the legal submission with cogent argument supported by authority that his pupil had prepared, rushed with him to court where he read the prepared script as his basic argument. It was successful, the court holding that in any such case one looks at the main object while laying aside the others. In the case of Introductions Limited the business of rearing pigs and inviting the public to invest was *ultra vires,* that is outside the legal power of the company to be engaged in, with the necessary implication that the activity that the company allegedly carried out in its name was that of the directors themselves who became liable for the losses. Fouad was proud to see the case and the judgment published in the law reports as a leading authority.

Those were happy days for Fouad and Helen. He had a good relationship with his pupil master, was full of pride for seeing his work and his legal potential appreciated. There was the prospect of being offered a place in chambers at the completion of the pupillage, and he was now earning more as a tutor. He was in favour with the tutorial agency while his new status of a trainee barrister on top of his academic qualifications opened the door for more exalted and better paid assignments. One such brought Fouad into contact with the English aristocracy. It involved his spending a week in residence at Hoddington Hall in Hampshire as tutor to Freddie, aged 19, and so help him secure a place at Cambridge. Freddie was the younger son of Sir Edmund Stockdale, first Baronet and former Lord Mayor of London. Freddie did not distinguish himself as a scholar and, coming to the end of his years at Eton, wanted to follow his elder brother Thomas to Oxford and to membership of the Bullingdon Club; but failed to gain a place. It was the same with the Cambridge college of his first choice. His uncle was a close friend of the Master of Jesus who then offered him a place to read law on condition that he passed the Cambridge Law Test.

As Fouad got off the train at the Hampshire railway station, he was met by the family chauffeur who carried his bag to the car and drove him to Hoddington Hall. The only conversation during the drive was initiated by the driver, and it related to shooting grouse in Scotland. He was met affably by the family, Thomas picked up his bag, took it to what was to be his bedroom, returned, sat down and took no part in the conversation. There was an animated talk about the glider that had dropped out of the sky in the morning, and of the pilot who came out unhurt and was revived by a glass of sherry as he waited for the club's rescue team. It was a balmy afternoon; they were sitting in the garden with the swimming pool nearby. Anne- Louise, the only daughter of the family, asked him if he fancied a swim; she said that Tommy would lend him a pair of swimming trunks if he had come without. He declined the invitation while Thomas did not react. Thomas was seven years older than Freddie and a barrister in Lincoln's Inn. He was quietly reserved; one got the impression that he was not keen on the law, may not have had serious plans to practice it long term while he waited for the time when it will fall to him to be the 2nd Stockdale Baronet and to look after the family's estate. He was married to Jacqueline, a Vietnamese and they had a house in London. He had come to spend the afternoon at Hoddington Hall. Sir Edmund who was wary at first became visibly more relaxed once he learned that his younger son's tutor and mentor was not a roman catholic. Lady Stockdale referred to her nephew Alexander who was brought up a catholic and, spoilt terribly by his mother, ran away from Ampleforth. Freddie defended Alexander who looked up to him as to an older brother. He said, looking towards Thomas, that once Alexander was 21 and in control of his money, they will be starting some new as yet unidentified enterprise, with him Freddie in the lead, that will make him rich. The unspoken but inferred sub-text was that the envisaged enterprise and wealth would compensate him as a second son for missing out on the baronetcy and the major part of the family's wealth. His father reminded him that he had twenty thousand acres in his own name next to the royal Balmoral estate; Freddie protested that his land was worth no more than one pound an acre. Anne-Louise said that she was blissfully poor as an artist and member of the Chelsea Arts Club. She and Marcus were living in penury while he toiled as a barrister in the Temple.

The tutor had an immediate rapport with his pupil. Freddie was a keen learner, enjoyed the lessons and made copious notes. He passed the Cambridge Law Test and got a place at Jesus. Fouad was invited to spend a further week in Cambridge to oversee Freddie's preparation and progress. Fouad also saw it as an opportunity to provide Freddie with a different outlook on the world than the privileged one he had experienced and observed at Eton and its extension at the then men-only Pitt Club. The Pitt Club had premises in Jesus Lane and its facilities were only available to the members and their guests. Freddie attended on some evenings with Fouad as his guest and introduced him, with a measure of showing off, as his personal tutor. Coming away from the Club and sensing what his tutor felt about the experience, Freddie confided to him that both he and Anne-Louse had voted Labour at the last election without telling anyone. The Pitt University Club was founded in 1835 in honour of William Pitt the Younger who had studied at Pembroke College. It continued over the years as a bastion of wealth, privilege and Toryism. It is often described as Cambridge's answer to Oxford's Bullingdon Club, which the Cambridge men dispute.

The tutor was lodged for the week at the University Arms hotel reputed to be one of the top five hotels outside London. One morning as he sat down waiting for his breakfast Freddie and Alexander came to join him; Alexander had driven from Easton Neston to see how Freddie was getting on as a true and serious Cambridge undergraduate. It so happened that a big, tall, loudly speaking American came in from the street to tell everyone of the amazing sight he came across on his walk: One of my tankers has overturned, he announced. Alexander ordered his breakfast in a fake American accent, and ordered his eggs to be fried "sunny side up!" Thomas Alexander Fermor-Hesketh, Baron Hesketh, inherited the title when he was only five years old. The family fortune had then been depleted by the inheritance taxes that became payable in respect of two successive deaths, It was rebuilt by the time Alexander got hold of the money in 1971 aged 21. He had always been interested in cars and he came into public prominence in the 1980's as an eccentric figure of the world of Formula Racing. A fervent supporter of Margaret Thatcher he became Conservative Party Chairman and John Major's chief whip in the House of Lords.

Fouad further supplemented his income by holding classes in law for some of his friends of the Middle Temple's Junior Common Room. Known for his acuity as a lawyers' lawyer they came to him for advice and to seek his help as they prepared for the examinations. Ursula said he was mad to do it for free when the others were well off and willing to pay a modest tuition fee. He got in touch with a Frenchman who ran a language school in Charing Cross Road and who had the lease of a whole building. As he was not using the top floor he agreed to let Fouad have the use of one room for one evening a week. Fouad started his own informal law school in the name of The Mentor, holding two one-hour classes every Friday with a break in between. Before long there would be up to 15 students in attendance.

The relationship between Fouad and the Stockdale family continued long after he ceased to be Freddie's tutor. Anne- Louise was vulnerable; she was unhappy, felt despised by her father, unloved by her husband Marcus; and she was addicted to amphetamine and other drugs. Freddie who had a brotherly love for her blamed his parents for sending her away to a public school at a tender age; it was bad enough for him as a boy. She was a good painter but her paintings tended to be bizarre representations of the degraded female body and to rampant sexuality. One evening in the Pitt Club, Fouad had to intervene to defend her reputation when some base specimen of a toff with some grudge against Freddie referred to her as a nymphomaniac. The tutor, on his first day at Hoddington Hall, had recognised Anne-Louise's unhappiness and vulnerability but had to rebuff her advances. He was there as a paid employee and felt even more vulnerable to manipulation and abuse than he perceived her to be. After his return to Chiswick he received a note from Lady Stockdale praising Anne-Louise's house in Acton and urging him to visit it. She implored him to befriend her. She also invited him and Helen to dinner at her London Club. She saw where her daughter was heading and she wanted to do all she could to save her. Marcus and Anne-Louise had a beautiful Victorian town house in Acton which was not far from the Caswell basement flat. The two families became friends and exchanged visits. Anne-Louise admired the paintings that Helen had acquired from Harrods and Bentalls, while Marcus and Fouad had the law as a common interest. One day while taking lunch at Middle Temple Hall Marcus asked Fouad what he had learned as a pupil about the ways of modifying and breaking up a trust under the then widely used provisions of the Variation of Trusts Act.

Fouad explained and Marcus concluded that it was of no help in his case because Anne-Louse's life was not insurable. A little time later Fouad telephoned Marcus and asked after her. He said she had passed away in the night. Fouad wrote to Lady Stockdale offering his condolence and to tell her that he loved Anne-Louise. She wrote back saying that she had been cremated and that the ashes were in an urn that will be embedded in one of the pillars at the entrance to Hoddington Hall. Marcus had Anne-Louise's pictures auctioned. Most of them were bought by Freddie.

When Fouad and Helen later moved to Leeds Freddie would drive from his Thorpe Tilney Hall in Lincolnshire to stay with them, and when he got married, his first, they were invited to the wedding reception. When Fouad, then Matthew, had a court hearing in London he would use Freddie's house in Chelsea. That was where he met Arabella Churchill, another unhappy member of the privileged class with a rebellious unconventional streak. She bemoaned her lack of achievement and poor prospects; and she was already leaning towards Bhuddism. She died in 2007 aged 58 leaving as her lasting legacy the major part she played as the co-founder of the Glastonbury Festival. Freddie Minshull Stockdale became a big name in the arts world as an opera impresario. He founded Pavilion Opera that became celebrated as a touring opera company which performed in private big houses. He took pride in informing his past tutor that he had written his first book "Figaro Here, Figaro

There". That was followed by others, all on the opera theme. He died in 2019 aged 71, survived by his second wife Adele, a soprano, and two children by her, five children altogether.

Towards the end of his pupillage Alan Heyman took on another pupil. Michael Kennedy arrived by way of Rugby and university to start his one year's pupillage. He got on well with Fouad and the latter did not see in his arrival a threat to his prospects of being offered a place in chambers. Fouad was treated as the more senior pupil and it was natural, as he saw it, for the chambers to be looking ahead and lining up another prospective member to succeed him. Fouad had the unqualified support of his pupil master and the clerk, an important member of chambers, who beamed to him every morning as he arrived. He was sufficiently encouraged to go out with Helen to look for a modest London house. Then as he came one morning and went to the clerk's room, it was a frown instead of a smile. There had been a chambers' meeting the evening before, and they decided to pass over him in favour of Michael Kennedy. He had misread the situation. A barrister's chambers is a serious business. What is looked for in a candidate, in addition to ability, is the potential by dint of image, background and connection to attract more business. That and the ever present nepotism in a small elite profession excused as it is expressed by the statement: Better the one you know than the one you do not know! Michael Kennedy was the product of a top English public school and belonged to a rich family, his grandmother the owner of one of the most prestigious department stores in Princes Street, Edinburgh. By contrast, little was known about Fouad other than his legal knowledge and ability. He was reserved and private, some would say secretive, by nature. After the forty years that he was to spend as a practising barrister there remained to many of his close colleague's gaps in his biography relating to background, upbringing, state of finances, political orientation and religion. Later it occurred to him that the chambers decision might have gone his way if he had played the Jewish card. Alan Heymaan was disappointed by the decision of chambers and did all he could to help his favourite pupil secure a place in an alternative good set of chambers. Told that Helen was from Yorkshire he used his contacts extensively which resulted in Fouad going up to Leeds to present himself to an old and well-established set of chambers at 6 Park Square. He was interviewed and he left a contact telephone number while he awaited the decision. He was at his in-laws's house in Royston when the news came that he had the offer of a tenancy to commence forthwith or as soon as he could make the necessary arrangement to transfer the family to Yorkshire. It was the 5th of November 1968. He went outside, could hear the fireworks streaming in the cold Yorkshire air and see the distant bonfire in the valley. He went to the public call box and told Helen the good news excitedly: He could now say he was a barrister. They were going up North. A note from Jeff Hackney: Well done, London's loss, Yorkshire's gain.

Roundhay

"That's just what we wanted", she exclaimed, as it came in view, an imposing stone clad house which reminded Helen of Anne-Louise's house in Acton: A garden in autumnal colours ending in stone steps rising to a small terrace then a stone archway bearing a classical head topped by a violin crossed with a scroll supporting an oriel window. But the glory of the house was in the wide open spaces and distant views of Roundhay Park that unfolded across the road. Standing on the top step one could see in the distance the cooling towers of a power station, more than 20 miles away. The husband, now Matthew Caswell, had been working as a barrister for four months while living in Huddersfield as a guest of the Maynards. During that time he took the London train every Friday to spend the weekend with Helen and the children, and to manage at the same time to keep up the two-hourly sessions of law mentoring. Now the time had come to bring the family over to Yorkshire and to find a house that was suitable for their needs and which they could afford.

It was constructed in the first days of the 20th century on a corner plot, and it comprised six bedrooms on four floors including the basement. It had its frontage in Old Park Road and a long flank with a back door extended along the side street which was The Drive. At some time in its life, it was divided into two houses by the erection of a breeze block partition at the foot of the stairs, thus separating the ground floor and basement from the rest or upper floors. The split occasioned substantial changes to the lower part and only minimal ones to the upper. They were now on offer as one lot; a purchaser intending to have it as a spacious family home would need to expend a lot of money and effort to reconvert the two houses to the one Edwardian original. But the couple had no money; they were only able to find the £6,000 purchase price by means of a 100% mortgage, and that was based, not on their then income, but on Matthew's hoped for future income of a practising barrister and member of Leeds chambers at 6 Park Square. Their optimistic calculations assumed a steady growth of that income over the years that would also allow for the work of re-conversion to be carried out piecemeal. The first thing they did when they took possession was to have the breeze block partition demolished, and for the bedrooms on the ground floor turned to an open living space. The topmost floor was set aside as guest rooms.

The first guest was Freddie Stockdale who was in the process of selling some land in Scotland and acquiring a small country house and estate in Lincolnshire. It was a purely social visit, an easy drive in an Aston Martin from Thorpe Tilney Hall to 73 Old Park Road; he stayed two nights. He was soon followed by some of the Bar students who had been attending Matthew's mentoring classes. As it became impractical for him to travel to London every week it was arranged for them to follow him to Yorkshire and be accommodated in his house as his students and guests until it was time for them to return to London to sit their examinations. It so happened that five years later Matthew and Helen met them in the course of the celebration of the 500th anniversary of Middle Temple Hall. Many judges and barristers in the North went down to join in the celebration. Matthew and Helen were sitting with members of his chambers when a succession of young barristers came over to greet him and pay respect to her by kissing her on the cheek. Matthew's colleagues who had not known of the past relationship of mentor and students were led to speculate about Helen's social background; that added prestige to the feelings that were had towards Matthew as a colleague. In the county that one could not then represent at cricket unless one was Yorkshire born, Matthew was seen as doubly an outsider; he was not even English born. They would tell you proudly that they were Yorkshire born and bred, discomfit you by their strange rendition of the Yorkshire anthem 'On

Ilkla Moor Baht'At', and enlighten you with the fact that Yorkshire was the biggest county in England containing more acres than there were letters in the Bible. But the xenophobia was also a cover for deep seated suspicion and racism that was embedded in every level of society including the lawyers and the judiciary.

Matthew had a taste of that in his first month in chambers. John Hichin, a senior colleague, had been instructed to represent a company that was defending a wrongful dismissal claim by a former employee. The matter went before an industrial tribune sitting in Leeds. After the conclusion of the evidence the hearing was adjourned to a later date for further legal arguments. In due course a date was set for the resumed hearing and notice of that was sent to the defendant company's solicitors, but for whatever reason it was not communicated to chambers. When the tribunal reassembled on the appointed day there was no sign of Mr Hichin who at that moment was starting another case in Teesside. An anxious telephone call from the tribunal's secretary informed chambers of the ghastly situation. There will be a time for finding how that had come about, time for investigation, accusation, and retribution. But for now one had to do what could be done to manage the crisis. It so happened that Matthew Caswell was the only barrister in chambers when the call was received and the clerk Charles Easton asked him to hasten to the tribunal to express regret and at the same time give an explanation that would protect chambers and its clerk from blame. He added by way of reassurance that the chairman of the tribunal was a past member of chambers for whom he had clerked for several years before he received his judicial appointment. Matthew hastened to the tribunal as a bearer of an explanation. He knew nothing about the case, and had no instruction from either solicitor or client. The director of the respondent company was present but there was no sign of a solicitor.

Expecting the chairman, past member of his chambers, to receive the explanation with equanimity, he was soon disabused. The chairman tore into him before he had heard the full explanation. He accused him personally of disrespect for the tribunal, for behaving in a cavalier manner with little concern for the wasted time of the tribunal and for the costs thrown away. In vain did Matthew Caswell indicate that he had no part in the matter, knew nothing about the case, was only the bearer of a message with an explanation from his chambers, and that he was in no position to add to the explanation. That provoked the chairman to insult the fledgling barrister: "They sent you here as a silent comic, a dumb comic in a pantomime!" he blurted out, paused to await a response, and there being none, twisted the knife as he added gleefully: "What are you asking us to do?" Matthew explained, pointing to the company director sitting behind him, that he had no instructions to ask for anything, but that the tribunal might consider re-listing the case for another day to allow John Hichin, whose case it was, to appear before them. The chairman thought it fit to twist the knife further: "No, we are not adjourning. The case was listed to proceed and we are here to see it proceed, so I ask you again what are you asking us to do?" Matthew Caswell turned to the company director and asked him if he would instruct him to do what he could, and the director nodded. Matthew Caswell asked the chairman to suspend the hearing for fifteen minutes to allow him to read the papers. That took the chairman by surprise; he had not expected the new unknown barrister standing in front of him to have the stomach for argument after the blows that he had rained on him. "Ten minutes", he barked, then with one of the wing members leaning to whisper in his ear, "Very well, fifteen" he added churlishly.

When the tribunal reassembled Matthew got up to address them. He had barely concluded his first sentence when the chairman interrupted him: "That was not how the matter was put to us by Mr Hichin at the opening." Matthew indicated that he had not discussed the matter with Mr Hichin, and that all he could do was to deploy what in his own submission was the respondent's company's answer to the claim. As he continued to develop his legal argument it seemed gradually to make an impression on the wing members and to engage the attention of the chairman. They rose to discuss the matter, came back and the chairman pronounced judgment for the applicant "after full consideration of the arguments so ably deployed on behalf of the respondent company." It is ironic that some ten years after that encounter the chairman who had a personal property dispute with his neighbour was happy to see it resolved satisfactorily with the assistance of Matthew Caswell as his counsel. The manner in which Matthew's first case was resolved in the industrial tribunal was received with relief by chambers as well as the respondent company's solicitors, and that notwithstanding that the judgment went against the client company. It was based on the merits of the claim, thereby avoiding what sanction including a wasted costs order might have been imposed if the hearing had simply been aborted. After Matthew had made two more appearances in an industrial tribunal he was taken aside by the president of the industrial tribunals of England and Wales who offered him appointment as one of the tribunal chairmen. That he was an Iraqi was working to his advantage without it being spoken of. It was the early 1970's and there was a lot of talk about the desirability of diversifying the legal system by recruiting and appointing more ethnic lawyers and judges. Matthew Caswell fitted the requirement: He was white, could almost be taken for an Englishman, spoke elegantly with a hint of an Oxford accent, carried distinguished academic qualifications, was a clever lawyer, and he was an Iraqi. The offer of a judicial appointment so early in his legal career was tempting. It would be a notable honour conferred on a refugee and would provide for him and his family a secure regular income with a pension to follow. Yet he was reluctant to accept it. His leanings throughout his training for the Bar and as reinforced by the year's pupillage was to develop a chancery practice that involved serious law rather than theatre. He felt that life as a chairman of an industrial tribunal would not be intellectually stimulating. He consulted the chambers clerk as well as George Hall whom he highly respected as a senior member of chambers. They advised him to decline the offer; they thought him capable of attaining a higher ranking appointment as a circuit judge. Another reason for declining the offer was that he was already earning as a barrister with an expanding practice almost as much as the salary of a full time industrial tribunal's chairman.

Matthew Caswell soon acquired a reputation as a Leeds chancery lawyer dealing with complicated civil cases; and he was virtually the only such in Leeds when he started. However, chambers at 6 Park Square was a set that dealt overwhelmingly in criminal cases. Matthew Caswell had to help out by accepting briefs to appear at quarter sessions for the prosecution or for the defence. He never felt at ease doing that while he preferred to appear for the defence rather than the prosecution. He was ever exercised about the possibility of making a mistake; and felt that a mistake he would make while defending was more pardonable than one made in the course of prosecuting which would or might lead to the accused being wrongly convicted.

It was in the fourth year of his practice as a barrister that he had his first case in the court of appeal, and it got his name in the law reports. He was sent to Teesside to defend a man charged with the robbery of a painting. The facts of the case were that one Durkin who styled himself a social reformer entered a local authority's art gallery in the middle of the night and stole a valuable picture which was then on exhibition. He did not intend to keep it nor cause the gallery to be deprived of it permanently. In fact he was so concerned that it might come to harm while in his possession that he was anxious to see it restored to the gallery. But not before making good his protest. He intended to put forward four demands in return for giving it up. Those demands, as evidenced by a 'ransom note' found on him, were: the installation of burglar alarms in the authority's art galleries; the opening of those galleries on Sundays so that a working man would have the opportunity to take his children to visit them on his one weekly day of rest; the payment of sums of money by the authority to two named charities; and, farcically, the raffle of a pair of the mayor's underpants with the proceeds to go to a third charity. He pleaded guilty to damaging the gallery and was convicted of burglary. On the advice of his counsel Durkin pleaded not guilty to the major charge of removing the painting without consent, contrary to section 11(1) of the Theft Act 1968. The trial proceeded and those in court were bemused by the manner in which the chancery lawyer with little experience of criminal proceedings cross-examined the prosecution star witness, the curator. He asked about the building, its locality, its age and what security measures were in place. He next asked about the contents: What paintings and other works of art? How many paintings were there and how they were rotated for different exhibitions? He lastly asked about the very painting that was removed. By the end of that cross-examination it was established that the painting had been removed on Sunday when the gallery was not open to the public. Further, the curator stated in evidence that the local authority had a permanent collection of paintings, the individual items of which were exhibited sometimes in one gallery and sometimes in another; that the entire collection was seldom on view at any one time; but that all the paintings were exhibited at least once a year.

At the conclusion of the evidence Matthew Caswell submitted that there was no case for the accused to answer, that the admitted removal of the painting by Durkin did not on the evidence constitute an offence within the meaning of section 11(1) of the Theft Act, 1968. That section provided, so far as was relevant, that where anything removed from a building ....is there otherwise than as forming part of.... a collection intended for permanent exhibition to the public, the person removing it does not thereby commit an offence under the section unless he removes it on a day when the public have access to the building.

Caswell submitted that Durkin removed the painting on a day, being a Sunday, when the public had no access to the building, and that the painting, forming part of a collection which was to be exhibited at least once a year, was not part of a collection intended for permanent exhibition. The submission failed, Durkin was convicted, but the trial judge gave leave to appeal and certified that the case raised an important question which was fit to go to the court of appeal for authoritative guidance.

After a long and lively hearing the court of appeal by a reserved judgment dismissed the appeal while holding that as a matter of construction a collection that was available all the time for exhibition from time to time can be said to be intended for permanent exhibition. The case attracted a wide scholarly interest, was reported widely and discussed in legal and academic circles as well for its facts as for the performance of the appellant's counsel, Matthew Caswell, which was variously described as scholarly and bold. To the editor of the worldwide circulating SAGA journals "the impudence of the appellant was matched only by the boldness of his argument." Matthew Caswell enjoyed his appearance in the court of appeal. His first, while the judges were fully engaged in the argument, asking questions and making notes such that at times the hearing seemed more like a dialectical discourse, with Lord Justice Edmund Davies asking Mr Caswell to acquit him of discourtesy for disagreeing on a certain line of argument. Caswell's opponent, Maclusky, giving his account of the hearing to the robing room at Teesside, generously described Matthew's performance as a tour de force. An account of the case and of the court of appeal hearing coupled with the information that the appellant's counsel was an Iraqi led to the attorney general putting Matthew Caswell on his list for junior counsel for the crown in criminal cases in the North Eastern Circuit. Thus it was that Matthew Caswell whose main interests were in chancery, and who felt uncomfortable dealing with crime, and as prosecuting counsel in particular, was now at the heart of criminal law and practice. He was instructed and was led in nearly every case of murder in Yorkshire and the North East and so became close to the leaders of the North Eastern Circuit with his name appearing in the law reports next to theirs. And it was materially rewarding. As a junior counsel his fee was two-thirds that of his leader. That, in addition to his income from all the other mostly civil cases, made him one of the biggest earners of the junior barristers on circuit, and the biggest earner in his chambers.

With the future looking bright and secure, and with the children growing up, he reviewed the situation with Helen, and they cheerfully looked to acquire a holiday home. They saw the advertisement in the Sunday newspaper, got in the car and headed north. After the dark days of Teddington and the austerity of Chiswick they now could look to the future with optimism. The past misfortunes were not spoken of but some memories were still fresh, none more so than the loss of their first house in King Edward's Grove. Going now prospecting for the luxury of a second, holiday house was to draw a line over past failures. They got up at dawn, got the children ready, packed the small NSU car, checked the tyres and the petrol gauge and set off looking for Shangri-La.

Ardrossan's main street was not a cheerful place to welcome you after a five hour drive. Straight rows of solid brown ochre terraces with not a single tree or blade of grass to be seen; no sight or sound of bird or gull; no shops or shoppers carrying bags; a seemingly obsolete railway line at the end of the street added to the desolation. As you came to the end of the street and crossed the railway line you had a view to your right of the quay opening up to receive you, and a glimpse of a sad and solitary café nestled coyly in a side-street to your left. As you parked your car and got out to stretch your legs you had your first view of Arran 15 miles away and of *The Caledonia* in mid-distance cutting the waves as it came towards you. The car attendant agreed it was a good day, then pointed to the island and added with a sardonic Scottish humour "That's Goat Fell over there. If you cannot see it, it's raining; but if you can see it, as you can now, it's going to rain!" A little later as the car was stowed away and everyone was aboard, one could hear the engine come to life, emit a muffled roar as it strained to leave the shore and head out towards Brodick. The Ayrshire coast was slowly disappearing. The start of what was to be a romantic adventure.

Ardlui

rdlui, a name on a board fixed high up on an iron pole
standing next to an opening as of a farm's entrance.
Board and name also intimated a passage in an easterly
direction from the Whiting Bay to Lamlash main road
across farmland to the sea and the Clyde. An unmade road
for a start, wide enough for a car, it followed the line of the
beck until they came to a sharp bend. The road disengaged,
turned away, passed close to the house then went away and
down on its own in line with the steep contour of the land,
getting progressively stee, and its surface rougher, the nearer
it got to the sea shore, its destination. Before getting there the
road had become a footpath that dropped precipitately into
a thick, dark, sinister looking wood, and disappeared from
view. A person would then plunge into the wood, negotiate
it cautiously with the thought that the adder was a native to
such as this as to other parts. Then the relief at the view of
a clear expanse of water hemmed in channel-like between
two islands; the bigger Arran nodding to Holy Island on

the other side. One has now arrived at King's Cross; the water in the channel is reputed to be one of the deepest in the Clyde, while surface craft come to shelter from storm and swell, benefiting from the protection provided by Holy Island. Over the years in the dim past many a brig came to drop anchor and allow people to embark and disembark. For a time the road was the only gateway to Arran. That was before the Brodick ferry terminal was established. Since then King's Cross has served as a base for small leisure craft attracted by its amenities. Those amenities would also have certainly held attraction to the Vikings in their heyday as a warring maritime power. The Viking Fort at King's Cross Point is a prime vestige of their presence, as do the remains of their ship funerals. A large stone hidden in the trees on the shore between Cordon and King's Cross with Viking writing on it would have been a commemorative testament to a long settled community, while it takes but a little to surmise that Whiting Bay was once known as Viking Bay. By the year 800 AD Arran had entered a long period of Viking domination; by 870 Olaf the White, Viking king of Dublin, had the whole of the Clyde in his dominion.

Ardlui is the house, but it is more than a house, rather a cluster of houses. The main house is stone built in a traditional pleasing style. On the ground floor: a door and two windows, one on each side; three windows on the upper floor; all of them identical, and all look to the front. One larger window on the stairs is the only one that looks over the back, straining to capture a glimpse of the sea. That the windows look away from the sea was a common feature of the houses in Arran; a rumour once circulated mischievously blaming it on the laird who it was alleged did not want the crofters to have the distracting pleasure of a sea view. But in modern times that feature is taken to be consistent with the practice of building at a level below the brow of cliff or mound to benefit from the protection they afford as shelter from the gales blowing in from the sea. At the front of the house: a fair size garden with a wych elm and flower beds; a lawn extending to a simple iron railing separating it from the road. Across the road, a smaller triangular lawn, part of the house's sixteen acre cartilage of trees, bushes, boggy fields and purple heather.

The house has two satellite cottages attached to it, one on each side. As one comes from the direction of the Whiting Bay to Lamlash main road one first passes the first and larger of the two, the other nestles on the other side of the house, next to a free standing barn. The cottages do not appear to have been built at the same time as the house or to have been added the same time. A branch footpath starting just before the larger cottage goes all round the back where it passes an independent small, one-room cottage. It may have been intended to provide accommodation for a single person or a couple of employees such as a guardian and a housekeeper. Beyond that a mound blocks the view of Holy Island as it provided shelter from the elements.

It was mid-winter when they first cast their eyes on the exotic island property they had come to view, and it looked desolate with no sign of life in the buildings or in the fields. A gate in front of the bigger cottage had come off a hinge and was hanging piteously down on one side. Pebbledash had come off the other cottage in patches, exposing wet bricks. Loose slates on the roof of the house with suspicion of worse. They took possession in the summer when the first urgent remedial task was to see to the roof. They searched for a good roofer and Alec McKinnon of Lamlash, Arran's only professional roofer, came to have a look. He negotiated the terms of his engagement and went up the ladder to get on with the job. That took him two days to complete. He reported that the roof was generally sound, that he had secured the loose slates but had to replace four which were split. The replacements could not match the original. Those earlier ones were high quality Westmoreland that could only have been brought over from the mainland. Slate of that quality was very expensive; the last time he enquired they demanded £30 a square metre and he would not wish to hazard a guess what they would have cost when the house was built. He could not say how old the house was but would not be surprised if its history went back to the clearances or the period that followed. Musing about the Arran clearance he thought the Hamiltons as lairds were not as bad as they were made out to be; the worst excesses were by their agents who made a lot of money in the process. Very little is known about the first people who lived in Ardlui. One of the oldest inhabitants of Whiting Bay had heard it said that the end cottage, the smaller of the two, was once used as an office. That may have had something to do with the human and goods traffic passing along the road, footpath and through the wood on the way to and from the King's Cross gateway beyond the wood. Some time after the Caswells had taken possession of Ardlui, Helen, minded to turn the two wing cottages to use as holiday lets, bought items of furniture from second-hand shops in Leeds and Bradford. She was overseeing the arrangement of the new pieces in the smaller end cottage when, looking in a wall niche, she discovered an old pile of papers among which was an illuminated address marking the retirement of one Muir. It consisted of a high blown panegyric, lauding the great selfless service that Angus Muir Esquire had rendered to the community over many years. No further information could be gleaned from that single coloured sheet of paper.

While the furniture was being unloaded a young man arrived drawn by the activity. Matthew judged him to be in his twenties: short, slight, fresh suntanned face, and ginger hair. He was carrying a lawn mower. He sought out Matthew, greeted him with respect, and engaged him in conversation. He said he had seen him arrive in Whiting Bay with the family several months before when they stayed at the *Cameronia*; said it was good that they decided to buy Ardlui which will now come back to life after several years of neglect. He said he liked the house. As for the end cottage he pointed to the furniture being taken into it and told Matthew that they should disregard some silly talk about it by some silly old women in the village. He did not believe it to be haunted, nor would he mind sleeping in it whether it was or wasn't. He was very proud of his circular lawn mower, the only one on the island and a rarity on the mainland. To demonstrate how efficient it was he started it and pushing it with a long handle proceeded to mow the grass in the triangle shaped lawn across the road. He declined the offer of money, said it was the first time and he would not charge for it. He said if he was required in the future his name was Sandy Taylor, his parents were the owners of the boarding house next to the *Cameronia*. Matthew had a favourable first impression of the young man, which did not tally with the description of Sandy Taylor given him by the post office mistress. Matthew asked her about the level of crime on the island; she said there had been no serious crime after the notorious historical Goatfell murder. There had been a spate of minor ones in recent years, she said, such as taking cars for a joy ride without the consent of the owner. But they had stopped, now that Sandy Taylor had grown up and settled down.

The Goatfell murder which took place in 1889 has continued to be in the news because of its strange location and the air of mystery and doubt surrounding it; just as it continues to engage the interest of lawyers, criminologists and dramatists. Two young men John Watson Laurie a Scotsman, and Edwin Rose an Englishman, met each other by chance on the ferry taking them across to Arran. A few days later they set out rock climbing and walked up Goatfell, the island's highest peak. Only John Laurie came down. Edwin Rose's body was discovered a few days later hidden under a boulder, face horribly mangled. There was in that a compelling circumstantial evidence pointing to Laurie as the murderer. He was convicted but the death sentence was commuted to imprisonment for life. That murder became one of the most notorious events in the history of Arran, only surpassed for notoriety by the Arran clearance, the bitterness of which has never lost its rawness entirely.

The Arran clearance took place during the years 1829-1840. It was embarked upon by the 10th Duke Hamilton (1767-1852). Its object was to dispossess a large number of small tenants and convert their crofts into a single farm to make allegedly a better use of Arran's economic resources. One notorious and well documented part of the clearance was the uprooting of many families and their transportation to North America. It was the 29th day of April 1829 when 89 souls gathered at the seaside in Lamlash to embark on the brig the *Caledonia* (196 tons). The reverend A. McKay preached from what has since been known as the Mound, and gave some comfort to the departing anxious people by the exhortation "Cast all your care upon Him for He careth for you" (1st Peter, ch 5, v7). The *Caledonia* arrived in Quebec on 25th June 1829. A memorial now stands facing the Mound. It reads "Erected on behalf of Arran descendants across North America to their brave forefathers who departed their beloved island home to Canada during the clearance years (1829-1840).

He dropped in at Lamlash Bay Hotel and carried his drink to a table at one end of the lounge. As he sat down he noticed two men in earnest conversation at the other end. He thought he recognised one of them. After a while the two men got up, shook hands and separated. One of them walked out. Alec McKinnon came across to join Matthew. He asked and was reassured how the roof at Ardlui had stood up to the recent big wind and rain. He said the business was good; he had been much in demand as a roofer. Asked about the other man he said he was a journalist from London writing a review of the Arran clearance, it being 150 years since the *Caledonia* sailed from Lamlash with 89 people bound for Canada. The journalist was aiming to sell the review to a Quebec newspaper; but was taken aback when Alec suggested he wrote about the second more recent clearance. Not by a Scottish Duke and his minions on this occasion, but by so-called Glaswegian bankers and moneylenders who were not true Glaswegian nor perhaps even Scottish. The Great Depression which started in 1929 and lasted well until the late thirties wreaked havoc on the economy of Arran. Some small farms went out of business altogether while others survived by borrowing money secured on their property. The Second World War helped businesses in other parts of the country to stage a partial recovery; but not in Arran whose population contracted during the war as the young men were conscripted in the armed forces while the girls sailed to the mainland to work in munitions factories. Several of the people who fell behind in the repayment of their debt saw their properties sold as they were evicted. That happened notably in the King's Cross area which included Ardlui. The bankers had in mind combining the different holdings to create a big one that would be used for a housing estate or, so it was rumoured at the time, a holiday resort to rival the *Auchrannie* in Brodick, while the proposed new one would have had the edge, what with its unparalleled location and views. But, as is the workings of predatory capitalism, the predators themselves became victims of the perennial recession, and they could not generate sufficient interest in their initial public offer and had to abandon the project. The roofer went on to talk of the present day Hamilton clan. Lady Jane was one of the two heads of the clan and was held in high public esteem. Her predecessor, the Tenth Duke, did initiate the Arran clearance but it was well intentioned and carried through with a degree of humanity. The Duke paid for the passage of the people across the sea to North America and saw to it that each family had some little money to tide them over on arrival, and to start a new life in a new country. Warming up to his theme he said that no one was caused to die in the clearance. One could not say the same about the new clearance. It cost the life of at least one innocent girl. Alec McKinnon would go no further, while Matthew was keen to learn more. He went and asked the sub-post mistress in Whiting Bay what she knew about the death of the young girl. She said the person in question was not a young girl but a woman in her forties. She had been born with a Down syndrome. When her parents died her aunt took her in at Ardlui, and she was given one of the cottages to live in. When the date was fixed for the whole family to leave, she was informed so she got ready. What happened next was shrouded in mystery but according to one reconstruction of the facts the poor woman got up in the early hours of the appointed day, put on her best dress, went out quietly and walked down the long path to the sea never to be seen alive again. As to the story that the cottage was haunted, that was simply based on what Don McKenzie said he saw. It was a dark cloudy night, and Ardlui was deserted, He was walking on the path leading down to the sea when some noise made him look towards the cottage. As the moon came out of a cloud, he said he saw behind the pane of glass in one window an apparition in the shape of a female in a white dress and a grey bonnet.

The Glasgow bankers, now joined by a Glasgow Corporate solicitor, having seen their grandiose plan to develop Ardlui and its environs frustrated, turned their minds to ways of extracting their initial investment. When Tom Chorley came along enquiring about acquiring a building plot he was welcomed with open arms. Tom Chorley was a single man, a colonial. A big man with a florid complexion he had spent his life in East Africa as a colonial administrator. Now that he had retired he was looking for a place far away from Africa and African tribal politics where he would spend the rest of his days in peace and quiet. He was prospecting around the King's Cross area when he took the Ardlui road. He walked past the unoccupied houses and barn down towards the sea. As he came to the wood his colonial experience and instinct stopped him from plunging into it. He turned left and followed an indistinct narrow footpath made by others before him who were probably also curious of what lay in that wood for the unwary. Going a little further down he saw what he was looking for, a plot of land with a ledge overlooking the water of King's Cross with a view of Holy Island face on and a side view of Lamlash. He was soon to have his retirement home on that plot. The house caused quite a stir as it was carried on two trucks through the streets of Brodick and Lamlash before it was seen with stupefaction by the farmers and tradesmen of King's Cross and Whiting Bay. Stewart Mackenzie who farmed next to Ardlui went about describing Tom Chorley's house as two caravans stuck together. Yet the end product was an elegant colonial style house with a large sitting room leading to a veranda. That was where Tom Chorley would see the sunset, reclined in a wicker chair with Johnnie Walker for company. He was an imposing figure who had held an important position in the colonial office. His speciality was the African elephant, and he lost no opportunity to make that known. There was nothing about the elephants that he did not know: their numbers, family life, herd instinct, eating habits and diet. To Chorley their diet was a big headache. A vegetarian diet, the elephants could consume grasses, small plants, bushes and even fruit. But it is the bark that was their favourite food. Their tusks were used to carve the trunk to get at the bark which they consumed in strips while damaging the tree beyond recovery. That set the farmers against them and put the colonial administrator in a quandary. He had to listen to the complaining farmers and be sympathetic to their legitimate concerns while his main remit at the same time was the protection of the animal from the illegal poachers who killed them to get at the ivory. Tom Chorley was a man of authority that he had exercised over a long distinguished career. He carried that with him to a small, remote Scottish island. Whenever he went walking authority oozed from every heavy and deliberate step he took. He became much talked about as an English 'character' that demanded respect and was given it. He was an honoured guest at the annual Arran Highland Games, and he held by invitation the position of honorary president of the fishermen and sea-anglers association. The main duty of his office was to preside over the annual competition. He would sit on a stool at the Lamlash pier, next to him the weighing scales and a member of the association who operated them. As the fishermen came with their catch to be weighed it fell to Chorley to cast a cursory glance to ensure that they were legitimate. He made a speech at the end of the day as he announced the names of the winners.

The Power family were next to come to buy a plot from the bankers. It was at a higher level than Chorley's, at a point just before the level road was succeeded by the precipitous footpath as it merged with the wood. Mr and Mrs Power had two teenage children who went to the local school at Lamlash. The parents were private persons and revealed very little about themselves. But the little that Bryan Power said told a lot. He said they came to Arran to get away from the rat race. Arran was full of people who had come across to get away from the rat race. They were nearly all seeking to turn a new leaf over earlier failure. Tom Chorley was an exception; he came over to turn a new leaf not over failure but to get a respite from the debilitating love hate of the African elephant.,

Nobody knew what or where Mr Power's job was on the mainland. He now had the semblance of a forge by the stream that marked the boundary between Lamlash and Whiting Bay, but it did not give the impression of being a serious business endeavour. He had no one else working with him or for him; no customers were seen about; nor was there sight of anything being forged. The general impression was that it was not a continuation of an earlier established business but of Bryan Power trying on a new profession. He did not talk about the business nor went about soliciting custom. Mrs Power was reticent, rarely seen in the village, and she responded with reserve to Helen Caswell's neighbourly invitation. But no reticence, social awkwardness or reserve could keep apart two normal fourteen year old boys. The moment they set eyes on each other they became a gang of two looking for adventure. They were to share one dramatic adventure redolent of mystery, conspiracy, robbery on the high sea, shady criminals and the police.

They walked down together along the road and footpath through and beyond the wood to the small seashore to see what there was of mussels, interesting seashells and coloured stones. They were amazed to find instead a large, red royal mail bag. It had a slit as if made deliberately with a knife. After a moment's hesitation they picked it up and using all their combined youthful strength carried and dragged it all the way up to Ardlui house. Matthew and Helen were in; they peered in the slit and discovered that the bag was full of post office savings books with loose banknotes in each; a substantial sum in total. There was no police station nor a policeman about, so Mathew reported the matter to John Terry who had a garage in Whiting Bay and also acted as a sworn police auxiliary. Three days later a post office van came on the ferry with three men, one of them a detective. The bag was taken away and John Terry reported the sequel. A police enquiry concluded that it was the product of a criminal conspiracy engendered in Northern Ireland

and put together with a great deal of sophistication giving rise to the conjecture that a political hand may have been behind it. The bag started its journey in Stranraer. It was then loaded on the ferry taking it to Glasgow. One or more of the conspirators followed on board. The central plan of the conspiracy was that at a certain predetermined point in the course of the passage the conspirators on board would fling the bag overboard to be picked up by their confederates waiting in a boat. Something must have gone wrong in the timing or some other twist in the story; the bag was missed and, carried by the tide, ended up where the boys found it. The explanation for the slit was that it was likely to have been have been made by the conspirators on board the ferry to make sure that it was the right prey. John Caswell and Neal Power each received a letter of thanks from the Postmaster General with an envelope that was a first day issue cover.

Ardlui is the family's holiday retreat. Each trip, they get up in the early hours and get ready for the journey. The mother would be fussing about and makes sure to pack the things that were missing at Ardlui as they left it the time before. They pile up into the car, not forgetting the cat looking bewildered in the wicker basket. Six hours later they are on the ferry looking towards Goatfell coming progressively into clearer view. They anticipate the pleasure of the days to come. But it is not all bliss as far as the parents are concerned. There will be work to be done as they acquired Ardlui; having to call in a builder, plumber and glazier; and to get a report from the caretaker who had been left in charge of the business of holiday lettings of the cottages and what, if any, complaint made or satisfaction registered. Those were not things to concern Rebecca and John. Their excitement knew no bounds. They did all the things that teenagers did on holiday: walking to the shops to buy knick- knacks, to the post office to send postcards to their friends back home, cycling to Corrie and riding and pony trekking at Glen Rosa -- and sailing. The most exciting event was the acquisition of a used GP14 boat that was kept in the barn and driven on sailing days to Whiting Bay. Sailing the GP14 exposed the youngsters to a dramatic, at the time frightening, experience. They were sailing just off the coast when the boat attracted the attention of sharks that came to circle it. They were enormous sea creatures that swam close to the surface so could be seen very clearly. A knot of onlookers stood on the shore observing the scene. The father was among them and was visibly alarmed and distressed until he was told and assured that they were basking sharks that are not considered dangerous to the passive human observer. They had tiny teeth but did not use them to bite. They were filter feeders, their diet being the plankton that they harvest in abundance by swimming close to the surface with open mouth. Because of its enormous bulk and weight the basking shark would be a hazard to any small boat that came too near to it. Rebecca and John returned unharmed and better informed about the denizens of the sea.

Ben was too young to participate in his siblings' adventures. To him Ardlui was the stuff of which dreams were made. He saw a lot of the island as he went about in the company of an adult. Years later he would recollect a glorious day when Phyllis the caretaker took him to Lamlash; there to board the small boat that ferried them to Holy Island. They walked along the cliff top until they came to where they could see Ardlui. In passing through the memory the past becomes a poem. Ben never lost the wonder of what he saw, heard and sensed as a child in Ardlui. For the next nearly half a century he made many trips to Arran and not once did the poetry lose its potency in mind and heart.

Ardlui is a framed aerial photograph of the house. The picture hangs on a wall in Joseph's room at 73 Old Park Road, Leeds. Joseph is Ben's son. A third generation of those who over the years fell under the charm and magic of Arran.

Miscarriage of Justice

A s a junior crown counsel, Matthew had an important part in the preparation of the several murder trials in which he was instructed. All the statements in the case came to him with the brief. They could run to hundreds of pages, to more than ten thousand in one particular notorious case that had been widely investigated by the police. He would have to read all of them and advise on evidence; what to include for use at the trial, and what to exclude; to draw out a list of the prosecution witnesses and the order in which they would be called to testify; and to advise what was to be disclosed to the defence out of the mass of evidence in the possession of the prosecution. That was an important part of the process calling for the exercise of fairness as much as judgment. Several cases of wrongful conviction were the result of failure by the prosecution to disclose material favourable to the accused. Matthew Caswell was particularly alive to his duty in that regard, which was influenced by his experience as a chancery lawyer. In the preparation of a civil case for trial there is a strict requirement that each party disclosed and made available to view by one's opponent any document that was in any way material in the case. It struck Matthew that there was no parallel disclosure requirement in criminal cases; nor could one be obtain. The pre-trial investigation is carried out by the police and the reports and statements are then passed on to prosecuting counsel, while the accused cannot be required let alone compelled to disclose such other evidence as he might have. Accordingly, it was the duty, as he saw it, of prosecuting counsel to identify what evidence ought to be disclosed to the defence, and do so by looking at the mass of information as though one was doing it with the eyes of a lawyer acting for the accused. It was ironic that a most notorious case of wrongful conviction was on Matthew Caswell's watch as junior prosecution counsel.

Stefan Kiszko was the son of a Slovene mother and a Ukrainian father who had fled to England after the Second World War. They were hard-working ordinary people who lived in Rochdale and were proud of their son when he got a job in the tax-collector's office. Stefan was a large child-man. Although of average intelligence he was grossly immature sexually and psychologically due to testosterone deficiency. His scrotum was poorly developed, contained no testes and his penis was abnormally small. His face was smooth and hairless, while some of his features and bone structures tended to the feminine. He was over six feet tall and walked with a waddling gait. His imposing pear-shaped physique contrasted with his apparent meekness, smooth pallid skin and high-pitched voice. He had no friends, no social life beyond his parents and his aunt Alfreda. When his father died he was left with only his mother and aunt. At school and at work he was sneered at and made the butt of people treating him for what he was, a mother's boy. At the time of the events leading to the court case he had been, and that was an important feature in the case, receiving treatment that consisted of the administration of testosterone injections. The effect of the treatment was noticeable. His voice broke, he acquired muscular growth, started to grow facial hair, and there was even a noticeable change to the hip bone structure. The changes were accompanied by a sexual urge that he relieved by masturbation.

Lesley Molseed was a small eleven-year old girl who lived in Rochdale with her mother and step-father. She went down to the shop to get some bread and did not return. Her lifeless body was discovered three days later on the moors nearby. She had been stabbed twelve times. Her clothing was undisturbed, but her killer had ejaculated over her knickers and dress. The semen when analysed was found to contain an unusually low sperm count.

What led the police to Kiszko initially was another complaint. It was of a man indecently exposing himself to some girls at about the time of the disappearance of the small girl. Two of the girls pointed to Kiszko as being that man. From that moment his fate was sealed. He fitted the profile of the man likely to have killed Lesley Molseed. The police then pursued such evidence as might incriminate him and overlooked others that tended to exonerate him. There was nothing that implicated him unequivocally and by the time that he went to trial on a charge of murder the only hard evidence against him was his confession to the murder made to the investigating police officer, and which he retracted soon after, He was to say at his trial that he did not make the confession under threat nor that he was offered any inducement. It was simply that he thought that once he confessed he would be allowed to go home to his anxious mother.

The tragedy in Kiszko's case was that it could have been proved all along that he was not the murderer. He suffered from hypogonadism; he could not produce sperm so he could not have been the man who ejaculated over the girl's clothes. But that fact was withheld from Kiszko's lawyers as well as counsel acting for the prosecution. Both sets of lawyers were seduced instead by what they perceived to be a plausible scenario: an innocent docile sexless Stefan was got hold of by the doctors who over a period of months pumped testosterone into him that engendered a sexual urge that he, an immature man-child, did not know how to cope with. He resorted to surreptitious masturbation at home, to indecently exposing himself to young girls in the street, to then taking the girl Lesley Molseed in his car to the seclusion of the moor where he ejaculated over her without attempting to penetrate her. The last ghastly act of stabbing her was forced upon him by the shameful act that had preceded it. He had to do something with the girl. He could not leave her on the moor. He could not drive her back home when she would have told everyone, including his mother, what he had done.

In accepting that assumed scenario one was also left with some sympathy for Kiszko. The doctors who treated him bore some of the blame. He had not been unhappy in his sexual backwardness. The testosterone injected into him turned a gentle, docile man into a sexual predator. The analogy with the Jekyll and Hyde syndrome was complete, and there was an enticing beauty in the drawing of that analogy. Further, in doing so, Stefan's lawyers had the satisfaction, so they thought, of being able to assist their client by arguing that at the time of the killing he was, by reason of the injections, suffering from such abnormality of mind as substantially diminished his responsibility for the killing, so that he should be convicted – not of murder which would incur a mandatory life sentence, but of the lesser charge of manslaughter.

The trouble with that approach was that in order to plead diminished responsibility Kiszko would have had to admit to the killing; but that he was not prepared to do for the simple reason that he had nothing to do with it. Further, his mother would not accept that he was guilty at all because she knew for a fact that he could not have killed Lesley Molseed. At the time of the abduction of the girl from near her home Stefan, in the company of his mother, was making his weekly visit to his father's grave. However, Kiszko's lawyers, holding steadfastly to the Jekyll and Hyde analogy attributed his refusal to admit guilt to the influence exerted over him by his mother. When confronted by a statement from an endocrinologist rejecting the proposition that the injection of testosterone could have the effect of raising the level of aggression in a recipient, Kiszko's lawyers dismissed the statement with a shrug. He would say that wouldn't he! They further allowed themselves to be deluded by the low count of sperm on the victim's clothing, Instead of investigating whether the presence of sperm at all was consistent with Kiszko's medical condition, they took the presence of a low count to be consistent with the condition and its treatment, In reality the low count was due to the deterioration of the semen under the effect of a three days' exposure to wind and rain.

In the eyes of his lawyers Kiszko had to be saved from the mandatory life sentence. They had to raise the defence of diminished responsibility even if they were to do so contrary to their client's protestation of innocence and his refusal to admit guilt. Thus it was that Kiszko's leading counsel David Waddington asked the trial jury to consider Kiszko's defence in two stages: They were urged to find him not guilty altogether; but if they did find him guilty at all, then they were further urged to find that he did the act when he was suffering from diminished responsibility by reason of the medical treatment he had received. That was a dangerous course to follow. It left the jury with the clear impression that Kiszko's own lawyer was accepting that he did the killing even while Kiszko himself was asserting to them in his evidence on oath that he was entirely innocent. That was a terrible miscalculation. Kiszko was found guilty of murder. He then languished in prison for sixteen years before the court of appeal quashed the conviction once it was revealed that he was incapable of producing any sperm at all.

It was further revealed that while Kiszko was in custody awaiting his trial a sample of his semen was examined by Ronald Outteridge, senior forensic scientist, and he found it free of sperm. When Outteridge disclosed that to Superintendent Dick Holland who was in charge of the police investigation the latter asked him time and again to examine further samples "until you get me at least one sperm". Sixteen samples were examined by Outteridge and not a single sperm was found. That crucial evidence was not made known to prosecuting or defence counsel. In 1994, two years after the discharge of Kiszko from prison Dick Holland and Ronald Outteridge were charged with perverting the course of justice; but further proceedings were stayed given the length of time that had elapsed since Leslie Molseed's murder and Kiszko's arrest and trial.

Chancery Unbound

M atthew soon acquired a busy practice as a lawyer dealing with traditional chancery cases including trust, company law, probate, land law and other arcane corners of the law. A chancery practice is not circumscribed within strict defined topical limits, and it was in the sixth year of his practice that he was instructed in a big case of compensation following a compulsory purchase. That was in an area of the law which was complex and specialist; researching it involved a tortuous journey through obscure statutes and conflicting case law. It came to him because he was perceived to be the only one in the North who could handle it, and because the solicitor and the client had no wish to venture out of Yorkshire. The client was Wakefield Metropolitan District Council. It had acquired by means of a compulsory purchase order an estate in West Yorkshire consisting of several acres of farmland. That was pursuant to a scheme to develop it into an industrial estate, and which was duly to become the Normanton Industrial Estate. What remained in dispute was the amount of compensation that was to be paid. Mathew Caswell was instructed to represent Wakefield Council before the lands tribunal. The hearing lasted several days with many witnesses, a lot of legal arguments and a site visit. The Council's case on the main point, which prevailed, was that the compensation should be the open market value of the land without taking into account any increase or decrease attributable to the scheme of the acquiring authority. That argument was based on a 1947 judgment of the court of appeal in the Pointe Gourde case. The tribunal dealt at the same time with several ancillary matters of valuation that were also substantially decided in favour of the Council. The land owner appealed, and the Council instructed Sir Derek Walker-Smith QC to represent it with Matthew Caswell as his junior. The choice of Sir Derek was made after much hesitation by, and internal conflict within, the Council. It was labour controlled, while Sir Derek was a well-known Tory politician who had recently been a minister in the conservative government of Edward Heath.

The appointment suited Caswell. Sir Derek was one of the highest paid QC's and Caswell's fees were fixed at two-thirds of his leader's. It was well known in legal circles that Sir Derek's idea of a leading counsel was to leave it to his junior to carry out the research, preparatory work and even the substance of the arguments and submissions in court, so that Sir Derek's contribution would consist of his high-profile presence, impressive voice and the consummate skill of a politician to use those assets as well as the choice of words to embellish whatever argument he was deploying. It suited Sir Derek in turn to have in Caswell a willing and able junior to bear the responsibility of preparing the case and to do so assiduously and with a sound judgment. They had an introductory conference in Sir Derek's chambers in the Temple followed by Sir Derek coming up to Yorkshire to view the site. There was nothing remarkable about a flat area of grass covered Yorkshire soil. Caswell did the driving and Sir Derek was bemused by the sights of Yorkshire streets, shops and people. "I suppose they all have votes!" he exclaimed. He spent the night at The Queens Hotel in Leeds and that accounted for two days to be added to the brief fee and as was customary he as leader hosted a dinner for his junior. In the course of the evening Sir Derek expanded on the stories that were circulating in Westminster and on what Sir Derek thought of some of the leading politicians of the day. He thought Ted Heath was dour and Ian Macloud flippant. He had nothing good to say about Tony Barber. Anthony Barber, as Chancellor of the Exchequer was a gambler, went for broke in adopting a lax control of the money, created the false dawn of an economic boom which then went out of control resulting in insupportable inflation and wage demands by public sector employees. Too late was the danger spotted and the policy put into reverse. The Prices Commission and Pay Board was then set up which led to general unrest and to the Tories going out of power. The Barbour Boom had been well-intentioned, Anthony wanted to break the cycle of stop-go, but "you do not make a silly gamble like that if you are the Chancellor of the Exchequer!" Sir Derek reserved his highest praise for Enoch Powell who was being traduced for his 'river of blood' speech. His fault, a Greek scholar, was in the choice of words, in using inflammatory Roman imagery instead of a measured classical Greek discourse. Yet according to Sir Derek Walker-Smith, Enoch was right in his basic premise concerning uncontrolled immigration and foreign incursions. He was more charitable to his political opponents while referring to Harold Wilson as shifty. Throughout the whole of that evening very little was spoken about the case that was due to be heard in the court of appeal. Sir Derek asked his junior what arguments were deployed for the landowner in the course of the proceedings in the lands tribunal; leader and junior then broadly agreed how the matter was to be addressed in the court of appeal.

Their routine at the court of appeal's sittings was that Caswell would sit behind Sir Derek and make notes of the proceedings. As the court rose at the end of the day leading and junior counsel would separate, the latter going to the library to look up the relevant authorities and to make notes of the references. He would next go over the notes of the hearing and underline the important parts, then have the pages photocopied. In the evening he went to join Sir

Derek who would be waiting for him at his room in the House of Commons. Caswell would then be left to himself, to work on what was required by way of preparation for the following day. That would include a short advice and a draft of the proposed legal arguments and submissions to be deployed on behalf of Wakefield Council. Sir Derek would return at the conclusion of whatever business had occupied him as a member of parliament. They would then go out to the underground and separate. Sir Derek's secretary would have the draft of his speech typed and made ready for him to take to court. One such evening was memorable. It was about eleven and as they were crossing a yard on the way out they heard someone call out in a soft, cultured voice, "I see that you have been immured till a late hour", and Harold Wilson stepped out of the shadows and came across to engage them. Wilson had resigned as Prime Minister not long before. It may have crossed his mind that while the fate of the nation was being discussed in the Chamber a fellow politician was busy making money as he was immured with another lawyer in a small room in the Palace of Westminster. Mathew Caswell was introduced to Harold Wilson who became animated when he learnt that he was from Leeds. He said with obvious pride that he had been appointed Chancellor of the then still new Bradford University to add to his involvement in the Open University. On their way to Westminster underground station Sir Derek referred to

Wilson's sudden resignation and the wide speculations as to the real reason.

It was a good brief. It ended well for Wakefield Council. Matthew Caswell found it intellectually stimulating and materially gratifying. He received a handsome cheque and had the added pleasure of seeing his name next to that of Sir Derek and those of other eminent lawyers cited in the specialist Property, Planning and Compensation Reports. And there followed the bonus of his son John and his friend Cyrile having the privilege of a private guided tour of Parliament.

Entente cordiale

⸺ ✎ ⸺

Emmanuel and Nicole Beau had two children, Cyrile and Stephane. They lived in an apartment in Levallois-Perret, a smart and expensive suburb of Paris; but not as smart or as expensive as the adjoining Neuilly-sur-Seine. Nicole would have dearly loved to be living in Neuilly-sur-Seine. She would often tell her husband how she would have loved to be living in Neuilly instead of Levallois, and Emmanuel would say they could not afford it on his salary of bank manager. He would add that Levallois-Perret was desirable and highly rated at or near the top of the Parisian satellite communes. The Beau was a bourgeoise family. Cyrile was coming up to the end of his studies at high school and had set his heart on securing a place at the business school ESSEC. That was one of the most prestigious business schools in Europe, a French selective "grande ecole." He was receiving private lessons in English in order to improve his chances of admission and an arrangement was made for an exchange visit of one week with an English schoolboy of a

338

similar age living in Leeds. The exchange started by John going to Levallois-Perret and having his first experience of the French educational system as he accompanied Cyrile to the school. Having been fed on the notions of the rebellious Frenchman and of the Gallic revolutionary spirit, John was struck by how regimented the school was, how strictly structured the lessons and how serious were the students and how respectful of their teachers. At the weekend John was taken to the main tourist attractions including the Louvre, Notre Dame and, at the particular urging of Madame Beau, La Sainte Chapelle, a 13th century gothic royal chapel close to Notre Dame often overlooked by the tourists and the guides. But the most remarkable impression that John took back home was the table manners of a French middle class family. Madame Beau would set the table, dictate the seating, lay the tureens and other serving dishes on the table and would insist on keeping to herself the task of serving the food by ladling portions from the common serving dish to the individual plates. John was inwardly dismayed by the small portions but it was impolite to ask for more. After one week he returned to Leeds with some better knowledge of Paris and France, a slightly better pronunciation of a few more French words, and one kilogram lighter. In retrospect the highlight of his week in Paris was the Sunday lunch with generous 'American size' helpings' at La Coupole.

Lacking the attractions of world renown that Paris had there were still attractions and experiences aplenty in Leeds on offer to a 15 year old French youth on his first visit to England. He went with John to Leeds Grammar School where he was seen as a distraction by boys of his age who teased him and befriended him at the same time while they played humorously with the French version and pronunciation of his name. Out of school there were the walks in the Park, boating on the Nidd, Betty's in Harrogate, the mystery of cricket at Bradford's Park Avenue and, most glorious of all, a 'dinner' at lunchtime of haddock and chips at Bryan's that filled the big plate with the incomprehensible mushy peas added. At the table for 'tea' in the evening one was left to help oneself, take as much or as little of the one thing or the other or others as one wanted, and to consume the lot in whichever order or pace one desired. A day in London was included. Matthew Caswell approached Sir Derek and he arranged for the two boys to be received by his secretary who showed them round the Palace of Westminster including the House of Commons and the House of Lords followed by afternoon tea on the terrace overlooking the Thames. At the end of the week Cyrile was seen to have put on weight appreciably. Asked in the last evening what he thought of Leeds he said the best and most memorable experiences were Betty's afternoon tea and Bryans fish and chips. How did it compare with John's week in Levallois-Perret? Here, Cyrile stood up for France in the historic Anglo-French rivalry: Leeds good, Paris twice as good; a week in Levallois-Perret should be requited by two in Leeds. Helen took that to be a compliment.

There was another exchange six years later between Ben and Stephane. But on this occasion Ben's arrival in Levallois-Perret was followed by his accompanying the family as they drove to spend their annual summer holiday in their Alpine chalet in Nevache. By this time the two families had become friends as they got to know more of each other. After the second boys' exchange Emmanuel and Nicole flew over and stayed a week at 73 Old Park Road. In return Matthew and Helen went to spend a few days with them in Nevache intending to follow it by continuing to follow the road to Turin. The route looked straightforward in the Atlas but was not for the fainthearted motorist as one left Briancon and headed into the mountains – an interminably twisted road, sharp vertiginous corners, inadequate road markings and discontinuous roadside crash barrier. As one crept a few inches away from the drop to one's right a car would suddenly emerge from behind a bend and come hurtling at speed down the slope to one's left. The pass at Mont St. Senis was particularly unnerving. One would sigh with relief as one came out of it only to be further unnerved by the long twisting road making the steep climb into the Hautes Alpes. Eventually one arrived at the scenic Vallee de Clairie and Nevache, a small hamlet hard against the Italian border. Nevache was like the end of the world; situated on a high ridge overlooking the valley far below it had hardly a level ground on either side of the narrow road that would climb further towards Italy and Turin. Remarkably for such a small population of about a hundred souls the hamlet had a church and two chapels, apart from a tiny private family chapel which belonged to the Beaus. In addition to the Caswells there was another guest; the Beau's father confessor had accompanied them in the drive from Paris. The priest was rather solemn, had a few words, hardly any English. He did not enquire about England or what impression the Caswell couple had of France. His conversation was limited to asking about the journey, while he could say nothing about Turin. He had never been there, nor had he any personal knowledge of the state of the road snaking towards it over the mountain. The meals were taken in a respectful economy of words bordering on solemnity. After the evening dinner the priest pulled out a violin and played a Vivaldi while Emmanuel joined with a mouth organ. On Sunday morning they went to St. Marcellin as did most of the people of Nevache. There was the shaking of hands of peace at the conclusion of the service. That included some Italians who had come down from the next hamlet across the border. A small Sunday flea market close by the church was a popular attraction. Emmanuel explained that the Vallee de Clairee including Nevache was occupied and claimed by Italy upon the defeat and surrender of France in 1940, but was resituated to France four years later. He added that the changes of sovereignty were achieved seamlessly. The presence of a few soldiers as agents of the Italian occupier state was not resented much because they were respectful throughout.

At the end of their stay in Nevache Matthew and Helen gave up the idea of continuing further to Turin. After the nerve racking drive from Briancon to Nevache Helen felt that she could not stand the anxiety and perils, as she saw the situation, of plunging further into the Hautes Alpes. They drove back to Briancon then turned towards Gap and the warm south of the Alpes Maritimes, the Mediterranean, Nice and Cannes.

League of gentlemen

⟨⟨⟩⟩

When Matthew joined 6 Park Square it was a conservative set of chambers. It maintained all the traditions that were accumulated over the centuries that defined the profession and those who practised it. A barrister was a gentleman; in accepting a brief he did not negotiate a fee in person, would rather show a measure of insouciance about the money while pretending that the relationships with client and instructing solicitor were not transactional. Most important, he did not solicit custom either expressly or by the way he dressed, carried himself, or by the intimation of his profession in public such as by the red-taped brief held in hand or the rosette in buttonhole. All those sordid things were below his dignity as a lawyer and a gentleman. Except that what he seemingly disdained to do, he left to the chamber's clerk to do while expecting him to do it well and to his satisfaction. That the barrister was a gentleman was carried to the extent that there were very few lady barristers in practice nationally, and none at

6 Park Square. Further, the barrister gentleman that was admitted to chambers was expected to arrive by way of a top university. When Matthew Caswell was offered a tenancy he was to join a set of seven, all but one of them Oxbridge graduates. The odd one out was George Hall who had an extensive knowledge and experience of the practice and laws of insurance which facilitated his progress to qualify as a barrister at a relatively advanced age. He was rich, and that compensated for whatever was perceived as his formal qualification deficit.

The epithet of 'conservative' attached to 6 Park Square described the conduct as well as the political support of, if not an actual affiliation to, the Tory party. In the long history of the chambers extending over several generations, there had not been among its members anyone who was of obvious non-British ethnicity; in fact everyone was Yorkshire born. That Matthew was admitted to membership notwithstanding his Iraqi heritage was mainly due to the initial interview he had with George Hall who was impressed by his qualifications and demeanour. George was well off, his wife having brought a substantial inheritance to the marriage; theirs was the household of a contended and benign English gentleman; so to him the common bond of gentlemen across frontiers counted for more than national differences and racial or ethnic diversity. The bond was further affirmed by George inviting Matthew to join him in the Leeds Conservative Club and, with Matthew assenting, proposing him for membership.

Halcyon days

The 1970's were the halcyon days. Matthew's practice was growing exponentially, and so was his reputation as a clever lawyer who was prepared to deal with complicated cases and never lost any; which was untrue. He won many more than he lost, and rarely lost one on appeal. He liked to appear in the court of appeal to which cases were raised for their legal complexity and importance. He felt more at ease arguing a point of law before a bench of three senior members of the judiciary who were prepared to be engaged in the legal argument than to do so before some judge of a lower court who might be more open to be persuaded by the theatrical turn of phrase and the flowery language. Raising a judgment from a lower court to the court of appeal called for good judgment as well as knowledge of the law. Matthew Caswell had several cases which were reported in the learned journals and law reports for their importance in defining and expanding the law. He became so well known that he would receive instructions from solicitors as far afield as Norwich,

Brighton and Carlisle. In 1975 he had his first pupil, Jennifer Heath later Kershaw, a graduate of King's College London, followed by David Rose, a Cambridge graduate, and by others who went on to join other chambers. The busy practice left little time for Matthew to spend with the children; he rarely left chambers to go home before eleven. The burden of caring for the children and seeing to their needs as school children fell mainly on Helen. She inwardly regretted missing out on a university education, but her role in which she willingly indulged was that of a loving wife and devoted mother. The improvement of the family's financial position also allowed her to indulge her impeccable taste in furnishing and embellishing the family and holiday homes, and in calling on antique and junk shops to discover, discern and acquire collectibles. In the meantime the children were doing well at top fee- paying schools: Rebecca at Leeds Girls High, John and Ben at Leeds Grammar School.

Dreams of Oxbridge

Rebecca was managing well academically in her all-girls school. In addition to a great deal of guidance and support from her mother, she was fortunate in having English teachers who were sympathetic and encouraged her work. Her sixth form teacher in particular, recognising her potential, urged her to aim high, thus reinforcing her confidence and self-esteem. Having considered an English degree, Rebecca eventually decided to study Law. She hoped to be a barrister, following in her father's footsteps, and she aspired with his encouragement to apply to Oxford.

Important changes were taking place at the time. Until very recently Oxford consisted of 33 same sex undergraduate colleges and halls of residence of which only five were exclusively for ladies. That was clearly unfair to the women who would have to be competing for far fewer places than were available to the men. Then, a few years before it was time for Rebecca to apply for admission four out of the total broke ranks and opened the doors to both sexes. Wadham was one of the four, a historically men's college it opened its door to women as well without any gender bias. Another college was St Anne's which was founded as an exclusive ladies society or college and was now admitting men as well. Rebecca went own to have a look at Wadham and met the law tutor. Rebecca made a good impression that was to endure. Jeff was proud of the fact that Wadham had gone mixed and particularly pleased with the very recent success of the innovative Wadham ladies boat on the river; he hoped that Rebecca might one day add to the prowess of the ladies eight!

In due course Rebecca attended the formal Wadham interview. She thought it went well and was minded to return to Leeds when she received a call to go to another interview at St Anne's. At first she took that to mean a rejection by Wadham. But going before Ruth Deech she was assured that such was not the case; it was just that she was also under consideration for an offer by St Anne's. That made her no less despondent. Wadham was her first choice and there was now the risk of a St Anne's offer with a scholarship that will outrank and hold sway over Wadham's. The despondency lasted until a few days before Christmas when Rebecca received a telephone call from Oxford confirming an unconditional offer from Wadham. Leeds Girls High gloried in that; it was one of the first offers ever by a mixed Oxford college to one of its girls. It was celebrated by a plaque displaying Rebecca's name and commemorating the event.

John envied Rebecca's success while he doubted he had sufficient ability to emulate her. His leanings were towards the sciences rather than the arts. Modest and self-deprecating by nature he tended to hide his light under a bushel while he was not sure if he was good enough for a place at Oxbridge. However, encouraged at home and with some encouragement from the teachers he thought of trying for Oxford to study geology. One of his teachers mentioned University College Oxford and the name of a leading academic in the geology department. John mentioned that to his father, and Matthew suggested he wrote to the Oxford academic soliciting a visit. That was agreed, and John got on well with the professor who after a friendly chat in his study took him to the refectory for coffee and to resume the conversation. Two geology undergraduates happened to come in and the professor introduced John as one who will be joining them the following year. That said, John returned to Leeds uncertain of his prospects; those words could have been taken as a settled intention to make him an offer, or they could have been a slip of the tongue. In any event an offer would have to be subject to John doing well in the college's admission examination. John sat the examination and came out thinking he had not done well enough, which filled him with gloom. Relief came with an offer of a place at Imperial College of Science and Technology. That was a high ranking world class university and could be said to be a better destination than Oxford for someone intending to study geology. It would allow one to pass seamlessly to the associate School of Mining so as to qualify as a mining engineer. But when a formal offer by University College Oxford arrived in the post all thoughts of going to Imperial College were set aside. The allure of Oxford, the name, the collegiate system, achieving parity with Rebecca actually and Ben potentially was irresistible.

By the time it was Ben's turn to apply for a university place Rebecca and John had already graduated from Oxford. Some of Ben's friends were applying to Cambridge. He gave a little thought to that and chose Oxford to read law; the question next was which colleges to list in his application? The Oxford colleges of father, sister and brother had been St Catherine's, Wadham and Univ. respectively. His father had suggested St John's; Ben looked at it and decided to list Wadham as his first choice. The school supported his application; that was followed by an interview and his passing the A-level examination with top grades in all the subjects. He was awarded a place, one of four in his year to read law.

The three children graduated from Oxford in law, geology and law respectively with a further MA in each case. Later, John further gained a Sheffield MBA, while Ben followed his Oxford years with a year at University College London where he completed a master's degree in Philosophy. In 2001 Fuad Matthew Caswell returned to Oxford (Wadham) to complete a doctorate in Arabic, the doctoral thesis appearing in print as *The Slave Girls of Baghdad – The Qiyan in the Early Abbasid Era.*

QC

—— ✺ ——

QC (Queen's Counsel), two letters that are highly coveted. They denote an upper grade barrister invested with substantial advantages. A QC is entitled to wear the silk in court, hence one is commonly referred to as 'a silk'; has precedence in court to include sitting at the very front, nearest to the judge's ears, while supported by a non-QC barrister commonly referred to as a 'junior' who would be sitting behind his 'leader'; the right to decline a brief unlike the juniors who are bound by the cab rank system to accept whatever case came their way; the fact that senior judicial appointments are made from the pool of QCs; and most significant of all, a silk commands higher fees. A senior, long in practice junior barrister can see his fees trebled overnight upon his appointment to QC. However, upon his or her appointment the QC gives up taking on the cases of lesser importance or of relatively small sums in dispute. Where a case of a particular importance or of a big worth justifies the resort to a silk, most of the preparatory work will then be carried out by their junior to include such things as reviewing the evidence, researching the law, and settling the draft proceedings. The QC presents the case in court, hence he is also commonly referred to as a leader or leading counsel. As against those advantages there is a risk in taking silk in that one gives up the bread and butter cases forthwith while waiting for the far fewer but better paid cases to come one's way. That risk is mitigated by the fact that in any one of the six circuits covering England and Wales the number of QC's is limited, fixed at a level that is big enough to meet the need but small enough to provide sufficient employment as it stifles competition.

In order to make the transition from junior to silk one is not required to sit an examination or attend an interview, nor even evidence an exceptional ability or earning power. The process is akin to being admitted to a gentleman's club and with a high degree of opacity added. The round of appointing a silk is carried out once a year with the result announced around Easter time. A candidate would submit his application to the Lord Chancellor's department, a copy would be forwarded to the leader of the circuit Bar, to be followed by the leader consulting discreetly the senior members of the circuit, in effect its silks. At the conclusion of the consultation the leader of the circuit would submit to the Lord Chancellor a list of the candidates recommended for the award; and that is normally accepted and acted upon unchanged. It almost invariably happens that those consulted and invited to express a preference would choose those whom they knew, to whom they were related or were otherwise similar to them in attitudes and beliefs. In consequence many if not most of the QCs, taking the North Eastern Circuit as an example, existed in shadowy clusters of freemasons, Jews, Catholics or members of 11 King's Bench Walk. That last was a circuit set with chambers in the Temple that over the years saw many high court judges, leaders of circuit and QCs pass through its doors. A member of those chambers applying for silk can count on a lot of support.

Thinking of applying for appointment to QC Matthew Caswell was disadvantaged; his being an outsider was to endure for upwards of his forty years in practice as a barrister. He did not play the Jewish card and to the very end nobody knew for certain what was his religion, his background, beliefs, or political orientation. He was ever so busy that he had neither the time nor the inclination to socialise and network; he very rarely attended the circuit Bar dinners. Being the originator of a chancery practice in the North Eastern Circuit he had no chancery predecessors let alone in silk to lend him a vote or support. All the QCs on the North Eastern Circuit practised in criminal law, while the Lord Chancellor had not yet made a provision for a slot to be filled by a chancery QC. Notwithstanding those handicaps Matthew put in an application for appointment at the urging of members of his chambers; they wanted him appointed as a silk thereby to leave the way clear for them to apply in turn. The leader of the circuit at the time was Peter Taylor QC who was highly respected and influential in the upper reaches of the judiciary; he was to rise in time to become the Lord Chief Justice. He had led Matthew in several murder trials. He now telephoned him to let him know that his name was not in the list of the candidates recommended for appointment, others having received a greater support. He then added, which may have been the main reason for the call, that he will fully support him for appointment as a circuit judge. So encouraged, Matthew Caswell applied to be considered for appointment, and he received a reply from the Lord Chancellor's department assuring him that his name will be in the next list of new appointments, with an intimation of the date, some six months later, when the list will be published. That was intended to allow him time to clear his diary of part heard cases and to decline accepting new lengthy cases. The period was also used by the Lord Chancellor's department to carry out the normal statutory enquiries and consultations. He happened to meet Alan Heyman, one of his two former pupil masters, who told him that he had been approached for a reference, and that he responded with an unqualified letter of support. Just before the end of the period of consultation he received a letter from the Lord Chancellor's department advising him in a few curt words that he should not make plans based on the expectation of a judicial appointment. No reason was given nor any explanation. He surmised it was due to his past, historical appearance at the Old Bailey on a charge of fraud. He had done nothing to conceal that fact, and he had actually disclosed it fully when he applied for membership of the Middle Temple. At his Old Bailey trial he had defended himself in person and was acquitted. That had been twenty years before and now Zilkha, his former partner and adversary, was exacting his revenge. It was a brutal letter. He could have protested, called for an explanation or sought an interview. He could also have referred to the unusual and murky circumstances in which his former partner brought the charges against him maliciously; and he could have referred to a transcript of the judgment in which the judge stressed in his summing up that even if every point in contention were to be decided against Mr Zelouf that would not have constituted a serious case of fraud. Now Matthew Caswell did briefly consider applying for a review of the decision, then dismissed the notion. He would have found it embarrassing, painful and it might have been fruitless. The disappointment was mitigated by the fact that as a junior barrister his earnings at the time exceeded the fixed salary of a circuit judge.

With the door of judicial appointment firmly shut he felt free to renew his application for silk. The leader of the circuit at this time was Gilbert Gray QC, a prominent advocate and criminal lawyer with massive earnings. He also had a side business of breeding pigs in a big way. It so happened one day that he was in the Cubana restaurant, where lawyers often had lunch, and was heard to bemoan the dire state of the market in pigs, the losses of which weighed heavily on him. He said he was only able to continue the business by covering its losses with his heavily taxed earnings as a barrister. He also bemoaned the fact that he could not set off the losses of the one against the earnings of the other because, so he had been advised by his accountant, they were two different business activities. If a set off had been possible that would have substantially reduced his tax bill. He followed that by saying rhetorically that if anyone could find a way of allowing the set off he would gladly let him have half of all the tax that was saved. Matthew Caswell overheard that, went back to chambers, looked up the point in the tax statutes and regulations. He telephoned Gilbert and after a few questions ascertained that the facts brought the case within an exception that allowed such a set off. Gilbert was as surprised as he was pleased to hear the news and, referring to the promised reward, was told that all that Matthew wanted was a cup of tea when they next met. In due course the Inland Revenue allowed the set off, a serious amount of income tax was saved, and Matthew Caswell was rewarded with a lunch at Terry's in York (Gilbert Gray was leading him in a murder trial) instead of tea at the Cubana in Leeds. As regards Matthew's application for silk, Gilbert Gray discussed it with Arthur Hutchinson QC, then the head of chambers at 6 Park Square. Gilbert said, by way of excuse for passing Matthew over, that he was earning so much as a junior barrister that he would have assuredly suffered a big loss of income were he to become a QC.

Yorkshire cricket

I t was in the first summer after the family had moved to Leeds that Matthew Caswell became a member of Yorkshire County Cricket Club. He had never played cricket nor was he a true cricket follower. He knew the rules of the game and enjoyed watching it played on some balmy summer's day at Headingley or a relaxed Sunday afternoon at Bradford Park Avenue. He mixed with other spectators, true Yorkshire cricket enthusiasts, who held strong opinions vigorously expressed about the state of Yorkshire cricket as they rehearsed past and present events, grievances and controversies. In nearly all the discussions one name kept on cropping up, Geoffrey Boycott. Caswell met him briefly at some cricket function to which Caswell had been invited as a guest speaker. Almost everyone at the function was a Boycott supporter but surprisingly the man himself was not at the high table nor was he even present in the body of the hall. Matthew could see him beyond a doorway to the bar. Geoffrey was not drinking but was engaged in earnest conversation with others. He only broke off and came to the doorway to listen to Mathews's speech before retreating back to the bar. Afterwards it was Matthew who went over to introduce himself and engage him in a friendly conversation. That gave Geoffrey all he wanted to know which was that Matthew Caswell, a Leeds barrister, was on his side. To Matthew it was the privilege of making the acquaintance and exchanging a few amiable words with a sporting hero and a Yorkshire legend. Some time later Geoffrey Boycott and his solicitor Duncan Mutch called on Caswell at his house in Old Park Road. It was an informal visit which had not been booked at Matthews's chambers. Nor was it a pure social visit. Neither Geoffrey nor Duncan had ever been inside Matthews's house before. They came for advice in relation to Geoffrey facing some threatened disciplinary proceedings. Duncan Mutch lived in Barnsley and practised as a solicitor in the firm's name of Dibb and Clegg. He was highly regarded for the wisdom, wide knowledge and practical approach that were the hallmark of his extensive and successful legal practice. He was utterly devoted to Boycott and was ever ready to defend him publicly and to use trenchant logic and language in decrying the wrong decisions of the Yorkshire cricket and general committees that were calculated to diminish an exceptional batsman who was a great asset to the club. In the course of the visit, it was Duncan who engaged Matthew in conversation to explain the purpose of the visit and give an outline of the dispute. Boycott stood apart gazing out of the window overlooking Roundhay Park. There was a moment when he turned round, pulled Duncan aside and seemingly expressed concern at how much Duncan was divulging because Duncan was then heard to tell him that he should have full confidence in Caswell as a barrister and friend, and to tell him all there was to tell. Caswell was flattered that Geoffrey Boycott with all his eminence and all his contacts had come to him for advice. Matthew did help as an adviser thinking that would be the end of the matter, but one thing led to another and he got deeper and deeper into the whole controversy surrounding Boycott and the club 'civil war' that ensued.

Caswell had no contact with the Reform group before; now they came to him for advice. His first impression of the Reformers was underwhelming. They did not know what's what. With the aid of a lawyer, they had put together an application to the court for an order that Geoffrey Boycott be restored as captain. That was hopeless; no court would do that. Instead, when Geoffrey's contract was cancelled the Reformers, on the advice of Caswell, requisitioned a special general meeting of the club and Caswell drafted cautiously two special resolutions. One was that Geoffrey be reinstated as a member of the playing team. The other proposed resolution was a vote of no confidence in the cricket committee. That marked the beginning of the club's 'civil war'. There were the loyalists supporting the administration; and there were the pro-Boycott rebels. Caswell's front room overlooking Roundhay Park became the centre of the latter's organisation. The club had a membership of 13,000, each having a single vote, and it was now a struggle to garner as many votes as one could to one's side. As is often the case with revolutions the establishment would be complacent while the rebels would have fervour on their side; and so was it at this rebellion. Several of the committee members were past Yorkshire cricketers by dint of which were very influential. They seemed to simply stand on their reputation while the Reformers were far more willing to get their hands dirty. Matthew Caswell was cheered on by the fact that he was on the side of the rebels against the Establishment. He became in effect the leader of the rebellion assisted by Reformer's secretary Tony Van who had contacts with the Press Association and the local media generally. Tony would call on Matthew at home every day to get a dictation to give to the press.

Caswell thought the Reformers were winning the battle when two ladies came during their luncheon break knocking on the door of his house in Old Park Road. When Helen opened the door they had a list of the members in the Leeds district; one name on the list was 'Mr M. Caswell'. They urged Mrs Caswell to encourage her husband to vote for Boycott. "But I do not need to do that", said Helen, "Matthew is certainly on the side of Geoffrey as everyone knows". The penny dropped; "So it is <u>that</u> Matthew who is on the list". The ladies left happy with exchanges of 'well-done' and 'good wishes'.

Matthew was in the Cubana when Brian Walsh came to him and said with reference to the Yorkshire conflict: "Matthew, how do you think we are getting on?" Matthew said "I think we have a good chance" so Brian became interested in joining the Reformers, which was important because he was a QC and a recorder, and what the Reformers lacked was social weight. All Brian wanted was if the rebellion succeeded, he would be the most suitable person to lead the whole thing, as chairman, president, the lot. Matthew then organised a meeting between Brian and the leading members of the Reform group. They came to his house and Matthew made the introduction. He attempted a little bonhomie but to little effect. The Reformers sat on one side of the room while Brian stood by Matthew just inside the door. Apart from Matthew no one had anything to say and the atmosphere was somewhat glacial. There was no glossing over the social gulf between the Reformers and Brian Walsh QC and recorder of the crown court; nor hiding the fact that this was a marriage of convenience in which the Reformers were using Brian just as Brian was using them.

The committee hired a London agency to produce a glossy brochure. The Reformers had no funds to fall back on, so their response could only be by leaflet. There was a meeting one evening at Caswell's house attended by the leading Reformers including Reg Kirk and Peter Charles.

Caswell had got together a text for them to approve. There were a few suggestions about what to add and leave out. Then Boycott arrived, read the draft and liked it. That settled the matter. The production and distribution of the committee's brochure would have cost the club thousands of pounds. By contrast the cost involved in the production and distribution of the leaflet was near minimal because that was done by the members of the Reform group and their supporters and friends. In any event the Reform group being no more than a loose association of a few men of moderate means had no money to spend. The only thing that could not be avoided was the cost of the stationary and the postage. That amounted to £2,200 which had to be found somehow. Peter Briggs called on Caswell and suggested an article by Geoffrey to sell to a leading newspaper. They sat at the kitchen table, Matthew composed the article which Peter took down to London, returning with a cheque from the *Daily Star* for £2,400. He could perhaps have got more for the world exclusive front page article by Geoffrey Boycott but £2,400 was all he demanded. Once brochure and leaflet were distributed everyone thought that the Reformers response costing a fraction of the committee's brochure was more professional.

The turning point in the war came when the 3rd of December special general meeting had to be postponed. Until then the committee were expected to hold sway. At issue was the failure of the club to send ballot papers to a number of members. The list of members was not up to date. Some people had left, others came in and were not recorded, others had died. In normal circumstances nobody would bother but because the club was in a big civil war it was a matter of deep concern that about 680 members had been disenfranchised. David Thorpe of Huddersfield and Kevin Birks of Leeds then consulted Duncan Mutch who issued a High Court writ in their names requiring the committee to include them in the vote. The committee took fright; they had a meeting at Headingley and decided to call off the vote and start all over again. The Reformers tried to push on with the SGM regardless. A large proportion of members had already cast their vote, so if you started all over again it would be like cheating. When the matter went before Vice-Chancellor Blackett- Ord he dismissed the committee's submission to call off the meeting and start again. He ordered that a new date be set for the current SGM, such as to allow time to deliver the ballot papers to those who had been missed. A new date was 21 January. That was a victory for the individuals who had brought the proceedings and they were entitled prima facie to an order for costs. Caswell who appeared for them did not ask for such an order because the Plaintiffs incurred no costs such as could be recovered from the club or the committee. Duncan Mutch, the firm Dibb and Clegg as solicitors, and Matthew Caswell as counsel were acting for the Plaintiffs free of charge. David Thorpe and Kevin Birks took a frightful risk in starting the action. They could have been facing a big monetary liability if the court decision had gone the other way and they were ordered to pay the committee's cost of employing a solicitor and a top team of London Barristers who commanded high fees.

At the SGM the Reformers won the votes for all their demands including the reinstatement of Geoffrey Boycott as member. The committee resigned; a new election was held when the Reformers' candidates had a clean sweep giving the Reformers, Geoffrey Boycott's supporters, control of the club. A new Yorkshire County Cricket Club was born.

Matthew Caswell had no ambition to be on the committee. He was very busy as a barrister and had no wish to be involved directly in the affairs of the club now under the control of his faction. He was happy after the change to see Boycott awarded a three year contract, and his friend Peter Townend installed in the position of club treasurer. He was also involved in the choice of Viscount Mountgarret as president. The tradition was that you had Lord Hawke and other lords at the top. After the Reformers had taken control Matthew Caswell discussed the position with Peter Charles. They knew there would be a counter revolution. Matthew calculated it would be good to have a prominent or lordly figure at the top as cover for any mistake or mishap. Their first choice was Huddersfield's Lord Hanson, founder of multinational industrial management group the Hanson Trust, and a club life member. Duncan Mutch knew him, his firm had acted for him and he even arranged for Geoffrey Boycott to give permission to the use of a photograph of him batting to be displayed in American newspapers alongside that of the great baseball player Mickey Mantle. Hanson's purpose was to demonstrate that his businesses had an Anglo American interest. Boycott did not receive nor ask for any financial reward. Duncan now approached James Hanson on behalf of Boycott. Hanson declined the offer of the presidency because he spent half his year living in the United States. That is the official version. But when Duncan came back with the news he also confided to Caswell that Hanson wanted to know who was the club chairman with whom he would have to deal. When told it was Reg Kirk he declined the invitation. Not that he had anything in particular against Kirk; it was just that they were of a different class. It can be said that Yorkshire cricket's civil war had some of the trappings of a class warfare.

It was Roy Ickringill who suggested Mountgarret for president. Rumour had it that the viscount owed his new post to listing cricket among his hobbies in *Who's Who*. But the explanation was far more pedestrian. Roy Ickringill was running to be elected as Harrogate representative on the general committee. He had the list of members which included Mountgarret. He set out canvassing for every vote, and that brought him to the viscount's door. Disturbed in whatever he was engaged in doing he came out to the door and saw this young man, not more than a lad, having the temerity to tell him why he should vote for him. He responded in his usual gruff manner which confirmed to Roy that he was a real lord. Ickringill telephoned Caswell, "How about having Mountgarret as president? He is very rich and has a large estate?" Caswell knew nothing about him other than he was a viscount. He had a Harrogate solicitor who instructed him regularly and also happened to play golf a lot with Mountgarret. Caswell asked the solicitor what he could tell him about him and if he would sound him. He did, and Mountgarret said he would be honoured.

Boycott in France

∞

I t was an enchanted weekend; Geoffrey Boycott was
spending it at the luxurious Hotel de Cap in Cap d'Antibes
with his lover Margaret Moore. They had an argument
followed by an incident that resulted in Moore sustaining
bruising around the black eyes and bruising to the face which
was to be categorised by eminent specialists as a tracking
injury from a bang on the head. Whether she sustained
further injuries is uncertain. The incident happened on 2
October 1996, the facts of which were then contested and
have remained mired in controversy ever since. According to
Geoffrey his companion and lover was beside herself as he
spurned her advances for marriage; she flung intimate items
of his clothing including the underwear, also the toiletries,
out of the window. When she then grabbed one of his best
suits from the wardrobe he reacted, "You're never having
that!" They were struggling so hard over the suit that they
fell together, both crashing onto the tiled white marble floor.
Boycott badly bruised his left elbow, while Moore sustained

the bump on her head. Moore's account is different. She claims grotesquely that Boycott in his fury got on top of her pinioned her to the floor and went on hitting her repeatedly. He only stopped when the telephone rang. She claims it was the concierge who hearing her screams rang to find out what was happening. Later Moore made a complaint to a Magistrate Court in France charging Boycott with assault and battery.

In January 1998 Boycott was convicted in absentia. The conviction was affirmed in October 1998 by judge Dominique Haumont-Daumas at the conclusion of a full hearing in Grasse. The verdict was further affirmed in May 2002 by a three-judge court of appeal sitting in Aix-en-Provence. That was as far as the criminal proceedings got. The Boycott campaign to clear his name was costly, as one would have expected, and was so confirmed by his solicitor Richard Knaggs. Richard was fiercely loyal to Geoffrey and that was reciprocated by the appreciation and friendship of Geoffrey and Rachel Swinglehurst. Richard Knaggs had a solicitor's practice with offices in Redcar. Over the years he had acquired a loyal following in town including the friendship of Rachel Swinglehurst and her family. Rachel was later to be Mrs Boycott and with the title of Lady Boycott in her capacity of Sir Geoffrey's spouse. On 24 May 2019 Theresa May announced her resignation as Prime Minister of the United Kingdom. In her resignation honours list she nominated Geoffrey Boycott for a knighthood. The announcement of that raised quite a storm of protest by those who thought that so rewarding a convicted woman beater would be a setback to the campaign against domestic violence on women. In the event Boycott did get his knighthood at an investiture by Prince Charles on 14 February 2020. As he enters his eighth decade Geoffrey Boycott could look with pride at the recognition of his long career and contribution to cricket by the award of a long overdue knighthood. At the same time he must rue the fact that the honour is tarnished in the eyes of some by the conviction for a serious and nasty offence. As Sir Geoffrey he would still need to declare it when applying for a visa to go visit or work in other countries and he might in principal be denied entry to certain countries including the United States. He may ponder in hindsight whether any more could have been done in the course of the long and costly campaign to spare him the stigma of the conviction. Looking at the matter objectively and dispassionately it can be seen that with the best intention of all concerned some better outcome was within grasp but was missed. Boycott's campaign which was endowed with so much effort, zeal and expense can be said to have been deficient in one respect, it lacked strategic flexibility chiefly in making the wrong assumption as regards the court procedure in France, and failing, once one became aware of the error, to change direction and benefit from the patent weaknesses of the opposition.

In any conflict, be it an opening batsman facing a fast bowler, a solicitor negotiating with the opposing solicitor or a barrister arguing a case in court an essential part of the preparation is to find all one can about the law or the rules of the engagement, about the judge, about one's opposing barrister as well as the parties to the conflict; to note in each case their respective bias or prejudice, their strong points and weak ones, and so plan one's tactics accordingly. In the case of Margaret Moore her weaknesses as an opponent were clear for all to see; they were matters of public record. In 1997 she was declared bankrupt with a deficiency of £404,850, £250,000 owed to the Inland Revenue. At about the same time her company Rapid System passed into compulsory liquidation and the liquidator was pursuing Moore for explanation about moneys that had just disappeared. She had a summary judgment against her for £35,000 that she owed to her former solicitor Sims-Steward. She had traumatic experiences in the several court appearances when she was all but described as a compulsive liar. In 1999 a court of appeal of three judges described her as fraudulent and dishonourable. The conclusion that one would draw from those facts was that nothing would have tempted let alone persuaded Margaret Moore to be involved in any court proceedings in England. For one thing she as a bankrupt would not have had the means within the jurisdiction of the English authorities to fund a serious court case. She could not possibly have derived any benefit from the proceedings.

Were she to recover any damages, which was unlikely, her trustee in bankruptcy, the Inland Revenue, the company's liquidator and Ms Sims-Steward among others would have competed to get their hands on the money. After the incident in the Hotel de Cap Margaret Moore returned to England with Geoffrey, buying him a tie at Nice airport, then after a few more days returned to France to lodge her complaint with a French magistrates court. She could have done that in England which would have been more convenient since she and Geoffrey were English, Geoffrey's witnesses likewise, the hearing would have been in an English court applying English law and with the proceedings in English. But it was clearly beneficial, in fact essential for Margaret Moore to take her complaint to a provincial magistrate court in France rather than an English court. But there was no reason for Geoffrey Boycott to cede to Margaret Moore that strategic advantage. She lured Geoffrey to Grasse and he followed. His barrister friend Matthew Caswell told him not to go to France for a rehearing. Caswell's view of the matter was that Boycott should announce that he was not going to appear in a provincial French magistrate court of Moore's choosing; that if she had any genuine complaint he was waiting to defend it in England. Besides, Moore could hardly have objected to that. Dealing with that specific point she was to allege that she tried to register a complaint at Kensington Police who turned her away as the incident happened in France. She may well have been advised by the Police that their

French counterpart were the proper agency to investigate the matter. But it was incorrect to surmise that the English legal system could not have been seized of the matter, the proof of which was that Margaret Moore employed English solicitors and an English counsel to institute proceedings in the High Court claiming damages for the very same alleged assault and battery in France. Her counsel Mark Strachan telephoned Caswell offering to do away with the claim altogether in return of £1 million. For the reasons stated above Caswell did not believe that Margaret Moore would bring such an action or any action in England. In the telephone conversation with Mark Strachan the word blackmail was not used nor it needed to be. They knew what they were talking about. However she came by her injuries Moore could not by any stretch of imagination be awarded one million pounds in damages. Strachan sought to justify the figure by saying that Margaret Moore spent so much time as Boycott's friend and companion that she neglected her business affairs which suffered as a consequence. That was laughable; what he was suggesting in a round about way was that his client had invested so much in the relationship and in her expectations in that relationship that she now wanted to be recompensed for her failed expectations. Caswell got the impression that Margaret Moore's offer was negotiable while he expected that a stipulation would be added to the effect that the money be deposited in some account beyond the reach of the English authorities. As regards the general view of the picture Caswell's calculation was that in case of need Geoffrey could start an action for defamation charging Moore with making a false allegation against him. That would have gone before an English judge and jury. The only defence that would have been open to Margaret Moore would have been to justify the slander or libel by satisfying the court that Boycott did actually hit her. Caswell had no doubt that in such a contest Geoffrey would win, yet looking at the matter realistically he felt there could have been no risk of Moore even coming to England and be involved in such an action. Boycott would have had a judgment of the High Court in his case, almost certainly undefended, that would put in the shade the 'in absentia' judgment by the magistrate court in France. What's more, all of that could have been achieved at a relatively modest cost. Geoffrey missed what in effect was an open goal.

That can be said to be the view in hindsight. Such an outcome would not have appealed to Boycott at the time. It would still have left him with the French in absentia judgment while any outcome short of a complete clearing of his name he would have seen as a perversion. He knew he did not beat Moore; he had the evidence to put before the court in Grasse which, so he thought, would assuredly prevail. The trouble with that approach was that team Boycott were looking at the matter as if the conduct of the case in Grasse would be akin to the same in an English court. Yet they should not have fallen into that error. It was a well known fact that while a trial in an English court was adversarial with cross-examination a principal tool to get at the truth, that in a French court would be inquisitorial in which there was no place for cross-examination, and it was left to the judge in the guise of an inquisitor to ask the questions. Not only was the distinction notorious, team Boycott was to be led by a French counsel who knew the procedure under which he would be operating!

In the event the one point of disagreement as regards the strategy between team Boycott and Caswell was that they believed in getting the right verdict at a trial in Grasse while Caswell was sceptical of that and suggested a different approach.

Matthew Caswell was at his desk in the Leeds chambers when the telephone rang. It was Richard Knaggs who could hardly contain himself in excitement. Great news; a great development! An admirer of Geoffrey was determined to see him cleared of all criminal charges. The man asked Knaggs to do all he could to bring that about; go the distance in getting the lawyers, the witnesses and the experts, whatever it cost. He was a rich man and placed no limit on how much to spend. With that unconditional support behind him Knaggs instructed a leading Paris *maitre* and got together a formidable team of witnesses and experts. He had made a block booking for a flight to Nice and virtually reserved the whole of a hotel in Grasse close to the courthouse. He invited Matthew to join the team so he would add him to the aircraft and hotel bookings. Matthew Caswell said that he had not changed his opinion that it would be unwise for Geoffrey to go to France. But if Boycott was dead set on doing so and will not be deflected from that course then he would consider it his duty to be beside his friend Geoffrey to do what he could to help. He will not go as one of a team. He will book and pay for his own flight, stay in his own apartment in Cannes, then drive on the day to the courthouse in Grasse to meet the others.

As Caswell turned on the television he was dismayed at seeing the deployment of Boycott's team on the piazza outside the government buildings in Grasse. They stood in a line facing the cameras. Caswell felt that while that might go down well with Boycott's supporters and fans back home it will not cut ice with the judge; quite the reverse. A witness is supposed to come to court to give a true independent account.

Mixing more than a dozen witnesses as a close group living, eating, drinking together, and likely in those circumstances to exchange news and views, was liable to raise the charge that the evidence of each was contaminated by closeness to the others. Besides, Caswell thought it unwise and counter productive to turn an incident involving two lovers in the privacy of a bedroom in a hotel in the south of France into one attracting worldwide interest. Caswell thought a low profile was more appropriate and more likely to impress the trial judge. Boycott's French barrister, maitre

Cardona, was of the same opinion; he could not see what all the hyped fuss was about. He said that to the French people which by implication included the judge Margaret Moore's case was no big deal. He said in France one pays the woman some money and moves on; it happened all the time. Team Boycott tried to explain to the learned maitre that in the United Kingdom it was a lot more serious. Yet it was impossible to convince him, the same as they tried to drive it home to the judge, what the magnitude of the case was for Boycott and how different it would be judged in the United Kingdom.

Caswell sought out Cardona in the courthouse and asked how he intended to conduct the defence. A complete denial of the charge, said Cardona. Caswell suggested a better course which would explain the undeniable facial injuries was to posit that there was some innocent larking about, to use a Yorkshire expression, and that the injury was the result of an unintended accident. Cardona did not think that would work. He said that under French criminal justice system that would still count as an assault, equivalent to what is regarded as a strict liability offence in English law. Caswell next asked him what his views of the judge? Cardona said he had no direct knowledge of her but her reputation was of a strong character who was so severe that she had even put her husband in prison, He could not say more. Team Boycott would have had no knowledge of that at the time.

It was a big courtroom where lawyers stood mixed pell-mell with the accused, the witnesses and members of the public. A wooden bar marked the area where the judge sat on a raised dais. One would stand at the bar if giving evidence or addressing the judge. The room was at first full of people because the court list was long. Some barristers stood in knots about the room engaged in casual conversation or flirting. When the name of a case was announced the barrister whose case it was would separate from his companion and rush to the bar, deliver his prepared speech then turn back to resume the conversation. Caswell discerned that the judge appeared to react more positively to an oration by a female barrister; in one case she beamed to a young lady barrister as by way of encouragement.

Soon there were fewer about. All the cases but one were for mention, the accused appearing for the first time and the case being adjourned to another fixed date. The case of Moore v Boycott had to wait until all the others were disposed of. Boycott came and took a seat at the front to the left. Then Margaret Moore appeared meticulously groomed and fragrant. She was aiming for a seat to the right and passed close to where Cardona was holding a conversation with Knaggs and Caswell. Knaggs fixed Moore with a look of contempt as he turned his back on her.

It was quite late when the case Moore v Boycott was ready and all the witnesses were asked to leave the room but stay in the building. They were ordered not to leave until they had given their evidence and were discharged. They were led to the library next door and kept under guard by a warder. They were called one at a time, no witness was allowed to be and stay in the courtroom until one had given one's evidence. That was to ensure that a testimony of one witness will not be contaminated by being present to listen to that of another before one had given one's own. The library was a working library; three local lawyers were busy at their desks preparing their cases. Caswell got into conversation with one of them and that gave him the opportunity to ask about the judge and in particular the sending of her husband to prison. The French lawyer said it was not a big thing, then added with a smile that the husband had to spend a night in the cells because he was naughty! As it got late and the local lawyers left there was more room for the witnesses to expand and relax, one consultant with a bad back laid himself down stretched fully on his back on the floor; the warder came to remonstrate that such undignified posture was not allowed in the library and was pushed off with the protest: *J'ai mal au dos*. It was uncomfortable and after a long wait the 'inmates' were suffering from hunger and thirst. The warder agreed to go down to the street to get food and drink upon their word of honour as English not to try to get away.

Dominique Haumont-Daumas had a point when she referred to Boycott's witnesses as a collection of 'witnesses and supporters'. Her job as a judge was not an easy one. In the melee of facts, submissions and conjectures she had to find the answer to the one discrete question: Did Boycott beat Moore in the Hotel de Cap on the 2 October 1996? There was little in the statements of Boycott's witnesses that could help her find a definitive answer to that discrete question. Several women, former and current lovers of Boycott, testified to his character as a gentle lover with no streak of violence. However, no one was suggesting that Boycott was a man of violence in the way he treated his lovers or women generally, nor was he on trial for that. That evidence of the ladies was relevant to the sentence that would follow a conviction. It would suggest that the event of 2 October was a one off lapse by a man who had no propensity to violence; that would be reflected by a lighter penalty. There were the experts respectively explaining how a tracking injury can result from a bump in the head; a police surgeon's opinion that the swelling to face was more consistent with Margaret Moore falling and banging her head on a hard tiled floor than a blow with a fist; another expert concluded that Moore's account of the incident was intrinsically untrue; an expert in photography cast doubt on the veracity of the photograph. But none of those experts had examined Moore or discussed the matter with her. As judged by the judge, and hers was the only judgment that mattered, those statements were inconclusive and not such as to affirmatively provide the answer to the 'question'.

Max Clifford was another defence witness. A professional publicist, Moore went to ask him to act as her agent to sell her story. He declined and forthwith joined the band of Boycott's supporters. The judge got no assistance from that, while she may have considered it distasteful that the professional agent used against the would-be client what she had imparted to him in confidence. The judge may also have wondered what personal benefit Clifford was hoping to derive from attending the trial other than the free holiday in the south of France. But it should be said in fairness to

Max Clifford that he never treated Margaret Moore as a client and that before appearing as a witness in Grasse he had already given substantially the same true account in a television interview. His task was to protect the public image of Boycott back home and to think ahead to the time when his exceptional services might be required for rehabilitation. Matthew Caswell elected to read his statement in English with the interpreter standing next to him. The long and the short of his evidence was that in his capacity as Boycott's barrister and friend he was approached with an offer that on payment of £1 million Margaret Moore would drop all charges and accusations against Geoffrey. As the interpreter came to the end of the statement the judge exclaimed, "Et c'est tout (Is that all)?" Caswell replied "C'est tout, madame (That's all, my Lady)." She raised her eyes to the ceiling. The demand of the money was as consistent with the woman demanding it being a victim of the beating as of her making a false accusation. Among the defence team of witnesses and supporters there was one person whose statement was pure gold if believed. In 1995 Sims-Steward became Margaret Moore's solicitor. A year later she set up a firm specifically to meet Moore's needs. But within months her retainer was ended. Moore refused to pay her the £35,000 that Sims-Steward claimed to be entitled to. The firm ceased trading and Sims-Steward had to apply to the court for summary judgment. She faced hostility and a pack of lies; she got her judgment; but the money was not there and Margaret Moore was declared bankrupt before Sims-Steward could recover the judgment debt. Sims-Steward's testimony in Grasse was that Margaret Moore had told her that Geoffrey Boycott did not beat her, that she sustained the black eyes when in high heels she lost her balance and fell face down to the hard marble floor. The trouble with the credibility of that account was that Sims-Steward had a grudge against Moore, a score to settle. Even then Sims-Steward could have been believed. Except for one thing. She did not turn up in court as an independent witness. She was one of a team of supporters, travelling on the same flight, staying in the same hotel and joining in the parade in the piazza as one of them. Judge Dominique Haumont- Daumas did not need to be ultra astute to suspect that Sims-Steward's evidence may have been infected by what she as a close member of a team heard and discussed with the others.

Yet the judge might have been assisted in finding the right answer to the question if a real attempt had been made. There were so many relevant facts to be forensically examined yet some may not have been and were lost by default: Did the incident happen in the bedroom, and was the floor a hard white marble tiles or covered in a thick carpet? The incident happened on the 2 October; could there have been a change of floor covering with the change of the seasons from summer to autumn? Following the incident did Geoffrey Boycott and Margaret Moore sleep together for two nights and did they make love? Or did Margaret Moore spend those nights in the bath? What would the *femme de chamber* say about that? Following the incident was Moore seen sunbathing, and what, if any, marks were seen on her ? Did the doctor who examined Moore ask her how she came by her injury, and what did she say? Did the doctor make a note of the examination and treatment, and what happened to those notes? When and where was the photograph taken, and by whom? Did the management of the Hotel de Cap-Eden Roc keep an incident book? Why was it not produced in court?

Those questions point to the deficiency of the inquisitorial system. The evidence was in the possession or under the control of Margaret Moore. It needed to be tested by cross-examination as well as by an order for the disclosure of documents. None of that was available. Geoffrey Boycott was badly let down by the inquisitorial regime.

After the conclusion of he trial the judge Dominique Haumont-Daumas had a press conference in which she appeared to be self satisfied with the way in which she presided over the trial of a case of international interest; she then went on to talk of the struggle of women generally and the professional ones in particular to secure equal opportunities and respect, and how that could only be achieved by women rallying to each other worldwide to fight against discrimination and injustice. A militant feminist discourse which she concluded with a flourish: "The future is woman!" quoting Aragon. Louis Aragon was a darling of the left, poet of the Resistance, a star of the existential movement, a luminary of the French Communists for decades before he fell out with them in the 1950's to become a leading intellectual critic of the Soviet Union. More than 20 years after the Boycott trial in Grasse one finds the same feminist Haumont-Daumas responding to the news of the conferment of the knighthood on Boycott by Theresa May who admired him as an exceptional batsman. Hamont-Daumas said that her idol was Emily Pankhurst.

Geoffrey Boycott had no chance in France. He went to Grasse to gain the prize of having his name cleared completely of the nasty allegation against him. In reality that prize was unattainable and he lost. While pursuing that he turned away from the no less brilliant and also attainable prize of a High Court verdict and judgment in his favour in respect of the same incident and the same baseless accusation. But he did not give up; he persevered to clear his name with the determination and concentration which were the hallmark of his career as a great sportsman. Thus, assisted by friends, admirers and well wishers he secured the most brilliant of all the brilliant prizes winning the battle to clear his name in the minds and hearts of his countless admirers and adoring fans.

Envy and Prejudice

Matthew Caswell was not always fully conscious of the envy and the prejudice. He was aware of them below the surface, but he preferred to see them as manifestations of bad manners, and he tried to ignore them. He would have been seen as a foreigner come to make his fortune in the broad acres of Yorkshire, perceived as standoffish, immured in the isolation of the 'Boycott Room' at the back of the building, ever seen bent over a pile of paper making money with every jot of the pen, while his children were garnering the top prizes at school followed by easy passage to Oxbridge. And yet he had the time to make waves in the Yorkshire cricket scene, lead a successful insurrection against the establishment of Yorkshire County Cricket Club, while appearing on television in the company of Geoffrey Boycott, archetypal Yorkshire personality and rebel. There were instances when envy and racism popped out unexpectedly. Such was the occasion when Stephen Williamson QC, then the head of chambers, opened the annual meeting with the bare unprompted observation that "Matthew brings a lot of work to these chambers." On another occasion Stephen confided ruefully to another colleague Michael Lightfoot that he was not the biggest earner in chambers. That said, Matthew got on particularly well with two eminent lawyers, George Hall and Mr Justice Glidewell. They showed what he felt was real warmth towards him and even respect for his foreignness while mistaking him to be an Iranian of Persian descent.

Matthew Caswell was appearing before Glidewell in a civil case in Leeds when at the conclusion of the hearing Glidewell invited him to his retiring room. He and Peter Taylor were then the joint presiding judges of the North Eastern Circuit. Glidewell had before him a copy of Matthew's last 1985 application for appointment to silk in which he disclosed that his taxed income the year before had been £105,000.

Glidewell said by way of explanation that the slots for QCs in the circuit were assigned to those in practice as criminal lawyers and that he was going to suggest to the Lord Chancellor having an additional slot added for a chancery QC. He had discussed that with Mr Taylor who was also in favour. He then asked Caswell if he would try to expand the base of chancery lawyers by attracting others to his sort of work and to consider starting a new chancery chambers. Glidewell pointed to Fitzhugh having done just that in the Northern circuit. Fitzhugh had started in practice as a barrister in the Manchester chambers, acquired a chancery practice, took silk and now, as His Honour judge Fitzhugh, was sitting as chancery judge in both circuits. Caswell thanked Glidewell for his concern and encouragement and for the intimation that a new place for a chancery QC may be added.

There were two Leeds barristers that he thought would be suitable to join him in starting a general civil-cum-chancery chambers. David Rose had been his pupil, was now his colleague at 6 Park Square, and was in favour of the proposed new venture. John Behrens belonged to another common law chambers but was lukewarm when approached. Then on further consideration of his own position it became clear to Matthew that the idea of his starting new chambers was not practical. It would have required finding rooms close to the courts district in central Leeds, have them furnished and equipped to include the nucleus of a library; and to also employ a clerk and a secretary. The funding for a start would substantially have to be by means of a bank borrowing to be repaid over a period of time as the chambers grew and brought more revenue. Matthew's then income was supporting three properties in mortgage in addition to providing support to Rebecca in the purchase of her first house. That will need be followed by a similar provision for John. Most of all it did not seem feasible to add to the demands of a busy practice the consuming duties of being a head of chambers.

The notion of setting up new chambers was allowed to go to sleep, then fade away altogether. In the meantime there was trouble brewing at 6 Park Square.

Trouble at Number Six

— ⌘ —

When Matthew joined the chambers at 6 Park Square, he was given the use of a tiny room which contained a desk, a chair, a shelf and an old bulky central heating radiator. It had a window that overlooked the square and many were the comments by those who knew him and who after an evening out in town saw the light at the window and wondered if he had a home to go to. That arrangement continued throughout the period when Max Gosney was head of chambers, followed by George Hall. When the latter was appointed a circuit judge he was succeeded by Arthur Hutchinson who abolished the system of members having their own desks. That was replaced by a common room with desks and tables in common use. That arrangement made sense in that on any day of the week most of the members would be out appearing in different courts throughout the North Eastern Circuit. They mostly had no cause to call at 6 Park Square other than to collect a brief for the following day. Matthew was in a different position. The overwhelming part of his practice consisted of or involved concentrated paperwork which he could never bring himself to do at home. The chambers' tenancy included three rooms in the building, on the same floor but at the very end of the main part. One of those rooms was furnished with a desk and two or three chairs; it was intended to be used for conferences. The other two rooms were smaller and bare. Matthew's tiny room was lost in the reorganisation, it was added to the clerk's room, and he began to make use of the conference room as a substitute. It was hardly used as a conference room by anyone other than himself. There were a few occasions when Geoffrey Boycott and his solicitor Duncan Mutch came to consult him; hence it became known as the Boycott Room. That seating arrangement continued for a few years while Arthur Hutchinson was head of chambers, and continued after he was appointed to the circuit bench and was succeeded by Stephen Williamson QC.

One day Matthew arrived in the morning and as usual went first to his mailbox to retrieve a new set of instructions. He then went to the clerk's room to see if there had been any messages for him. He felt that something was not quite right; Charles Easton looked away while the girls looked embarrassed. He went along the corridor to his conference room and found Shaun Spencer in his seat with his feet resting on the half open drawers containing the briefs that Matthew had kept there to be dealt with in due course. Matthew looked at the scene quizzically while Shaun folded his two arms over his chest and looked at him defiantly. Nothing was said or anything done, and after a minute or so the odd tableau of silent challenge and unspoken defiance dissolved. Matthew picked up the brief that he had come carrying and walked out. He went to tell Charles that he was going home. The latter made no comment but looked pained and embarrassed; the girls stopped typing, Julia smiling nervously. There was a repetition of the same thing in the next three days. On the fourth day Shawn was not in but had left on the desk as from the day before the crumpled wrapping of a hamburger, a near full carton of chips and an empty tin of coca cola. Matthew cleared the mess and got down to work. When he turned up on the fifth day Shawn was there as defiant as before with brazen contempt added. Matthew went out to the Square, called at the next barristers chambers and asked if they would have a desk for him. He returned to No. 6 and told Charles that he was leaving and where he was going. Charles told him that he had a better plan for him.

Charles Easton as clerk to 6 Park Square chambers in Leeds had a close association with Arthur Blaney who clerked for 11 King's Bench Walk in the Temple. They were each engaged as a clerk on the basis of being paid 10% of one's receipts. Notwithstanding its London address Arthur's chambers, like Charles's, was a circuit set with the members practising and mostly having their home in the North Eastern Circuit, while the administration at 11 King's Bench

Walk consisted of Arthur supported by a junior clerk and an accountant. Charles acted as Arthur's agent on circuit; that was pursuant to some private understanding or arrangement. At the time of the confrontation raised by Shaun Spencer the position of Charles Easton was precarious, some of his members complaining that they were not getting enough work or not paid enough, while nearly everyone was against the continuation of the historical arrangement conferring on the clerk the right to a 10% commission. There was a growing clamour at the Bar generally for replacing the position of clerk by that of a salaried administrator.

While the trouble involving Matthew and Shaun was brewing Charles anticipating a rift discussed the matter with Arthur and measures were agreed to ease the transfer of Matthew from 6 Park Square to 11 King's Bench Walk. A significant element in that related to the moneys owed to Matthew by many solicitors for completed work. Arthur agreed to collect them free of charge and to account to Charles for his 10%. At the same time 11 King's Bench Walk as chambers welcomed Matthew as a new member and forthwith proceeded to acquire premises in the centre of Leeds to serve as circuit rooms. Matthew was to have a room to himself while Jayne Turner was now employed as a junior clerk and typist with a room next to his. Charles had raised the alarm with Stephen Williamson as the trouble started. He telephoned him several times at home urging him to take the matter in hand. Stephen's response was not to interfere and to leave it to Matthew and Shaun to compose their differences. When he was told eventually that Matthew had resolved to leave he rushed to chambers thinking of retrieving the situation. He treated Matthew to an expensive lunch and offered him the exclusive use of one of the then unused rooms at the back. But by then the elements of the agreement with 11 King's Bench Walk had either been implemented or were on the way to be completed, to the extent that Matthew felt he was already committed to the move, while he felt unhappy at leaving the company of good friends and colleagues. Stephen Williamson was a brilliant criminal lawyer with a razor-sharp acuity, but was quite inadequate as head of chambers. Not once during the lunch and the discussion that followed did he mention Shaun or indicate how things would work out between him and Matthew. With all his intelligence Stephen appeared to regard the fall-out to be simply a matter of two colleagues in an argument over the use of a desk and a room. He overlooked or chose to overlook what other reasons lay at the heart of the matter. And Stephen was cynical; he concluded the painful discussion with: "I shall say nothing against you, if you say nothing against me!"

The Call of London

H e had not planned to leave 6 Park Square. That was where he had started his career as a barrister and he will always think of it as his chambers. Time and again he will revisit the circumstances leading to his departure and wonder whether they could have been managed better. "You left it to Stephen to fight your battle," said Helen, and he had to accept the personal criticism while disputing the implied tolerant view of the part played or wasn't played by Stephen Williamson as head of chambers. Long after those events he will agonise what else he could have done to avert the rift, and wonder if that would have been likely to produce a better and lasting outcome. From the moment he allowed himself to be provoked by Shaun Spencer, which was deliberate, a train of events was set in motion that was out of his control. He felt the pain as he handed over the keys to Number 6 then walked out never to return. Yet there were compensations awaiting him as he joined what was to be his London set of chambers.

He now had keys to 11 King's Bench Walk, his new chambers headed by Franz Muller QC occupying a part of the first floor, while the rest of that floor and the ground floor comprised the chambers of the future Lord Chancellor Derry Irvine. The topmost floor was the town flat of Lady Butler Schloss, a senior judge and a scion of a distinguished family of lawyers, judges and politicians. Derry Irvine's chambers specialised in public law and included several leading and eminent members including Tony Blair soon to acquire a greater eminence as Prime Minister of the United Kingdom. When Tony courted and married Cherie Booth, they were both pupils of Derry.

That Franz Muller's chambers, as judged by the space it occupied, was the smaller chambers in the building was a reflection of the fact that it was basically a provincial set, its members covering the courts across the North Eastern Circuit. Rarely would a member be seen at King's Bench Walk and that would mostly be to attend the hearing in the High Court in London of an appeal of a circuit case. As provincial chambers with a London base Muller's chambers were highly regarded in the North of England and some very eminent barristers and judges were associated with it including the Newcastle barrister Peter Taylor who rose to the very apex of the judicial system as the Lord Chief Justice; also the Sheffield barrister Paul Kennedy who rose to the court of appeal and for a time was spoken of as a future Master of the Rolls.

For Matthew it was a privilege to be able to come down to earn a good living working in the Temple and be accorded general respect: A gated community of lawyers in the Middle of London, between Fleet Street and the River Thames where one could enjoy the open green spaces of Inner Temple, feast one's eyes on the historic buildings such as the 12th century Temple Church built by the Knights Templar or the spectacular Elizabethan Middle Temple Hall which saw the first recorded performance of Shakespeare's Twelfth Night and the adjacent Temple Garden where, according to Shakespeare's Henry VI, Part 1, Richard Plantagenet, Duke of York, plucked a white rose and the Earl of Somerset plucked a red one for the Lancastrians; that marked the start of the War of the Roses.

The Temple comprised the Middle Temple and the Inner Temple, two of the four inns of court, the other two being Lincoln's Inn and Gray's Inn. In many respects an inn resembled a traditional Oxford or Cambridge college, benefiting from a hall, a well stocked library, a senior common room for the practising barristers close to a junior common room for the novices and pupils. That provided occasions for the old and venerable to have beneficial contacts with the keen, vibrant and ambitious youth. One could have a light meal from the refectory or take a more substantial but hurried buffet lunch in hall. The latter was particularly the case with those who were appearing in court on the day and would have only a one hour break for lunch.

It helped that the High Court was on the other side of Fleet Street, and it was permissible for the barristers to cross it in the court dress of wig and gown thereby saving the precious time it would have taken to disrobe and re-robe. Those who had chambers in the Temple could also call during the hour break to rest and get the up-to-date news and instructions; and they would have the assistance of the chambers clerks who would carry their bags and law reports to and from court.

In addition to having a place in the historic King's Bench Walk Matthew now also had the keys to a newly established circuit annexe that consisted of rooms on the third floor of Goodbard House. That held a dominant position in the centre of Leeds, its windows overlooking City Square. He had his own room next to that of Jayne Turner who was employed as a junior circuit clerk liaising with the main administration at 11 King's Bench Walk. Next to his room he had the use of a conference room and beyond that a library which also served as a common room when needed. Rarely was it needed by the barristers other than him. In most days only he and Jayne were present, and she combined her duties of clerk with that of typist, door keeper and tea-maker as solicitors and clients came for a conference with him. On a daily basis Jayne was virtually his secretary and friend even while they lost none of the strict formality that their respective professional functions and ranks exacted. It was ever a case of addressing each other as 'Mr Caswell' and 'Jayne'.

The biggest recompense that he obtained following the change of chambers was that his income almost doubled overnight. Arthur Blaney knew how to fix the level of fees to extract the most and, no less important, how to get them paid. When Matthew made the move there had been fees owed to him by several solicitors for work completed, and which were allowed to remain unpaid for unconscionably long periods. Charles Easton was reluctant to press so hard as to cause a rift with solicitors who provided steady work for other members of chambers. Those outstanding fees were soon recovered by Arthur, money received by Matthew, out of which 10% was forwarded to Charles Easton as his clerk's commission. Arthur turned away the smaller insufficiently rewarding cases including the criminal ones. To him the basis for Matthew joining 11 King's Bench Walk was transactional. He was to provide Caswell with some good work through his contacts in London and the South East. At the same time Arthur made a direct approach to the scores of solicitors who regularly instructed Matthew Caswell and he expected them to instruct 11 King's Bench Walk in whatever criminal cases came their way, while asking them in particular to consider Franz Muller for any case that justified the employment of a QC. In the meantime, and with Matthew Caswell now a member of the circuit chambers in the Temple, many of the urgent applications and cases for hearing in London were received and accepted unseen by Arthur, which meant that Matthew had to deal at short notice with a variety of cases in respect of which he had no earlier involvement, hence no opportunity to form an opinion as to their merits in the law or upon the facts. Yet, his clerk having accepted the instructions he had no option in the matter; he had to do what he could, embarrassing though it was at times to try to push along an unsustainable claim or vindicate a hopeless defence. The new regime also wreaked havoc with parts of his practice as it replaced them by others. A substantial part of his practice as a chancery lawyer was advising often in heavy cases which required close application, time and effort. He needed to be out of court now and then to attend to a serious and demanding chancery case, and would ask that the day or days be kept free of court hearings, but that was to no avail. Franz Muller's chambers were a common law set where complicated commercial or chancery cases had hardly been known, while Andrew the second clerk who was in charge of the diary could not bring himself to turn away a court application on a particular day by saying that Caswell was otherwise engaged when that was not truly the case. Matthew Caswell was being driven very hard by his new chambers, but the effect was mitigated by the fact that by then the Scottish Ardlui had been sold and replaced by a London flat that combined well with his London practice.

24 Pennyford Court

In the evening of 21 August 1944 a 'Flying Bomb' (doodlebug) hit Wharnecliffe Gardens Estate in St. John's Wood with a tragic loss of life and extensive damage to property. In 1980 the site was cleared and seven modern four-storey blocks of flats were built to cover the site. The majority of the new flats were sold by Westminster Council on long-term leases. Number 24 Pennyford Court was one such that Matthew bought in the open market. It was a two bedroom flat on the second floor with the street entrance in Henderson Drive, while the rooms overlooked the prestigious St. John's Wood Road. The flat was blighted in its reputation for being thought of as an ex-council flat, yet it had a most enviable position. It was one mile away from Marble Arch as one proceeded in a southerly direction along the bustling Edgware Road. A similar distance to the east separated it from the fashionable St. John's Wood Terrace, Regent's Park and Primrose Hill. Looking north across the road one had a glimpse of Lord's Cricket Ground,

Abbey Road with the iconic recording studio nearby and Hamilton Terrace with its elegant Victorian villas and mansion houses. To the west one came to Clifton Gardens with its many shops, mini supermarket, the fashionable Raoul's Café next to The Robert Browning Public House named after the celebrated literary couple. Further along one came to the upper-class Clifton Nurseries and the trendy Warwick Castle public house with the picturesque Little Venice round the corner; smart houses overlooking the Regent Canal, home to long boats, water buses, quaint waterside cafes, cosy public houses and popular restaurants. One could take the water bus in Little Venice in the morning to cover the 8.5 miles run before linking up with the Thames at Limehouse. There is time to take lunch then return back for afternoon tea at Warwick Castle or Raoul's. The canal was at a lower level than the estate. One could go down the steps and be in an enchanting serene world free from the bustle and noise of the streets above. An easy walk along the towpath brought one to Camden Town and its popular market.

The family were excited at having their own London flat. There was the thrill on the first day as they set out in the morning to have a look at the surroundings. The flat became an important amenity for the children after finishing at Oxford; it became a second home while they embarked on new courses of study: The Bar School for Rebecca and Ben, the latter combining it with a Master's degree in Philosophy at University College London, while the flat and the many attractions surrounding it were where John courted Penina culminating in an engagement after an evening at the local Indian restaurant Akash! That proved to be a propitious engagement to the marriage that was soon celebrated at Wigan Parish Church. a happy union of the white rose and the red.

What Helen liked most about the flat was that it was within a walking distance of Church Street with its line of stalls offering antiques, curios and objects of vertu. Helen had a good eye and a good appraisal of the jumble of objects big and small. She would spend hours looking for bargains! She loved to furnish a newly acquired property, then adding to the furniture and rearranging it from time to time. When Matthew acquired a small Filey seaside flat for his own use as an occasional virtual retreat and the better to be able to concentrate on preparing a heavy court case, Helen had the thrill of trawling through the salesrooms of Filey and Scarborough to get the flat furnished and equipped; but once done that was the end of her interest in Filey while she dreamed of the next one. When some time later the family acquired an apartment in Cannes they had it adorned by articles that Helen spotted in Church Street including a 1972 painting by Clifford Hall that had been exhibited in the Royal Academy. Later, Helen became frail with the passing of years and the onset of Parkinsonism but that did not deter her from the forays in Church Street and Maida Vale now accompanied by her daily help and personal assistant Phylis. They would spend a few nights in the St John's Wood flat then return to Yorkshire happy with the Inter- county spoils.

But the flat was essentially required for Matthew's own use. He used it extensively and it became indispensable to his work. It had the additional benefit of a private bollarded parking space. Whenever the call came for him to go to London to appear in a case in the High Court in the morning he would get in the car, drive down all the way however late the hour, park the car, go to any one of a number of cafes and restaurants nearby. In the morning he would take the underground train at Warwick Avenue and get off at Temple, or the bus along Edgware Road with a stop in Aldwich. The flat also had its uses when he became involved in the affairs of Yorkshire County Cricket Club and embroiled in Geoffrey Boycott's many fracas. Whenever there was a test mach at Lord's some of Matthew's friends, cricketing fans, came down to London for the day. They would drop in at the flat for refreshments during the lunch break. At close of play Matthew would go with them to Seashell in Lisson Grove, one of London's best fish restaurants where they would betray their Yorkshire heritage by ordering haddock instead of cod, and with mushy peas added.

Those were years of achievement. Rebecca had graduated with an Oxford degree in Jurisprudence and married a fellow student Frank whose family farmed in Leicestershire. The newly married couple bought their first home with a little help from Matthew, a cottage in Burbage where their child Emma was born; Rebecca in the meantime had become a member of a Leicester barristers chambers. John graduated with an Oxford degree in geology and got a job with the National Coal Board. Identifying him as managerial material they arranged for him to attend a course of business study at Sheffield University where he added an MBA to his academic qualifications. He married Nina and they settled in Ashby de la Zouche, buying a house with a little help commensurate with that extended to Rebecca. Ben was soon to be on the way to Oxford in the footsteps of Rebecca to read Jurisprudence under Jeff Hackney at Wadham.

La Californie

"It's a piece of heaven" said the estate agent and many would have agreed with him. European royalty, northern industrialists, near eastern potentates and Indian maharajahs, they came, they saw and were smitten. So they built their villas on the slope of the hill overlooking Cannes that was La Californie and retreated there in winter, to get away from the burden of office, socialise, make friends and new alliances.

As an army officer King Zog participated in the declaration of Albanian independence from the Ottoman Empire in 1912, assumed leadership of his nation in 1922 and was declared king in 1928. In the same year he joined the rank of the other royals and potentates by having a villa constructed for him on a plot in La Californie, a relatively small one commensurate with the size of his new kingdom. By the time that Matthew and Helen were taken to view it had become Villa Anais consisting of five apartments with a semi- detached lodge or *maison de guardian* as a sixth.

The attention of Matthew and Helen had been drawn to an advertisement in the *Times* of a flat close to Antibes on offer for sale with an asking price of £90,000. They looked at their finances and thought they could afford it. They contacted the estate agent and he arranged for them to make a brief visit to the south of France where they were also invited to look at other properties. After viewing two properties they were taken to see what Villa Anais had to offer. Helen did not want to look at any other: "We are not going to see a better one", she said. It was a luxurious apartment with a good view of the sea at one end, the Esterel mountain on the other, and some stretch of sea, trees and buildings in between. It cost them the French franc equivalent of £230,000. Thus the family acquired an international property. It held an enviable position in one of the most sought after parts of Cannes. It stood at the Carrefour where the Avenue de la Californie came to link up with Roi Albert 1er. One is reminded that the latter was so named to honour the King of Belgium who stood up defiantly and courageously to the invading German Army in the First World War. There came a time when this part of the Californie was known as the Belgian district. Next to "Le Califonie", a venerable hotel now converted into apartments, was the street with the name of Reine Elizabeth, in honour of the Belgian queen, consort of Roi Albert. It was this queen who created a water trough right up against the flank of Anais. The water was from a mineral water source which Anaïs shared. Next to the Reine Elizabeth street stood the Anglican church that King Edward the Seventh built in memory of his younger brother who died in Cannes. An impressive memorial was constructed by the municipality of Cannes at the other end of Avenue de la Californie as an offer of condolence to his mother Queen Victoria. Close by the church was the Pavillon de Fleur where the Spaniard Pablo Picasso had a turbulent private life while enjoying one of the most productive periods of his life. The Avenue de la Favorite was next and it contained a big house of a Prussian Royal and the even more immense pile of the Maharani of Jaipur where Winston Churchill spent many holidays as an honoured guest. The Prussian house, stripped of its German name, backed on to that of Prince Michael Romanoff, brother of the Tsar and commander of the Russian Army in the First World War.

The five apartments in the main house were on three floors, basement, ground floor and first floor. Matthew and Helen chose a large apartment on the first or upper floor. they chose it for the views from the two terraces. The main terrace was at the back with a view of the garden, the sea, the bay and the two islands of Lerrins beyond. It was suffused all afternoon by the sun and the light of the south. There was also another smaller terrace at the front. It had the sun in the morning, and it gave good town views of La Californie.

Anaïs was a *coproprietee;* everyone had their own apartment and shared in the ownership and were responsible for the upkeep of the common parts of the villa. The six owners met once a year to appoint or confirm the reappointment of a managing agent and to set a budget. Each one made a contribution to the service charge calculated as a percentage of the total, the percentage depending on the size of their apartment. The only other apartment on the first floor, smaller than the one purchased by the Caswells, was occupied by a Belgian couple, Jacque Belfroid and his wife. They had no children, were well off with a boat in Cannes marina. The only other occupants of Anais at the time were Roger Fain and his wife Myrelle; they owned the *maison*. They were French, had started a business of couturier in Paris and moved to Cannes in uncertain circumstances. Because he was French, was the first in Anais and was well connected it fell to Fain to be the President of the coproprietee and that was inevitable because Belfroid deferred to him while the Caswells were absent most of the year and took little interest in the management of Anais. Theirs was simply a holiday apartment.

Roger Fain was a remarkable man. He had a perfect command of English and followed the financial news and the world markets keenly, was well connected and ever on the lookout for opportunities to make money. He and Myrelle had made a lot of money in Paris and were now in the south of France enjoying their retirement as millionaires. Roger was just the man to manage the affairs of the coproprietee. He had a razor sharp intelligence, an acute acumen, lacked nothing in savoire faire and was highly admired and respected as he moved among the Jewish business community of Cannes. And he was blatantly dishonest as was revealed when the Schaeffers appeared on the scene. Under the French state building regulations each unit of human habitation had to have a cellar. That was intended for the keeping of wine and for general domestic storage. Anais was not different. It was built with an independent cellar house straddling the foundations of the main house and the *maison*. The cellar house consisted of six individual cellars which were sold with the five apartments and the *maison* respectively. Fain as president of Villa Anais surreptitiously called in builders who had his cellar incorporated in his house for use as an office. That left five cellars in the cellar house. He then got the builders to convert the five to six by demolishing partitions and putting up new ones. The new sixth cellar was thus carved out up to one half of the Caswell cellar and even more drastically out of those of the three apartments that had not yet been sold. Fain with the connivance of Belfroid voted the transfer of the alleged 'additional' cellar to himself. Compounding the villainy he caused the cost of all the work to come out of the general account of Villa Anais.

The Schaeffers, Claude and Monique, were a French couple from the Alsace. Claude was a mid ranking manager of the French banking and financial services group Societe Generale; Monique dabbled in interior design. They had no children while Claude's job took them to different countries.

They were metropolitan, spoke perfect English to add to French and German, and they got on well with Matthew and Helen. Claude got a transfer back to France where they aimed to spend the rest of their lives. They had some savings and they thought of investing them in trendy Cannes with hope of income and capital appreciation. The three Anais apartments which were on offer answered to their plans. They purchased them and got on with the improvements to Anais with the support of the Caswells. A fountain that had graced the chateau of King Zog was disposed off. In its place they constructed at their own expense an 'infinity' swimming pool for the use of all at Anais. Monique then got on with redesigning the basement to create a luxurious apartment with all modern accessories. That included the construction of a patio beyond the line of the building, a corner of which was immediately below a waterspout that vacated rainwater as it fell on Caswell's main terrace. The attention of the Schaeffer couple then turned to the cellars, and they were horrified to see that they were one cellar short while the others were smaller than the ones shown on the construction plans that formed part of the title deeds, the original of which were held by the Land Registry in Grasse. Claude carried out a close investigation and discovered what Roger Fain had done. Claude the banker was made of a different mould than Jacque Belfroid. He expressed his outrage in no uncertain terms forcing Fain to disgorge what he had stolen, and to do it at his own expense. The Schaeffers

414

recovered their cellar. At the same time Fain was compelled to restitute the half cellar to the Caswells leaving them with two adjoining small cellars with the combined size of the original. The Schaeffers had only three apartments out of the six. They exercised control with the backing of Matthew and Helen. Claude became the president of the coproprietee and looked at the accounts with the keen eyes of a bank manager. He discovered that everyone had to contribute a just proportion to the cost of the water supplied to Anais, and did so contribute. That was so with the exception of one. The lodge had been receiving the water from the main building of Anais for years without a meter. When confronted Roger Fain said how was he to know that he had to pay for the water. Claude asked him sarcastically, "Where have you been living all those years?"

Matthew and Helen were having their afternoon tea when the doorbell rang. Matthew answered it and Monique came in sobbing. Claude had left her. He had attended some convention, met a Spanish academic who must have been of low morals else she would not have seduced a married middle aged man! Claude had gone to live with other woman leaving Monique on her own in Anais. Monique was distraught. The drama was the talk of La Californie for months on end. Monique kept on saying in the presence of Matthew and Helen while sobbing, "At my age who will be there to buy me?" while easing her distress by using a string of expletives against the other woman, in English peppered by vulgar French. She would not be consoled by expressions of sympathy or by well meaning assurances by Helen that sooner or later Claude will see sense and come back to her. Then Monique made a big mistake. She came back to Anais on the last bus in the company of the driver for a lover. That gave Roger Fain and Myrelle their schadenfreude; the rest of the denizens of Anais were scandalised, Monique's brother came down from Colmar a month later to put an end to the disgrace. Six months later Matthew answered the door and there was Monique begging him not to tell Claude. The other woman got tired of Claude and went back to her husband, and Claude has now made overtures to come back to Monique as erring husband and penitent. They sold the flats a year later and put the money in the purchase of an apartment in the 16th arrondissement of Paris. The basement flat was purchased by an Austrian by the name of Wayd, his wife an American. He was a bully and she a manipulator. They did all they could year after year to remove the waterspout that discharged water on their patio when it rained, unconcerned whether that would cause the water to accumulate on the terrace above with the attendant risk of flooding the apartment of the Caswells. Matthew stood up to the bullying and threats of the man Wayd, and countered the manipulations of the woman. The dispute nearly went to court before the Wayds admitted defeat, sold out and were gone away. As far as concerned the Caswells peace and good neighbourliness were thereafter restored for good.

Oxford

He was coming up to his seventies as his practice had started to decline; so many solicitors who had regularly instructed him over the years had either retired or died, and it was time for him now to assess his own position, and he started with a review of his preceding thirty years at the Bar. By many objective measures they were good, productive years during which he earned and amassed large sums of money that left him well provided for in his retirement. He was highly regarded and there were many cases in the law reports in which his name was cited as an advocate. Some of these were important law cases and were highlighted in learned publications and textbooks. Yet he did not receive the official recognition that he craved as he missed the appointment to Queen's Counsel while he was passed over for judicial appointment. Helen hoped he would retire so they would spend more time together in their old age. He did not find the prospect of complete retirement appealing. He felt that he still had the desire, ability and energy to yet make more of his life whether in the law or otherwise. Otherwise? And he remembered that he had an unfinished business at Oxford.

It was his second attempt to secure a doctorate; he started it hoping that its success would expiate for the failure of his first. There were preliminary requirements before seriously embarking on the project of working for a DPhil; thus an Oxford doctorate is designated, distinguishing it from the designation of the equivalent PhD at other universities. The most challenging requirement was the choice of a topic for research. It had to be sufficiently worthwhile academically and socially, one that was calculated to add to the sum total of human knowledge. It had to be original in the sense of it being new in its field or otherwise under-researched. There had to be the prospect of sufficient material to be researched, accessed and used.

Searching for a topic he directed his attention to the early part of the Abbasid period, the 9th century AD in particular, which saw the apogee of the extent, power and remit of the Arab empire in the east and the high watermark of its civilisation with Baghdad at its centre. Far reaching historical, religious and cultural events and controversies were taking place. In the course of his extensive reading about that period he chanced on peripheral references to women with strange or foreign names acting the courtesans while notorious in the performing arts as singers, instrumentalists and poets, commonly called qiyán (sing. qayna), expression meant to denote slave singing girls. There were passing references to them in learned and academic circles. To Charles Pellat, citing al-Jahiz, they were 'Les esclaves chanteuses de gahiz', while they made an appearance in Beeston's as 'The Epistle of the Singing Girls of Jahiz'. The Arab academic Mustafa al-Shak'a was the author of several learned reviews dealing with different aspects of Arab and Islamic cultures. The DPhil aspirant happened to come into possession of his review of the Abbasid civilization in al-Shi'r wa-l-shu'ara' fi al-'asr al- 'abbasi. It contained a chapter on Abbasid women poets with references to slave girls such as 'Arib and Fadl who had made their names as singing girls and poets in the cultural scene of 9th century Baghdad. But the portrayal by Shak'a of the qiyan was quite different from those of Pellat and Beeston. Al-Shak'a is an Arab nationalist, proud of what he perceives to be a pure Arab culture when not sullied by Persian and other alien intrusions.. When confronted by the material that was associated with the qiyan he recoiled from their openly immoral behaviour and grossly salacious language. Hence the chapter in which they were described was full of wide gaps in the narrative demonstrating the expurgation of whole sentences. The interest of the would-be doctoral candidate was engaged in the topic to the extent of expanding his search to include the works of other writers including al- Jahiz, al-Isfahani and al-Mas'udi. And he discovered a new world of international trade in slaves, slave markets in every town, of slave girls and concubines; of a society of aristocrats, rich men and bureaucrats who had the means, free time and inclination to enjoy and be engaged in leisure activities for their own sake; of literary salons, meeting places and brothels; of a language that combined the refined and elegant with the dross and the salacious. Thus it was that he found his topic for a doctoral thesis.

He discussed the matter with John Gurney and it was well received. Dr Gurney was a fellow of Wadham College, a tutor in Persian which was his speciality. He was also a member if the Oxford Oriental Institute. Through him, he, as Fouad Matthew Caswell was admitted to the college as a postgraduate student reading for a doctorate in Arabic. Gurney's next step was even more helpful to Caswell. He got van Gelder's agreement to act as the supervisor. That was a very useful and long-lasting benefit to Matthew in that Geert Jan van Gelder was the Laudian Professor of Arabic, one of the world's most, if not the most, eminent and respected of Arabists. And van Gelder was one to whom the epithet 'Renaissance Man' was most fitting – intelligent, knowledgeable, artistic with particular interest in the music of Bach, sociable, and with good temperament to cap them all. Based on the premise that Caswell already held a London first class degree in Classical Arabic awarded to him in his then name of Fouad Menashi Zelouf, and with the support of Professor van Gelder and of Dr Gurney the Board of the Faculty of Oriental Studies accepted Caswell's application to study for a doctorate, but with one stipulation. As it was more than forty years since he had obtained his London degree he was now required to work for and obtain an Oxford's Master of Studies degree before qualifying as a probationary DPhil candidate.

The Faculty of Oriental Studies which covered Asian and Middle Eastern studies was located in the Oriental Institute's building in Pusey Lane. It was a branch of the Bodleian Library with a reading room at ground level, rooms for lectures and seminars on the upper floors, in addition to individual studies for the professors and other leading academics. The basement included the common room and a bar serving hot drinks and light snacks. The building was accessible to anyone holding a Bodleian card and at the time of Caswell's time a woman porter ensured that all she deemed undesirable were kept out. The street door was always locked; she sat at a window overlooking the entrance and pressed a button to open the door electronically as she acknowledged a legitimate arrival with a smile. The research for a higher degree in oriental studies was carried out at the Oriental Institute, or in the Oriental Reading Room at the main Bodleian building in Parks Road, or in the library of one's college plus one's own college room. One could borrow books from the Oriental Institute library while most college libraries served also as reading rooms. Wadham's Ferdowsi library, modern, well stocked, comfortable and open day and night is a superb example of a good university library. It was built and equipped with a generous bequest by a member of the Pahlevi royal family of Iran.

When he was admitted to Wadham as a postgraduate student he expressed a preference for a room in the main college building in Parks Road. Instead, he was allocated a room in Merifield. That was a purpose built modern annexe situated in Ferry Rod close to the shops and amenities of Summertown and within a short bus ride to the city centre. It provided accommodation for 146 undergraduate and postgraduate students each one having an individual room while sharing a common room and kitchen with others on the same staircase. The new research student liked his room: cosy, clean, centrally heated, quiet with a pleasing view of garden and flowering trees. In addition, he had the benefit of the complex being adjacent to a ticket operated public car park which he would use when he arrived from Leeds or London by car. He soon discovered that he could easily reach the Summertown bustling high street by crossing the car park on foot. The only drawback that he saw in this arrangement was that almost every other student he came across was an undergraduate and so very much younger than him. That drawback, if one could properly call it that, was remedied after the first year by his agreeing to have his room exchanged for another room that formed part of another Wadham college accommodation in Lathbury Road, Summertown. That consisted of five rooms on the upper floors of a Victorian house; the rooms intended primarily to accommodate mature DPhil students. As it happened one room came to be occupied by a young male undergraduate to whom it had been allocated in default at the time of any other available college room. The young man was delighted to make the exchange thereby moving to a room in a purpose built student accommodation having all the modern amenities including an internet connection, while he would enjoy being close to other young undergraduates. As for the older barrister turned a student the room in Lathbury Road was ideal, answering to all his needs. The room was big with a high ceiling, and he would spread his books and papers on desk, shelves and carpeted floor as he worked in near isolation, free from intrusion. The big window faced south and overlooked a mature garden with an ample ancient pear tree; he could almost touch one of the branches.

Mrs Ishak was the part owner of the house and had the exclusive use of the ground floor including the garden. She was the widow of Dr Ishak, a fellow of Wadham College whose academic interests were in economics and politics. He was a remarkable character who added a little mystery to the life of Wadham. For a start everyone mispronounced his name as 'ee-shaak' whereas the correct name and pronunciation should have been 'is-haak or is-haaq', the oriental version of Isaac. The name pointed to an Assyrian heritage by ethnicity and probably a Nestorian by faith. He spoke Persian and a variety of Kurdish. This came in handy as he dealt with the princess, sister of the Shah, when she came on a visit to Oxford. This princess had an international reputation as a hedonist, a man-eater who pursued men for pleasure. Dr Ishak acted as her guide and consort, many would add lover, during her visit. Wadham derived a great benefit from that. Ishak persuaded the princess to make a generous gift to the college specifically to create a state of the art library in the name of Ferdowsi (940-1020 AD) considered to be the most influential figure in Persian literature, author of the Shahnameh (Book of Kings) reputed to be the world's longest epic poem composed by one man. Dr Ishaq was also part of the new left movement of the 1960's and added to the reputation of Wadham as a radical college. Then came the time after the events leading to the creation of the Ferdowsi library that Dr Ishak wanted to buy the house in Lathbury Road while the college was keen to retain him as a fellow. He could not find the full amount of the asking price, so the college advanced half of it to become a joint owner. The arrangement survived the death of Dr Ishak, his half share passing on to his widow. She was guarded at any mention of her husband, knowing full well that he had been controversial in the political views that he held. A mere mention of his name in the basement of the Oriental Institute would be met by glum faces. They were mostly there after years of doing service as diplomats, journalists, delegates to united nation's agencies and senior civil servants. Dr Ishak did not hold back on his left-wing views which were seen by some as extreme, by others as unpatriotic, by yet others as subversive. There could have been an element of racism in all that. Van Gelder is a good judge of people, free of prejudice and any trace of racism. His student did not know what to make of an observation he made after reviewing a piece of work in which Persian influence on the Abbasid polity was mentioned. Van Gelder commented that the Iranians had a significant presence in the university, and added that in his experience all Iranians were troublemakers. That could not apply to Dr Ishak's wife and widow who was English to her fingernails. Mrs Ishak was a gracious woman and a good neighbour. She maintained good relations with the students. At the start of each academic year, and with it the change of the mix in the upper floors, Mrs Ishak would invite the students to dinner; and when the pears were picked in their due season she would send a big quantity upstairs in hampers. She also continued to have a special regard for Wadham which was reciprocated. She was noncommittal when talking about her late husband. Asked what sort of a Marxist Dr Ishak was she would say that he believed in the redistribution of wealth.

A similar arrangement for a house purchase obtained when the van Gelders purchased their Oxford home. Geert Jan was a Dutch academic married to an English woman Sheila. The venerated Laudian professorship of Arabic had always been held at St John's College and when van Gelder succeeded to the professorship he thereby became a fellow of the college. When an elegant housing development was created in north Oxford the van Gelders became interested in buying a house in Merrivale Square. They had some savings supplemented by a gift from Sheila's parents. That still left a shortfall and St John's provided it in return for a share, it being understood that upon Geert Jan retiring at sixty the house would be sold as he and Sheila would then want to return to Holland where their two daughters had their homes. St John's contribution to the purchase price was of minor significance to it in the context of its wealth and its wish to have and retain van Gelder as a fellow. St John's was a very rich college with large endowments; there was a saying that one could walk from St John's of Oxford to St John's of Cambridge without having to step outside the lands of the former.

The life of a research student is a solitary one. There were five in the house at Lathbury Road who were working for a DPhil, each on a different discrete subject. The subjects did not touch each other while the contact between the individuals was minimal. A room at the front overlooking Lathbury Road was a kitchen with a table and hard dining chairs. It could have served as a common room if the desire had been there. In fact, there would be some occasional contact as when one went to make oneself a hot drink or a snack. One might then see Ursula examining, choosing and rearranging the many jars of vitamins which filled one side of a shelf. Her subject was in geography, supervisor a lecturer at Somerville. Ursula complemented her income by going to spend one day a week at Southampton University to teach undergraduates, and there was the promise of a full-time appointment once she got her doctorate. Kate was a few years older, a northern chemist with a supervisor at Keble. She was more advanced in her research and already in the early stages of writing her thesis. That made her feel superior to Ursula the Slovene and Gregory from Portugal. She did not like Gregory and the feeling was reciprocated. He was generally finding life hard in Oxford. He did not like the weather, found English bread indigestible and the sliced white a disgrace. He was hard up and wondered if he had made a mistake by applying to Wadham instead of some other better-endowed Oxford college. He was not getting on well with his supervisor and wondered if he had chosen the wrong discipline and the wrong subject for a thesis. He disliked and mistrusted Kate in equal measures; and with a touch of paranoia. One evening he bought a Kentucky fried chicken which he was keeping to the following day. When he looked in the fridge the following morning there was no trace of it. He went about telling anyone who would listen that the disappearance must have been connected with Kate's nefarious ill feelings towards him. On Kate's last visit home she returned from Sheffield with a set of sharp knives. They were made of stainless steel slit- cradled in a block of wood. She placed that on a corner of the working top with a notice in her neat handwriting, "You may use these knives provided you do so carefully and d0 not lose them. THEY

ARE EXPENSIVE". Arthur occupied the top floor; nobody knew what his subject was. Practically a recluse he indicated his presence by the noise he made as he heavily trod the stairs.

Matthew Caswell was still working as a barrister, attending chambers to collect briefs and new instructions as well as meeting solicitors and clients who came to him for advice. In addition, he attended court hearings on circuit and in London. Consequently, the work for a DPhil could only be accommodated within the constraints of his legal practice. He had to meet his supervisor at least once a month on a date fixed in advance. The venue for the meeting was always at the van Gelder house at 48 Merrivale Square. Geert Jan had a study on the second floor and Caswell would sit across the desk facing him as they discussed the work that Caswell had already done and submitted, for example, a chapter on the qiyan in the early Abbasid era. Midway through the meetings Sheila would appear unfailingly with tea, shortbread biscuits and a broad welcoming smile. The meetings would be concluded by identifying the nature and scope of the next chapter and fixing the date of the next meeting. Caswell would then spend all the remaining time that he could spare in Oxford that day, researching the topic in the library of the Oriental Institute, making copious notes which he would take to Leeds to form the basis of the material of the next chapter that he would post to van Gelder to look at in advance of the next meeting.

He loved being a student again. On his Oxford days he would take the bus at Summertown, get off at St Giles then go spend the morning in the reading room of the Oriental Institute then walk out with books he borrowed. He liked to go back to the college, make his way to the Middle Common Room to meet some friends and read the newspapers, thence wend his way to the college's beautiful garden to breathe the fresh air, walk or sit at one of the benches with book in hand. Some fellows who saw him always holding a book wondered at the assiduity of a man who, advanced in years, was engaged in a serious academic project, and that after he had practised and made for himself a distinguished career in the law. He was privileged by an invitation from the Master to dine at his lodge and by other invitations to drinks and dinners hosted by the Senior Common Room. In addition, he was allowed as of right as a senior research student to dine at high table in hall once a term. Of the people he met in the Middle Common Room he easily established a rapport with two American Rhodes scholars who were doing Philosophy, Politics and Economics (PPE). Amiable and respectful they needed little encouragement to stand for election as the common room's president and secretary respectively. They followed that by serious, professional canvassing. They seemed knowledgeable, talked politics in measured terms which corresponded to a grave and serious mien. They were once heard to argue with Gregory vociferously about the history of Portugal and the excesses of the Salazar regime before betaking themselves to the popular and lively King's Arms next door where more than one American presidential campaign was reputed to have started. One such and fairly recent was by a Rhodes scholar at University College who admitted to smoking cannabis but without inhaling.

The Master of Studies (MSt) had a bad start. He was required to carry out research on some suitable topic leading to an erudite dissertation. As it was envisaged that the MSt would likely lead to a DPhil it was agreed that the research and the dissertation could be such as be part of the doctoral thesis in due course. He chose for a subject al-Imá' al-shawa'ir (The slave women poets). When the dissertation was ready Wadham as the candidate's college submitted it to the Faculty of Oriental Studies for consideration by two academics, one of whom had to be an external examiner; Julia Bray was nominated as the latter. She held the position of Professeur de Literature Arabe Medievale at the University of Paris. She travelled to England for the examination and a date was set for it to take place at the Oriental Institute. As soon as Caswell appeared before the examiners Professor Bray tore into him saying that the dissertation was poor and badly researched; that the observations it contained were hackneyed while many of the really good points were overlooked. In vain did Caswell try to defend his work while the other examiner appeared to be shocked by the ferocity of Bray's onslaught and was tongue tied throughout. Coming out of the room the student was met by Dr Gurney who asked him how it went, although the question was superfluous, the answer was in Caswell's face. He said it had been a terrible experience. Gurney reacted to that with outrage, "Why do they do such things!" he exclaimed. Caswell then walked into van Gelder's room for comfort. Geert Jan van Gelder came straight to the point. He asked him how he got on with Julia Bray and Matthew Caswell acknowledged that she had been right to find fault and to criticize but not in the manner that she did. That drew a smile from van Gelder who was secretly pleased to hear those words. He judged Julia Bray as ambitious and self-assertive, attributes that carried her progressively through Manchester, Edinburgh, St Andrews and Paris 8 Vincennes St Denis. She was now eyeing the big prize, the Laudian professorship which van Gelder was not going to let pass away from him before it was time for him to retire. Matthew Caswell made some improvement to the dissertation with the help of van Gelder. Resubmitted for consideration by two new assessors they approved it with no further questions asked. Their report stated pointedly that an MSt candidate's dissertation should not be required to be more than the equivalent of a single discrete article. Julia Bray did eventually succeed to the Laudian professorship upon the retirement of van Gelder in 2012.

He now applied for transfer of status from Provisional Research Student to DPhil. Two assessors were appointed, namely Dr Luke Treadwell and Dr Marle Hammond of SOAS, the latter as external examiner. The assessment was to be based on the submission by Caswell of a chapter of his proposed doctoral thesis followed by his attending a viva examination. He submitted a chapter on al-Ima' al-shawa'ir as eulogists that had been approved by van Gelder in the course of the supervision. The viva took place at the Oriental Institute on 13th April 2006 when the assessors had concerns about the submission and about the arrangement of the chapters within the framework of the proposed thesis. They suggested a number of changes and improvements. Dr Hammond recommended, among other suggestions, a citation and a review of a 1996 monograph by Mernissi, "Women's Rebellion and Islamic Memory". Fatima Mernissi is a Moroccan writer and an activist feminist. She posited that the inferior social status of women in the Arab and more widely the Muslim societies was attributable to the arrival into those societies in the course of the Abbasid era of a large number of foreign women, the jawari, who so subjugated themselves to their men masters and so ministered to all their whims that the men became spoiled and henceforth expected every woman to be their slave. The assessors indicated in the course of the viva and confirmed that in their official report that they could not recommend the transfer with the things as they stood but, with the candidate expressing willingness in the course of the viva to make the changes that they suggested, they would be willing to recommend the transfer upon resubmission of his piece of work with the changes actually made. The report included a list of the changes which were required; Mernissi's book was not in the list. Caswell made the changes with the help and approval of van Gelder and resubmitted his application for the transfer. That was considered and discussed at a new viva examination in June 2006. Dr Robin Ostle of St John's replaced Luke Treadwell as internal assessor with Dr Marle Hammond continuing as before. On this occasion the assessors recognised that the piece of work was much improved by the changes that were made but they still had some further concerns which they listed. Noting that the proposed doctoral thesis was complete in draft they concluded:

> We strongly advise the candidate to work through the complete draft of the thesis in close consultation with his Supervisor, paying extremely thorough attention to the recommendations as set out above. If this is done, he ought to be allowed to submit the thesis.

That was signed by both assessors, but Dr Hammond added a further personal note in which she attacked Matthew Caswell personally for ignoring some of her recommendations, referring to the Mernissi mention in particular. She all but made a charge of duplicity, as serious as it was wrong:

> While it is often appropriate for a student to reject certain recommendations made by an assessor, it is disingenuous to pretend to make the changes and then reverse them when you think that this reversal would not be noticed.

There was no factual foundation for this charge. Dr Ostle held himself at a distance while Caswell had the unqualified support of van Gelder throughout. By letter dated 30 June 2004 the university approved the Transfer of Status from P. R. S. to DPhil.

Mernissi's book was for the specialists; copies were not easy to obtain. Matthew Caswell borrowed a copy from the Oriental Institute library, wrote a critique disputing Mernissi's postulation, and added that to the thesis. It is ironic that in the view of many who read the finished thesis that critique was the most engaging part of the thesis.

His DPhil project now proceeded apace and he was growing in confidence all the time, Happy were the occasions that took him to 48 Merrivale Square. Sheila was always friendly and welcoming, while Geert Jan was ever his supervisor, protector in the face of academic intrigues as well as friend; and he had some knowledge of the law and of court procedures. A colleague and member of the Faculty of Oriental Studies was Dr Zimmerman who specialised in Islamic history. In that capacity he was appointed to supervise a research student of Asian descent. It did not take Zimmerman long to conclude that the candidate had neither the capability nor the application to persevere; he so reported and the candidate's status as research student was revoked. He sued Zimmerman and the university alleging racial discrimination and claiming as damages all the moneys he would have earned if he had been allowed to proceed with the prospect of getting a DPhil award. The ramifications caused a great alarm in the Oriental Institute, and van Gelder appeared in court to defend the university as well as Dr Zimmerman against the charge. He now had two concerns as supervisor of the barrister Matthew Caswell. He was concerned at the attitude of his student were he to fail to get his doctorate. Matthew assured him that he was not looking to use the award as a stepping stone to an academic appointment or to any other gainful employment; that all he would have lost would be an injury to his pride. Another concern for van Gelder was the blame he might get as the supervisor were his student's thesis to be a failure. The answer to that was in his own hands. He would not allow Matthew to apply for leave to supplicate for DPhil unless and until he felt it was good enough.

He felt quite sure as he advised Caswell to apply. That was to be followed by the appointment of two examiners. Dr Nadia Jamil, an Oxford academic and member of the Oriental Institute was nominated and she accepted the appointment as the internal examiner. Caswell as the candidate was entitled to have his own nominee as external examiner He left that to van Gelder who nominated Edmund Bosworth. That was a happy choice. Professor Bosworth was an erudite, highly respected retired academic, author of many works on Arab and Islamic subjects including several contributions to the Encyclopaedia of Islam. Van Gelder counted him among his friends; and Caswell had a good rapport with him on their first meeting when Bosworth mentioned with paternal pride that he had a son who was a circuit judge. Bosworth and Nadia Jamil were provided with copies of the draft thesis to consider before the date was set for the viva. Dr Jamil was to be found in the Oriental Institute almost every day, met up with Matthew Caswell and they discussed the thesis informally. She liked it, took great care in evaluating it and offered Caswell several constructive suggestions to improve it which he gratefully received and acted upon. And she would refer nearly every time to her own article published in Oxford Studies in Islamic Art; "Caliph and Qutb: poetry as a source for interpreting the transformation of the Byzantine cross on Umayyad coinage." That had no connection to anything in the thesis while Caswell was appreciative of her interest in his work, her useful suggestions and constructive observations. Dr Jamil had been so generous with her informal observations and suggestions some of which found a place in his thesis that citing her erudite article in the bibliography would be a show of appreciation. When he mentioned that to van Gelder the latter smiled and said, "Very well, give it to her", which Caswell was happy to do.

The viva started with Nadia Jamil asking Matthew Caswell what he had aimed to achieve in writing his thesis. He did not get the drift of the question and had no answer. The two examiners pointed to the copious translations which would almost qualify the thesis as an anthology of medieval Arabic poetry. They pointed to the way the Arabic verse was so treated as to produce an elegant meld of the medieval Arabic and the classical English; Nadia Jamil kept on exclaiming "It's admirable, really admirable!" Professor Bosworth was concerned that the draft thesis did not sufficiently indicate the source of the material. They would not recommend giving him leave to supplicate for a DPhil; instead, he was offered the choice of either accepting an M. Litt there and then or taking the opportunity of revising the thesis and resubmitting it for the degree of DPhil. He chose the latter option, made the requisite revision which was accepted. The examiners recommended granting him leave to supplicate subject only to making one minor correction. He had made a mention in the draft thesis of a passage in the al-Ima'al-shawa'ir and gave the page number. Nadia Jamil had a copy of the book where the page number was different; and Caswell was required to correct his draft thesis. He got down to resolve the conflict and discovered that there had in fact been three identical editions of the same book published in the same year in Damascus. The obvious inference was that there existed one genuine version and two pirated ones; but there was no way of telling which was which. Instead of correcting the reference in the thesis he introduced a note explaining the matter. That was accepted by the examiners and the university informed Caswell that he was free to supplicate for the degree of DPhil, which he did and it was formally awarded to him.

The thesis was published in 2011 in the name *The Slave Girls of Baghdad – The Qiyan in the early Abbasid Era*. That had been preceded by the publication of *Menashi's Boy*, the first of several wide-ranging and widely acclaimed books and plays that were to define Fouad's last career as a writer.